Praise for *Love Promised: A Future Life Revealed*

For over 30 years, I've been teaching how we're connected to each other and everything around us via cords…and now Kent has captured what cords looks like in photographs. Love Promised *will truly inspire and educate anyone who wants to know more about this milestone we call death.*

  —**Sonia Choquette,** *NY Times* Bestselling Author

Perfect in its timing, well written, and truly thought provoking, this book provides insight to those looking for answers about this journey we are all on. If you have ever lost someone you've loved, Love Promised: A Future Life Revealed *is a must-read. Incredibly comforting, it will change your perception and possibly your life. With its accounts of the past, the present, and the future, this book moves past boundaries and shows us how fragile they were. Further, it inspires each and every one of us to realize that anything is possible and that nothing is ever only as it seems.*

  —**Petrene Soames,** author of *The Essence of Self-Healing, Fifty Ways to Fix Your Life* & creator Positive Thought Cards© World-class psychic, medium, teacher, paranormal expert

Every now and then comes a story so surprising and riveting that we are prompted to re-examine our own concepts of reality. In Love Promised: A Future Life Revealed, Kent Smith opens a doorway to a world of incredible possibilities. Powerful, engaging, and heartwarming from start to finish, Kent's remarkable story of love, beyond the normal concepts of time, will keep you coming back for more. You won't want to miss it.

  —**Paul Elder,** Monroe Institute Facilitator & author of *Eyes of an Angel*

What an amazing journey…the first chapter will pull you into Kent Smith's world and you will end up taking the trip right along with her.

  —**Rita Mills,** publisher, *The New Era Times*

This is a remarkable, beautifully written spiritual journey of awakening and transformation, of love lost and then re-united in spirit, and the ongoing miracle of synchronicity. Kent Smith validates the tangible communication that exists between human beings and 'spirit' that transcends time and space, and shares fascinating insight into the 'life-line' that tethers the past, present, and future. This is truly a one-of-a-kind love story that chronicles the future incarnation of Kent, and her lost love Russell, as Mark and Eva Wexford... complete with specific details and a chronological time-line that predicts how Mark and Eva will fall in love and marry in Toronto, Canada in 2048; and, how, over a decade later, Mark and Eva will discover Love Promised: A Future Life Revealed in a small bookstore, profiling their past life as Russell and Kent! This is a compelling, wonderful must-read.

——**Kim O'Neill,** Author of *How to Talk With Your Angels* &
The Calling: My Journey With the Angels

I am a card-carrying library member and read ALOT. When I read Kent Smith's manuscript I literally could not put it down. This work is a very important catalyst in the shift of our collective consciousness to the reality of reincarnation, life after death and so much more. I have always called The Celestine Prophecy *a book on Spirituality 101*—Love Promised: A Future Life Revealed *is PhD level.*

——**Peggy Sue Skipper,** author of *The Art of Conscious Evolution,
Love Signs* & *Ancient History from Beyond the Veil*

Love Promised
A Future Life Revealed

A True Story

The Continuation of Life and Love in Spite of Tragedy

Three things that cannot be long hidden…
The Sun, the Moon, and the Truth
—Gautama Buddha

Kent Smith

Universal Life Strings Publishing
2012

ISBN# Hard Copy — 978-0-9851654-2-0
ISBN# MOBI ebook — 978-0-9851654-0-6
ISBN# ePUB ebook — 978-0-9851654-1-3

Second Printing — May 2013

Credits

Book cover design photograph is entitled *"Butterfly Emerges from Stellar Demise in Planetary Nebula NGC 6302."* Credit: NASA, ESA, and the Hubble SM4 ERO Team— September 9, 2009

Photograph of St. Thomas of Aquinas used in this manuscript was taken by user identified as Svencb on January 22, 2006, and is licensed under the Creative Commons Attribution-Share Alike 3.0 Unported. Permission is granted for public use under the GNU Free Documentation License. Its description is noted as is: *Sculpture of Thomas Aquinas, 17th century, at Slovenské národné múzeum, Bratislava, Slovakia.*

All other photographs used in this manuscript were taken and are copyrighted by the author.

Universal Life Strings, LLC
P. O. Box 58594
Houston, TX 77258
www.UniversalLifeStrings.com

Book Production Team
www.BookConnectionOnline.com
Rita Mills — Project Coordinator, Book Packager
Cover Design — Vicki Mark
Editors — Peggy Sue Skipper & Shirin Wright

This book is dedicated to

Mark Allen Wexford

and

Evangeline Marie Stone

To be Wed
On

Saturday, August 22, 2048

At
St. Paul's Bloor Street

Toronto, Canada

Table of Contents

Introduction   9
Chapter I — Growing Up — The Gift in a Song 23
Chapter II — A Moment in Time with Russell 54
Chapter III — Tragedy Strikes, But *He is Still Here* 69
Chapter IV — Spiritual Scavenger Hunts Reveal a Future Life 110
Chapter V — A New Year, Another Adventure … in Canada 141
Chapter VI — Past Lives — Our Irish History Comes Alive 170
Chapter VII — Cords! Our Link to Each Other and to Our Universe 206
Chapter VIII — Do You Have *Horizon Wireless* on Your Side? 234
Chapter IX — The Journey's End 253

Epilogue 288
Author's Letter. 294
Acknowledgments 297
For Mark and Eva — A "Clue" 300
End Notes 301
Bibliography 303
About the Author. 306
Index 307

Death may be the greatest of all human blessings. To fear death, my friends, is only to think ourselves wise, without being wise; for it is to think that we know what we do not know. For anything that men can tell, death may be the greatest good that can happen to them; but they fear it as if they knew quite well that it was the greatest of evils. And what is this but that shameful ignorance of thinking that we know what we do not know?
　　　　—**Socrates,** Classic Greek Philosopher
　　　　(c. 469 BC to 399 BC)

Some people would say that because we don't know, it can't be. I would say that because we don't know, we don't know.
　　　　—**Charles H. Townes,** Physicist & Nobel
　　　　Laureate, University of California, Berkeley
　　　　(1915-　)

Introduction

I t's interesting to note that two of the world's most renowned, intuitive, and intellectual thinkers of the past and of today, separated by over 2300 years, both agree...we simply don't know what we don't know. And if this is true, as with all science throughout history, does it not then leave room for the unknowable, unexpected, and unexplored to become that which we do know, expect, and explore?

Physicist Charles H. Townes, who designed radar bombing systems during WWII, says the *"laws of physics are very special, and the creation of human life is really quite striking. One has to believe that either it was planned or it was a fantastically improbable accident."* Townes goes on to say that science is exploration and the fundamental nature of exploration is that we don't know what's there... *"We can guess and hope and aim to find certain things, but we have to expect certain surprises."* He further states in an interview with Scott Carrier for *Esquire* magazine in 2001, *"We all know Columbus failed in his search to find India, but instead found the Americas."* At that time, he said, it might have been perceived as a failure but, of course, we all know that it wasn't. Townes says *"a revelation and an idea are essentially the same thing; for religion, it's a revelation, for science, it's just an idea, but both are one in the same."*

This book, *Love Promised: A Future Life Revealed,* is for the open-minded. Any book that is published, of course, is open to public scrutiny and that too is welcomed and, moreover, encouraged. I've always felt that healthy skepticism is good; however, it may be difficult to truly critique any material unless one has thoroughly explored and researched the subject at hand or had the same experience. Furthermore, I don't consider myself to be an expert on the subjects that will be presented, but only wish to share some insight into personal experiences with regard to these topics. Then I will share the information and knowledge that has been revealed, which has the potential to someday open the doors to the very real possibility that reincarnation is not just a theory. This idea is being speculated on more every day in Western society and the numbers of those who believe in the concept have jumped considerably.

The concepts of *reincarnation* and *spirit communication* are the main subjects of this book, which is being written primarily for two reasons. First, so that the material could be officially documented and put into a time capsule to be opened mid-year 2067; and second, to help anyone else who has had similar experiences and might be more at peace and even somewhat enlightened by reading the material.

The above terms are absolutely intuitive to most metaphysical students, but to others, some explanation might be necessary since one's basis of knowledge could be very different from another's. I will attempt to offer these concepts at a very elementary level. Webster's refers to the word *spirit* as "an animating or vital principle held to give life to physical organisms." The communication mechanism to which I am referring is *psychic* communication. Much like we accept that radio waves transmit signals from one location to another or from a sender to a receiver, a psychic wave, if you will, is the link that allows thoughts to be transmitted across space and time or, one might even say, outside of space and time as we know it. According to Webster's, one who is considered psychic is "a person apparently sensitive to nonphysical forces" and it's my guess the word *apparently* has to be used since it is not proven according to popular belief nor, thus far, by scientific means. And, of course, people are still trying to prove that they love each other too, right? The lyrics to a beautiful song by Allison Kraus stated it very clearly when talking about love:

> Old Mr. Webster could never define
> What's being said between your heart and mine
> You say it best when you say nothing at all.

Without a doubt, one can show or vocalize how much they love another. But the communication or *knowing* is not really something that can be proven, at least not on a scientific level. Maybe it's supposed to be that way with psychic communication. Words sometimes do just get in the way. I'll never forget hearing for the first time the well-known psychic Sonia Choquette, who said, "We are all psychic, though 90% of us are muted." What a simple but extraordinary statement, I thought. Hasn't science also told us that we use only one-tenth of our brain's capacity? So quite possibly we *are* muted, I thought—quite a few of us, which opens a whole new world for the potential that mankind could achieve.

I do believe we are a trifold being—i. e., body, mind, and soul—and as a tool, we can become a better receiver. To look at it another way, have you ever tried to tune in to a particular radio station and either the signal was too weak or there was nothing but static interference? Well, I look at the majority of humanity, including myself, as not having always taken care of the greatest gifts bestowed us, namely the body, mind, and soul. We all have moments or periods of time where we eat right, think positively, and meditate or pray, but do we do all these things on a consistent basis and for any length of time? Let's face it, we are creatures of habit and victims of victims and it can literally take years, decades, perhaps generations, for people or even cultures to drastically change. Possibly our receivers or physical antennas are not capable of getting the signal or message these days due to our own static interference or weak receivers. Perhaps Neale Donald Walsch, author of the *New York Times* best-seller series of books, *Conversations with God*, is correct in saying that God didn't stop speaking to us 1000 years ago; rather, we just stopped listening…and perchance, did we over the years inadvertently render ourselves incapable of listening? As a society, I feel the majority are way out of tune. But this can be changed and, furthermore, is changing.

With regard to the term *reincarnation,* we know this belief is quite accepted in Eastern philosophies. However, in most Western ones, the concept is still relatively new. The religion and philosophy that were brought over to the New World many years ago were the traditional ones of Western Europe, primarily the Catholic and Protestant religions. Therefore, any thought not accepted by these two religious authorities was at one time considered heresy and, even today, the concept of reincarnation is not accepted by the leaders and devout members of these organizations. On the other hand, reincarnation is a widely accepted belief among some very well-known Eastern religions, especially Hinduism and Buddhism. I've come to believe from casual study that, many years ago, those in England, as opposed to those in India, thought if they conveyed to their people that they had more than one chance to get it right, they wouldn't try hard enough. Whether through inspiration, protection, or simply disagreement over what some may have considered a fact, it is thought the subject of reincarnation was removed from the Bible, some believe in the early 1500s. Regardless, the knowledge that has been imparted to most of the generations in North America did not include the concept of reincarnation. Moreover, as with any religion, one is told *what* to think, not *how* to think. Is it not, therefore, a fair statement to say that our philosophical and religious beliefs up to now were possibly narrowed due to the limited knowledge that we have been exposed to in our studies? I think that they are and in order to really search for the truth, one must at least consider all sources of knowledge in order to form an *intelligent* belief.

A good foundation or starting point of understanding what a word means is necessary to convey the point being made to another. Many years ago, while studying a wonderful philosophy of life called Concept Therapy (concept meaning "ideas" and therapy meaning "working with") written by Dr. Thurman Fleet in the 1940s and '50s, I learned that all thoughts can be placed on your own triangle of knowledge. Furthermore, I learned we can take all knowledge, tossing any one concept into our fact corner, our theory corner, or our fantasy corner and, basically, the truth is not the same for all. Moreover, Fleet proposed that in reality there are many, many theories, and very few facts. A very simple analogy was provided in his philosophy. If a man were to travel to Egypt from the United States to see, touch, feel, and smell the Pyramids of Giza built thousands of years ago by the Egyptians, he would be able to say beyond a reasonable doubt, the Pyramids are indeed a *fact* to him. If this same man comes home to tell his sister, who has never been to Egypt, about the Pyramids, describing his own experience, this knowledge to his sister would then be only a *theory* and possibly one she believes in, since she knows that her brother would have no reason to lie about such a thing. Now, if the sister tells a friend of hers who has never heard about or seen pictures of the Pyramids and doesn't believe that such magnificent structures could have been built years ago with the technology existing in that day, this knowledge might only be a *fantasy* to the friend. So, here we have an example of an idea that is a fact to one, theory to another, and yet a total fantasy to someone else.

Therefore, each day we are either consciously or subconsciously accepting or rejecting ideas based upon the criteria that our mind has accumulated up to that point. And often, what we consider to be a fact is, rather, a belief based on someone else's unfounded knowledge. With the idea of "death," it would seem a fact which no one can deny, that our physical body at some point comes to an unexpected halt, can no longer sustain an illness, or just ages and decomposes. In other words, it just ceases to exist and what happens to the soul that inhabited the body is still being theorized by both science and theology. True, the ego of a human doesn't want to think of oneself as not existing anymore, whether we want to admit it or not. Even a lesser-evolved animal operating on instinct alone has a fight-or-flight reaction mechanism to protect itself from demise. Aside from the ego mind-set, it is my firm belief that we do in fact have a soul, and this is not merely to avoid thinking of myself being non-existent someday. As far as our understanding of death, I think Dr. Deepak Chopra says it best in his book *Life After Death: The Burden of Proof* when he states "our fault is not that we fear death, but that we don't respect it as a miracle."

As these quotes indicate, the concept of death is a mystery and something yet to be fully understood by the conscious mind of man. There are many, many theories, but to this day, scientifically we still don't know. And quite possibly, *scientifically*, we may not know for some time, since science today uses analyses based upon the five physical senses. However, there is a common thread of belief among most, if not all of the world's religions and philosophers, and that is "we don't die." The Christian Bible tells us:

> Behold, I tell you a mystery; we shall not all sleep [die], but we shall all be changed, in a moment, in the twinkling of an eye, at the last trumpet; for the trumpet will sound, and the dead will be raised imperishable, and we shall be changed.
> —*1 Corinthians 15:3*

Though the conception of Jesus was immaculate, as most Christians believe, he was a soul who possessed a human body that was released when the time came. Also, if you are a Christian and you believe in his resurrection, then did he not appear to humanity and show us that when we shed this physical body, we do *not*, in fact, die? Yet, for most Christians, death is still looked upon with fear and as somewhat of an ending unto itself and, therefore, for most it is an uncomfortable topic of discussion.

The Buddhist faith, as a different example, focuses more on trying to understand exactly what death is; only after understanding death can one know *how to live*. Oddly enough, I had this thought myself long before learning what I know about the Buddhist way of life. From what I understand, the Buddhist faith considers life to be impermanent; therefore, one is always in a state of becoming. Everything mental and physical is transitory and changing, so death as we understand it today cannot be.

> The soul that exists in the body of everyone cannot be slaughtered, therefore you need not have to lament over the death of any living being.
> —*The Bhagavad-Gita, The Yoga of Knowledge, Part 1*

To a Buddhist, all life is an infinite process and death is just a part of that process, therefore, one cannot exist or be understood without the other. Furthermore, this belief and also the Hindu faith teach that a soul can exist on many levels or planes of consciousness. And depending on how one lives his or her life, it may be necessary to come back to this physical existence and in a different physical body to live all over again, under different circumstances.

> Just as the embodied soul passes from childhood to youth to old
> age, it also passes from one body to another. The undaunted person
> therefore is not deluded.
> —*The Bhagavad-Gita, The Yoga of Knowledge, Part 1*

So, exactly what is this *transition* we call death if you believe, as I do, that we have a soul which, like energy, can never be destroyed? And if we don't die, is it possible that we can communicate with those who are considered dead, or, using the now popular term, crossed over? Though the concept has been around for centuries, it is still considered by some to be heresy or even "spiritism," as referred to by those in the Bible who feared and condemned it. Yet, the concept *is* becoming more widely accepted by many who are well respected in their own field of study, not to mention being the subject of two well-known television programs, *Ghost Whisperer* and *The Medium,* and many TV specials and documentaries.

Also, do we really come back? As one looks out into the world it becomes apparent that life is seemingly *not fair* to all. Why is it that in our society today we find a 10-year-old girl who has a mother addicted to cocaine, when you can also look out into the world and find another 10-year-old girl playing a violin at Carnegie Hall as masterfully as any adult could ever hope to? I watched this young girl on PBS one night and was totally amazed. Have you ever made this comparison or asked yourself why or how this can be? Do we simply continue to toss off the thought that we just don't know everything there is to know in God's world or the cosmos and leave it at that?

Most of my professional career has involved working as a NASA contractor, an exciting industry to say the least, and considered by most to be a very technical and scientific one. Though not an engineer, having received a Bachelor of Science degree, I was able to advance in technical support positions that required a general understanding of the aerospace engineering field. In doing so, some unique, fun, challenging, and gratifying opportunities opened. So over the past 22-plus years primarily working in Mission Operations Directorate for both the Space Shuttle and International

Space Station (ISS) Programs, my desire to know more about the unknown and about outer space has thrived in the leading-edge technology we have used to get there.

With the refurbishment of the Hubble Space Telescope (HST), its lens can now see 70 times more than it could see before. Hundreds of astronomers around the world are now lined up to use the space telescope, i.e., point it in the direction they want. We may be more surprised than Columbus was, since we are now able to look out at our universe in a way we've never been able to do. Also, the Goddard Space Flight Center plans to top Hubble with yet another space telescope called the James Webb Space Telescope (JWST) or Webb that will look out into the world only through the eyes of an infrared camera.

Additionally, scientific research is being done worldwide to determine the origins of our universe and understand its structure. NASA is in the process of designing and building a space-based telescope for the JDEM or Joint Dark Energy Mission, where they will try to unravel the mystery of supposedly empty space. Scientists now believe approximately 95% of our universe consists of dark matter and dark energy. Basically, it is called "dark" in the vastness of space because we can't see it with the human eye and we don't yet know what it is, though scientists are speculating that dark energy may be causing our universe to expand. It is also hoped that we may begin to understand more about these numerous not-so-stagnant black holes which light cannot escape, as observed.

Further, we are beginning some new, innovative research with what is now called NASA's Physics of the Cosmos Program, formerly called Beyond Einstein. Launched in 2011, the Alpha Magnetic Spectrometer (AMS) was deployed to the ISS on one of the last space shuttle missions. The AMS will stay on this orbiting laboratory more than 200 miles above Earth for its duration, hoped at a minimum to be until 2020. This international project, sponsored by the U. S. Department of Energy, includes a team of scientists, physicists, and engineers from 60 institutes in 16 countries. Together these experts will research particle physics in space, hoping to learn more about dark matter and antimatter and to measure cosmic radiation that may someday help enable future interplanetary manned spaceflight.

There is also the Supercollider in Geneva, Switzerland, at CERN, the European Organization for Nuclear Research, where A Large Ion (Hadron) Collider Experiment or ALICE, a huge atom smasher, is being used by particle and theoretical physicists to study particle physics. These experiments with subatomic particles subjected to high-energy acceleration may someday reveal the most fundamental particle of our universe, which has been called "the God particle." Scientists are now claiming that after the Big Bang (if you believe this is how our universe began) this first matter (antimatter) is believed to have traveled faster than 186,000 miles per second, or what we know as the speed of light. Furthermore, there are ongoing studies by physicists at Harvard University to try to slow down the speed of light using laser technology and freezing temperatures. Amazing new scientific encounters are definitely on the horizon. Additionally, I feel our thoughts about science and theology will slowly start to coincide with ongoing research and findings in quantum physics and the analyses of quantum mechanics, or how things may work, in this subatomic world.

I have to admit, though, my love of outer space comes second to my yearning to know more about our *inner space*. It was the afterlife that became a passion for me at a very young age...an inner search to understand personal experiences that I later found were classified as paranormal. And growing up in the 1960s and 70s in the small town of Fulton, Kentucky, answers were not easily found, even though I sat outside at night by myself just staring at the stars, hoping for an answer. This yearning to know more led me down many paths in search of the truth. And though studying and finding many satisfying ones, I never considered myself an expert in this area. However, I don't think spirit communication has been fully understood in past decades or possibly even centuries; basically, what we don't understand, many times we fear. Furthermore, much of what we fear, we totally reject on some level of thinking. Possibly there were people living in biblical times who deeply feared the unknown and, because of that, warned us in the Bible that such things should be avoided at all costs. However, it was *quite accepted* in the Bible that prophets were spoken to by God, his angels, and even Jesus once he left the Earthly plane of existence.

Now, even among those who may be prone to believe it is possible to communicate with someone in spirit, there may be some who feel we still don't fully understand the process. This may be true, but it doesn't negate the fact that a good number of people believe it happens. And, are there not just too many synchronicities and supposed coincidences not to pay more attention to what could be happening, and then explore, so we *can* know and understand?

It also stands to reason that one doesn't have to fully understand the source of all being to recognize and appreciate the beauty of Earth's creations that are far beyond man's ability to create. This omnipotent power has been given many names, e.g., God, Allah, Buddha, Krishna, and is sometimes even referred to as Spirit, or simply X. From here on, I will refer to our source of being as God, since this term is the most familiar. Wouldn't God want us to comprehend the source of all being so we could understand ourselves more? As the Bible (King James Version) tells us in Proverbs 4:7 "Wisdom is the principal thing; therefore, get wisdom; and with all thy getting, get understanding." I can still hear the echo of those words from my father. So, if spirit communication were not possible or, if possible, should be avoided, then how or why would biblical prophets or angels have spoken with us in the far distant past in order to impart their knowledge or prophecy that is also written in the Bible? Should we not have listened to them then? Should we then not believe these stories in the Bible? *Could there possibly be prophets among us today who are just not yet acknowledged as prophets?*

It is also implied that the finite mind of man will never be able to understand the infinite. However, as we begin to comprehend just how much more we are than our physical bodies, we recognize it is most likely our superconscious mind, the one we are still trying to understand today, which *is* connected to "all that is." On this other level, perhaps it really is possible to know the answers to those age-old questions such as… *Who are we? Why are we here? And what is life really all about when the unexplainable happens?*

These questions will definitely come to mind for anyone who has had what is classified as a true paranormal experience. And for those who do experience the unexplainable, they are usually their own worst skeptic and will not be satisfied with just any answer. Furthermore, they might even spend their entire life searching for answers and keep silent about their experiences for fear of being viewed as different, odd, or even crazy. Anyone going through life with blinders will look only for ways to convince themselves of what they believe to be true and may try to convince others of the same. However, when one knows in their heart that something is true, it is no longer a belief, nor is there any desire to *convince* anyone else of their truth. It is one thing to share knowledge and quite another to try to persuade, for truth needs no persuasion.

A real seeker will know that many possibilities exist. No idea should be discarded without careful examination and everything should be evaluated objectively. My father repeatedly used this quote: "When the student is ready, the teacher will appear." And I now know some experiences of mine, called out-of-body or OBEs, prepared me for being able to accept some later experiences in life that otherwise may not have become my truth.

It has been my belief for some time that communicating with those who exist in the *spirit world* or another plane of existence *is* possible. This belief became a truth to me when I lost someone dear to my heart in a tragic car accident, December 2005. His name was Russell Morris, and he was someone with whom I was deeply in love. Then, without warning, he was gone…*or so I thought*.

This book is primarily about our relationship before and after he "died." It will also include specific details that have been revealed to us (his father, Ron Morris, and me) about a future life Russell and I will share one day as husband and wife, father and mother, in a subsequent lifetime on Earth as Mark and Eva Wexford. We were also tasked to write a book; when we asked why, it was simply stated…*It is time for the truth to be known*. Reincarnation simply implies that as a soul, or spiritual being, we can experience many lifetimes, one after the other, in a different physical body. But on a daily basis, and on a conscious level, we are not cognizant of it. Also, for the most part, the unawareness is for good reason, as each life, it seems, is uniquely designed for specific growth patterns, fulfilling one chapter in our own book of life.

In this book, I'll share with you the path that eventually led me to Russell and the tragedy of losing him, but still having him in my life. You may also enjoy the exciting spiritual scavenger hunts we've been on with him and my father by our side in spirit. Included as well are some beautiful messages from my Spirit Guide, Thomas, who has steered me throughout this book, not to mention my life. Quantum physics will be touched on from a layman's perspective since it theorizes well this world of ether and may someday bridge the gap between science and religion. Also, I was encouraged to try to comprehend this theory even more in order to obtain a better understanding of the information being provided about the unique photographs gifted to me during an overseas trip.

In conclusion, I personally believe humanity is on the verge of some amazing new discoveries about life by continuing to explore both within and without. What I've come to know is that we *truly* have more help than most of us are utilizing or even aware of, from beautiful guides and souls not just on this side but the "other side" as well. Interesting to note is that when I shared my story with some friends, colleagues, a retired Air Force Colonel, a radio show host, an engineer, an astronaut, and an Ivy League professor, all of them told me of a significant paranormal experience of their own. Except for two who had shared theirs with a handful of people, each stated that they had never mentioned their experience to anyone else. In summation, I don't think our experiences are unique…in fact, it's my belief they are more common than most of us realize.

Love Promised: A Future Life Revealed

This journey begins with some background information about my life, provided only as a reference to show how personal experiences inspired my quest for more knowledge about the paranormal. I've tried to make the story interesting and fun with the primary goal in mind being the time capsule. When reading, do think outside the box, putting the ideas on your own triangle of knowledge. And whether fact, theory, or fantasy to you, please know these words are coming purely from my heart; they are my truth, and someday possibly yours or your grandchildren's, now that this seed has been planted.

Kent

Love Promised

A Future Life Revealed

A True Story

The Continuation of Life and Love in Spite of Tragedy

Chapter One

Growing Up—The Gift in a Song

We are more than the sum of our knowledge;
we are the products of our imagination.
—Ancient Native American Proverb

While on a family trip at the age of 11 in the 1960s, my siblings and I were each allowed to purchase a small souvenir in the gift shop of our hotel before leaving Hot Springs, Arkansas. I must have carried that dollar bill around forever, while my parents patiently waited and everyone but me was checking out. The little Indian leather pouches and dreamcatchers always caught my eye. Maybe that had something to do with being told that I was one-eighth Cherokee, who knows. Feeling a sense of urgency to find *something*, I stumbled across a small, square glass dish with orange writing painted on it. And, I was inclined to purchase it because there was something beautifully inscribed on it that touched my soul. Something inside me said, *"Buy this because you will need it someday."* Much later in life, I learned that this inscription was the "Serenity Prayer."

> God grant me the serenity to accept the things I cannot change;
> Courage to change the things I can,
> And wisdom to know the difference.

My growing-up years were some of the best of my life. I can still remember my father saying to me, "Honey, you can turn on the radio and get a message from God through music any time; just think of a number and turn to that station, then listen." And, oddly enough, during some of my most trying times, reassuring words or words of wisdom would come through on the radio station at just the right time. Words of inspiration and insight that guided my next decision, or comforting ones that helped dry a tear when I was upset and felt all alone. Listening to songs began my communication with God at a very early age, and this has continued throughout my life. Songs like "Ain't No Mountain High" by Marvin Gaye; "Get Together" by the Youngbloods; "I'll Be There" by the Jackson Five and more importantly… "Reach out" (in the darkness and I'll be there) by the Four Tops, ran through my head at nighttime on certain occasions…times that made me look at life just a little differently.

My out-of-body experiences (OBEs) started at a very young age and were frightening because I did not understand what was happening. I can remember lying in my bed with the lights out, drifting off to sleep. Then suddenly my body would begin to vibrate, very subtly but intensely, and I would gently begin to float up and away. What startled me was that I knew it was not a dream as I hovered over the body lying in my bed. When the fear set in, it would take me instantly back in my body, lying there with my eyes wide open, trying to figure out in my little mind what was happening in the darkness. After a few minutes of feeling sleepy, my eyes would close and again, the sense of drifting would start. Along with the fear, I quickly realized that jerking my body around would bring me back in an instant so this became my safety net. I can actually remember holding on tight to my pillow at night thinking this would keep me from floating away. More than once, my body seemed paralyzed yet I was awake. Terrified, I would try to scream but not a peep came out of my mouth. Fortunately, this did not happen too often. Several years later, it was comforting to learn that this paralysis is quite normal for one who experiences an OBE, according to a book called *Soul Traveler* by Albert Taylor.

When I was a young child, we used to live in a white wood-framed house and I shared a double bed with my older sister, Rebecca. The ceiling light was just a light bulb attached to a long string so I would stand on the end of the bed and jump off, hoping to catch the string and turn the light back on. Doing this, of course, would shake the bed and make a thud when my feet hit the floor, so each time my sister would awaken, asking me to turn the light back off. At times, sucking my thumb would help put me to sleep. As we grew older, our father, who was a real estate contractor, built a new house for our family. I then slept in a twin bed next to Rebecca's but she still adamantly refused, and rightfully so, to let me turn the light back on when these experiences happened. After all, she was trying to sleep. Not wanting to appear crazy, I did not tell her why the light consoled me. Some nights, my only option was to sit on the floor of our closet with this light on while reading a book to avoid the experience. Other times, I would go into my parents' bedroom and stare at them until they awoke and put me between them in bed. Or else, if they didn't awaken, I found some comfort falling asleep on the floor at the end of their bed, wrapped up with my pillow and blanket. Either way, with my parents, I mostly referred to these experiences as nightmares or "just one of those things happening again." It wasn't until we were adults that my sister told me she awoke during the middle of the night when we were teenagers and looked over at me sitting up in my bed, *and then also lying down at the same time.*

At the age of 11, I escaped the fear when spontaneously leaving my body so quickly. Flying through the air horizontally at a vast speed, feet first, was so odd and I just remember being amid clouds. But unlike the typical fear, I shared this beautiful and peaceful feeling with my parents the next morning. To their surprise, my final words were, "I'm not afraid to die." Fortunately, we were privileged to have the most loving parents one could ever have, so never do I remember them looking at me strangely or even saying anything to make me feel foolish. Even so, these types of experiences are not easily described, especially when you are afraid to speak out, so I never mentioned them even to my siblings. Typically, I was only cognizant of leaving and returning during these experiences and not so much of what happened in between. I can remember, however, thinking how nice it would be to grow up and get married someday just so I could have someone to sleep with and hold on to.

My four siblings would agree that we could not have had more fun growing up, thanks to our parents. First of all, what our father gave to us rang true to the old saying "The greatest gift a father can give his children is to love their mother." Gosh, were they ever a happy couple. Dad was a leader and Mom a follower—a perfect match. As kids, we never really knew what we had in our parents until we visited our friends. Only then did we realize that our house was not so much the norm. I can still remember coming home from college one weekend and hearing my father walk through the front door of our happy home. With a big smile on his face, he said, "Where is my bride?" Then he moseyed to the kitchen where Mom was cooking dinner and gave her a big hug and kiss. He then would work his way around to whoever was in our informal dining room to ensure each got their share of his attention, whether by telling them a joke or pretending he was punching them in the side. Dad not only had a dry sense of humor, he also looked like Rodney Dangerfield, never realizing he had said something funny. Our friends enjoyed staying over and if we were ever invited to someone else's house, we always wondered what we were missing at ours. Our parents never minded the noise, so we could play to our heart's content and even turned up our music loud, dancing away. Sometimes we danced with them. Dad and Mom loved music too and we were thrilled to hear stories of their winning a jitterbug contest before we were born. We still have a black-and-white 8mm video from 1961, now transferred to a disc, where Dad and Mom filmed us coming one by one through the doorway, dancing to the music on our new hi-fi. At the age of seven, you could make some really cool moves in cotton socks on a hardwood floor! Today, we cherish that short film more than ever. Dad loved electronics, so whether it was a stereo system, movie film recorder/projector (camcorders today), an electronic exercise bike, or the latest intercom system for our new home—you name it, we had it. And I adored listening to him on his ham radio, a love from his old Navy days. "K4UXN," he would say, "Anyone there, copy?" One night excited me so, as he was elated while talking to someone aboard the ship that recovered the Apollo capsules.

As we got older, family nights in the den were a big treat on weekends, as we huddled around the TV and fireplace to watch late-night movies. During commercials we would beg Mom to make some homemade fudge. If only there had been a pause button—she probably missed part of the movie just for us. She loved making us happy and was probably the most patient of all mothers. Like Mom, our father was generous in more ways than one, especially with affection and the words "I love you." About the only thing that would upset our parents was sibling rivalry, which, as with most families, did happen. We were disciplined with love, however, and Dad's stern hand never had to touch us because waving it in the air was all it took, along with a little eye-brow raising and some serious eye contact. Still, he could be a little harder on the boys in the family, who had a tendency to be rambunctious. But then again, we all were. I remember arguing with my sister over clothes when we were teenagers. Our discipline was sitting together at the dinner table reading a chapter on anger from one of Dad's philosophy books. Now, that is not easy to do, especially when you are mad, and the one you are mad at is the person sitting next to you. But all said and done, it helped the emotion to dissolve when you realized what you were doing…*to yourself.* Our dad was the only father I can remember who would come off the 18-hole golf course at the country club during the summertime and jump into the swimming pool with us. Our mom would scream, "They can't swim yet, Wick!" as he tossed my younger brother and

Love Promised: A Future Life Revealed

sister into the deep end of the pool, but she was not quick enough and he would just laugh and say, "Now they can!" Or, if we rode ponies on Sunday afternoon, he put us in the saddle, then slapped the pony's rear end so it would take off. During the winter when it snowed, he was a big kid himself, getting up early and building a fire in the fireplace. He then woke us up before dawn to get our snow boots on so we could all go play in the snow, many times pulling us behind the car in sleds tied one behind the other. He had fun swinging my brothers Bill and Jeff into the small ditch on the side of the road and then getting out of the car laughing. They loved it too, but our neighbors would say to Dad, "Wick, you are going to kill those kids!" And what fun coming home to the hot chocolate and marshmallows Mom had waiting for us as we sat by the fireplace thawing out our toes and fingers. Whether it was swimming, riding ponies and horses, or snow sledding, we learned quickly and with a lot of adrenalin. And this was how we learned to do everything in life.

Not long after getting my license to drive at the age of 17, I begged my father to let me drive while on a family vacation. It was fun going fast on the interstate actually doing something, not just sitting in the car for hours. As we got closer to the city of Chicago, however, I was ready to pull over and give Dad back the wheel, thinking that he would want to drive then anyway. But he said in a calm voice, "No honey, I'll just stay back here, you're doing fine." "What?" I thought to myself and then stated, "You're going to let me take this family of seven in our station wagon on what is becoming a fast and crowded road?" With a laugh, he replied, "Sure, you have to learn sometime. Just keep us headed north and look for signs to Milwaukee." Getting nervous now, I kept asking the same question for a few miles and finally thought to myself, "He is serious!" Very soon, the roads were crowded, ramps were ahead, and there was no time to think about pulling over. Though stressful, it was a real accomplishment for me and from then on, driving through large cities was more fun than driving between the cities. Fortunately, I realize now that with all my fun and challenging experiences growing up, the faith and confidence our father placed in us truly gave us more faith in ourselves.

During our adolescent years, Dad always had words of wisdom and wanted to share what he had learned. As a seeker of truth, he found a book by Louise Hay entitled *You Can Heal Your Life*. No longer could we come home from school and complain about having a sore throat. Or else, he would ask us, "Who were you mad at today?" or "What did you want to say but didn't?" so you'd best be prepared to answer those questions.

Dad would say, "It's okay to make mistakes, you just have to learn from them." As an example of just how compassionate he could be when you did make a mistake—well, while driving to school one morning I turned the corner too sharply and hit a parked car. How could this have happened? Oh, that's right, looking the other way while waving to a friend in her car, duh. How embarrassing to have this happen when you are a high school senior and it's your last day in school. My dad happened to be the last one to show up at the scene of the accident, after the police and what seemed to be a dozen other people were there. This was my first car accident in our small town and I was pretty shaken up to say the least, but fortunately uninjured. Dad proceeded to get out of his car, never looking at mine or the one I'd hit. He obviously could see I looked physically okay but more than that, he was concerned. He quickly moved through the small crowd after shaking a couple of hands to say thank you, and as he got closer to me he said, "Honey, are you okay?" Shaking, quivering, and in a voice about ready to break down, I said, "Yeeeaaahhh." He then put his arms tightly around me, kissed me on the forehead and with a smile, said, "Well, then, that's all that matters, isn't it? So let's go home." And not once did he mention that car accident again, knowing quite well my lesson was already learned. That experience set the tone for how I would one day deal with my own children's mistakes.

Dad and Mom were very forward thinkers and like many middle-class families in a small town during the 1960s, we belonged to a local church in Fulton, Kentucky. Ours was the Presbyterian Church but we often visited our other grandmother at the Baptist Church, less than a block away. However, I remember Dad speaking to us about one of the previous ministers in this Presbyterian Church, who had been killed. It had left my father thinking about how God would let something like this happen. Here was a great young preacher with a beautiful young wife and two small children, devoting himself to sharing God's word. Something just didn't seem right. So troubling was this event to our father that it spurred him to look even further beyond organized religion for answers that he had most likely wondered about for a long time. He knew these were not answers found just by listening or reading through scripture and singing hymns a couple of hours each week. Earlier, his thirst for knowledge had led him to request literature from the Rosicrucians Order in California and to become a local Knight Templar in 1952 like his own father, by then deceased, who had been a Master Mason.

Two of my father's favorite books were *The Power of Positive Thinking* by Norman Vincent Peale and the *Handbook to Higher Consciousness* by

Ken Keyes, Jr. I still cherish the note Mom wrote when giving them to us as Christmas gifts. *"Hope you enjoy this as much as we have if you are inclined to read it. It's not the destination but the journey of life that is so important."* Another favorite author of theirs was Emmet Fox, an electrical engineer by trade who became a popular spiritual leader in the early twentieth century. In the United States, he was one of the first to introduce the theory of reincarnation to the West.

Concept Therapy (CT)

A philosophy of life called CT, which my father stumbled upon and wanted our whole family to study, was not meant to replace our religion but to enhance it. This self-help philosophy teaches historical facts regarding science and religion, and also new ideas, presenting many theories from all the different religions in the world. I was never asked to accept any idea on blind faith, but to evaluate it, study it, and discover the truth for myself. The founder, Dr. Thurman Fleet, taught certain known universal laws, outlining good principles to live by based on what we know works and what doesn't. The CT philosophy was the first we knew that taught a correlation of science and theology all in the same course, presenting the thought that, in essence, these two main authorities in our world may not disagree with each other. Science doesn't deny the existence of God; it merely states that such cannot be proven by scientific means. The world is made up of energy, and religion teaches that God is everywhere. So Fleet thought this omnipotent power must be in each and every one of those electrons, protons, and neutrons. Not to advocate evolution of the species, but truthfully, he said, would it be any less glory to God if man descended from the ape, since before man, this was God's highest creation? What we do know is that, above all other beautiful creatures, humans were given the power of reason, the ability to reflect on self. Therefore, what we should study is not the evolution of man, but the evolution of consciousness.

At the age of 16 in the 1960s, these thoughts satisfied my thirst for knowledge beyond anything else I had ever heard. In the 1970s, though each of us paid for our own college education, our father paid for all our courses of study in CT, the knowledge of which we still use in our lives today. I learned more in these classes about life than while obtaining my college degree. Furthermore, it provided an ideal foundation for all the other knowledge I acquired later in life. As teenagers, we went to church less often during this time, and there were rumors in our small town that our father had taken his children out of the church. Some even ventured to say that we had joined a cult. When Dad organized a CT class, a derogatory remark was made on the local radio station about how someone was brought into town to talk about God outside the church. My father knew it was him they were talking about. It wasn't unlike small-town folk to be judgmental, particularly if something didn't fit into the mold of the all-American, 1960s "Leave it to Beaver" family. In my youthful mind, I wondered about the biblical principle taught in our church, "Judge not, lest ye be judged." My mind no doubt questioned their comments and actions as being contradictory to what they professed to believe. However, it really never bothered my father too much, or any of us for that matter. We were following our hearts, speaking our truth, and "walking our walk" or doing our best to adhere to our own principles. As Dr. Wayne Dyer, another great author of self-help books and spirituality today, also says, we must be independent of the "good" judgment of others. And, that we were.

During this Age of Aquarius in the '60s, '70s and even early '80s, we were growing up in more ways than one, having so much fun learning together as a family. In a course called Psychiatric Principles, we were being educated on how the mind operates, studying all the different human emotions. The power of suggestion was introduced and we learned how it plays an integral role in one's life. Known scientific laws were taught, as well as how those basic electrons, protons, and neutrons relate to one another and evolved throughout the different stages or phases of creation—electronic, mineral and chemical, vegetable, animal, and human. Dr. Fleet's laws of the body, mind, and soul were like life's little handbook, with detailed chapters on subjects like love, hate, and how they each affect the body. These laws also included knowledge of how to eat healthy and, in general, what it means to *Know Thyself*, the very motto of CT, based upon the ancient precept of Socrates. Not only that, we were learning about all the religions in the world in a course called Basic Principles. It fascinated me to hear what each culture, not just the one in which I lived, believed in. Dr. Fleet took a single thread of basic truths from all religions, and known science too, and wove his philosophy around those ideas and how they directly affect man in the evolution of consciousness. The information Dr. Fleet was given in his illumination put him on a path of research that eventually helped to deliver his perspective of understanding God's world as a whole. His philosophy, then and today, teaches simple and practical ways to live life to the fullest.

Love Promised: A Future Life Revealed

What I learned was the importance of positive thinking, how it impacted our lives, and how it attracts what we want into our life. We were not just told "Do unto others as you would have them do unto you" but we were also taught *how* to do this, as life is a "do-it-yourself" proposition. If one ever began to put Dr. Fleet on a pedestal by asking a profound question about life, he would simply tell them, "I don't know," wanting them to dig deeper and figure out the truth for themselves, for this is truly how we not only learn, but also understand. And in his mind, if it could not be understood, it most definitely would not be practiced.

Therefore, during this time, as a teenager reading scripture and not fully understanding it, my desire to attend two hours of a formal religious Sunday school class and church service was becoming less, yet I couldn't wait to hear 26 hours of CT instruction, all in one weekend. You know there had to be some fun interaction for a 16-year-old to sacrifice her Saturday nights in a classroom setting, listening to a speaker! My first class was taught by a fun-loving, older gentleman, Reverend E. L. Crump. He was an electrical engineer for 20 years, then went on to become a Methodist minister for 20 years before teaching CT another 20 years.

Fortunately, at this time in my life, I was actually being saturated with information for which my soul was yearning…some real practical data based on God's principles. This knowledge was directly applicable to my life at any given moment to help me understand more about human nature, so that any crisis could be dealt with. As a teenager, it was a good time in life to be armed with such tools. I learned to be responsible for my actions, for the consequences were truly up to me; if things were not going right in my life, looking in the mirror was on the agenda. Early on, and long before the concept became ever so popular, we were taught the Law of Attraction. But how wonderful that Jerry and Ester Hicks, along with Abraham and many others, have expanded on the concept and have made it more widespread today. Plus, with the scientific advancement of what we know about the subatomic world, it appears there is now a new age of enlightenment upon us.

Regarding CT, one can get continuing education credits through the state of Texas for these classes through their institution based in San Antonio. I'm grateful to Dr. Fleet and all the wonderful CT teachers. Blessed I was with parents who were soul-searchers and progressive thinkers in their day, not afraid to stand up for what they believed in. And though we were not in a church setting while learning, did not Jesus say, where two or more are gathered in my name, there I am also?

OBEs and My First Psychic Reading

It is sown a natural body; it is raised a spiritual body.
There is a natural body and there is a spiritual body.
—1 Corinthians 15:44

As much as I valued the CT philosophy, it only touched on subjects such as clairvoyance, reincarnation, and OBEs. CT was written to assist the layman on how to live a better life and it was not meant to delve into these more controversial topics 40 years ago. Also, how to live one's life in a positive, practical way was truly the most important concept to learn. The philosophy was all about the health of the body, mind, and soul; I could inspire you, *or bore you*, with many stories of how this philosophy helped me to deal with life's challenges. But for some who have had paranormal experiences, the yearning for even more answers was still there. I can still recall the barely hidden surprise of my high school English teacher when I chose the subject of extra-sensory perception, or ESP, for my Senior English paper in 1972. I did not profess to her my hopes of researching and finding more information on the paranormal, nor did she ask why this subject had been chosen. With a very inquisitive look, Mrs. Bennett only asked if I was sure this was what I wanted to write about. "Yes" was my answer, with no explanation.

When I was 18 years of age, my father drove me to the outskirts of Memphis, TN, to see a psychic, a sweet lady who lived in a modest brick home. Sadly, Dad told me she moved to the country because she had been shunned by society for doing what she did, yet the police would often come to her for help in solving murder cases. As we walked in, I noticed a card table set up in her living room with a deck of cards on top, which reminded me of my mom's bridge club. A second glance, however, let me know it was not a normal deck of playing cards. This was my first time to see Tarot cards which, I later learned, were made especially for some psychics, who used them to predict someone's future. For privacy, my dad left the room when the psychic asked me to sit across from her at the table. I was very excited that my first real psychic reading was about to begin. And though the session was not recorded, I do remember five specific predictions that were supposed to occur in my life. Amazingly, three have.

The psychic first stated that traveling over water to distant lands was in my near future. I was surprised to hear this as my family had traveled before—we had even taken a month-long road trip to California—but not by plane and certainly never overseas. So, though I really hoped it would happen, such a trip seemed very doubtful. Almost one year later, in 1973, my older brother, Bill, joined the Navy and after boot camp was assigned to an American naval station in Morocco. While there, he would meet his future wife, the daughter of a naval officer, and my parents excitedly flew over for the wedding. The very next year, working through a difficult relationship, I needed space to regroup and dropped out of college for a semester to visit my big brother, whom I dearly missed, for a month. Making this trip required Dad's permission and although he finally agreed, he wouldn't let me travel alone since I had never flown before. That was just the excuse Mom needed to go see her first grandbaby. Very soon my beautiful palomino was sold for a round-trip airline ticket to Africa. Mom and I were thrilled to be traveling to Casablanca via Lisbon, Portugal, to see my big brother, his wife, and my new nephew. In my wonderment as we crossed the ocean that night, I recalled what the psychic had told me and indeed, it was a surreal moment.

The second thing the psychic told me was that one day I would marry someone with blond hair. "Are you sure?" I asked her, as my dream was to marry my high school sweetheart, a brunet. "Yes, I'm sure, sorry if that is not what you wanted to hear but I see one who is blond," she said. It wouldn't be until after my engagement in 1975 when the realization hit me that I had fallen in love with a blond-headed man, much to my amazement.

The third prediction given was that a place where I would be living one day would catch on fire due to faulty wiring. It would, however, be many years before this happened. In 2004, when a traffic cop prevented me from getting to my condominium because two of the buildings next to mine were on fire, that prediction immediately came to mind. Fortunately, the fire was extinguished before it reached my building. A barbeque grill burning on a patio was thought to be the cause until a newspaper article reported a statement from an investigation that attributed the fire to faulty wiring.

College life in the '70s was enjoyable and my OBEs had all but ceased on a conscious level as I became more involved in school, sorority life, and relationships. And was I ever glad that they had when convincing myself that seeing *The Exorcist* one summer at the movie theater with my sister and a friend would not bother me because of my age. Wrong! The three of us shared a room at a Kentucky State Resort Park where we worked as lifeguards. That pitch-dark night I hardly slept a wink and fortunately had no OBE. Though I had always felt protected, the unknown can sometimes leave you in doubt when you don't fully understand your own experience of being out of the body, especially if you are watching a movie that involves the possession of one's body, and a grotesque one at that. To the others, the storyline was funny but it was more than frightening to me, and I was not able to admit why. A few years before, I had memorized "The Desiderata," a piece of prose, which included the words, "do not distress yourself with dark imaginings" to comfort me at times like this. In the 1920s, Max Ehrmann wrote:

> Go placidly amid the noise and the haste, and remember what peace there may be in silence. As far as possible, without surrender, be on good terms with all persons.

> Speak your truth quietly and clearly; and listen to others, even to the dull and the ignorant; they too have their story. Avoid loud and aggressive persons; for they are vexations to the spirit. If you compare yourself with others, you may become vain or bitter, for always there will be greater and lesser persons than yourself.

> Enjoy your achievements as well as your plans. Keep interested in your own career, however humble; it is a real possession in the changing fortunes of time. Exercise caution in your business affairs, for the world is full of trickery.

> But let this not blind you to what virtue there is; many persons strive for high ideals, and everywhere life is full of heroism. Be yourself. Especially do not feign affection. Neither be cynical about love, for in the face of all aridity and disenchantment, it is as perennial as the grass.

> Take kindly the counsel of the years, gracefully surrendering the things of youth. Nurture strength of spirit to shield you in sudden misfortune. But do not distress yourself with dark imaginings. Many fears are born of fatigue and loneliness.

> Beyond a wholesome discipline, be gentle with yourself. You are a child of the universe, no less than the trees and the stars; you have a right to be here. And whether or not it is clear to you, no doubt the universe is unfolding as it should. Therefore be at peace with God, whatever you conceive Him to be.

And whatever your labors and aspirations, in the noisy confusion of life, keep peace in your soul. With all its sham, drudgery, and broken dreams, it is still a beautiful world. Be careful (or cheerful). Strive to be happy.

Another time I was grateful to have memorized these words was when the headlights on my little navy blue '69 Volkswagen went out one snowy winter night while I was driving alone on a two-lane country road halfway through my 36-mile trek home. On the snow-covered highway, it was extremely difficult, if not impossible, to see the yellow line on the outside edge where fairly deep ditches lay. Anxiety set in as I began to feel trapped. Fortunately, there were not many travelers to collide with, but I wondered if my car would be seen if I landed in a ditch and needed help. Of course, cell phones were unheard of in those days. It would not benefit me to turn around and go back to my dorm and there was no place to stop and pull over. Nor did it look like the snow was going to subside. I remember clutching the steering wheel and straining to see just by the moonlight on the white snow, while my windshield wipers swooshed away the large, falling flakes. My heart now starting to pound, I prayed to stay on the road. Then I remembered *The Desiderata* which calmed me down as I recited it out loud. Suddenly, out of nowhere, there seemed to be the taillights of a car in front of me. I didn't know where this car came from or how it happened that it traveled the same route as I did for the next 15 miles to within a block of my house, where street lights helped the rest of the way. I had to drive slowly but, thankfully, so did the car in front of me. Although it was still a challenge to drive, those taillights were the only thing that guided me home. If only I could have let this person know my appreciation for what they did, even if they were not aware of it. Or was that really a car in front of me after all? The taillights were the only thing visible and when finally approaching street lights, the car was gone. How could they have turned so quickly in that snow, when I never took my eyes off the road in front of me? It amazed me at first while turning off the highway, and then all I could think about was how good it felt to be home. Could it have been divine intervention? Little miracles do happen for us every day, and most often when we are unaware of what is happening.

Life Continues, with a Few Challenges

It was also during the mid-seventies that our family began to spread out a little more, with my siblings and me getting married and establishing lives of our own. Soon, we would be saying goodbye to our grandmother, whom we called Perky. I can vividly remember sitting and talking to her when she was in bed and very ill, and not expected to live much longer. Surprisingly, she proceeded to tell me that my family would end up moving to Texas. At the time, that seemed very unrealistic so when I mentioned it to my parents, they assumed she was "talking out of her head," as the phrase went. Ten years later my parents would semi-retire just south of Houston and three of the five children, including me, would eventually follow over the next five years to make Clear Lake City our home.

Before moving to Texas, however, I would spend several years making a home for my own little family in two other small towns, one of which was where my children were born. The awareness of my OBEs was still rare during the early years of my marriage, but another miracle would happen when delivering my third and last child. When I was almost one month overdue, the gynecologists decided to induce labor. After several hours, however, they discovered the umbilical cord was wrapped twice around the neck of the baby, which meant the oxygen was cut off with each contraction. For fear I would panic, they didn't tell me this right away. All I knew was that everyone in the delivery room started moving around very hurriedly while more medical assistants and another doctor showed up. Metal banging against metal was all I heard except for my doctor telling me from across the room not to push, and that he was getting ready to perform an emergency cesarean section. My baby's head was down into the birth canal as far as it could go and I had stopped dilating at 7.5 centimeters. Natural deliveries don't occur until one is fully dilated at 10.

Later, I learned the doctor had rushed out to speak with my husband and my parents in the waiting room. The panicked look on his face was obvious as he ripped off his mask but they were not prepared for what he said. "We are in an emergency situation and I have to ask, which one do you want me to save, the mother or the child, if I have to make that decision?" Before my husband could breathe a word, my father yelled, "You save my daughter!" Back in the delivery room, I was sweating profusely and in a lot of pain, now both physically and mentally, and the urge to push was getting much stronger. Telling my doctor I wanted to deliver naturally seemed to upset him as he shouted at me, "Do *not* push." Needless to say, I knew something was wrong and began to feel scared. As my head slowly turned from the doctor, all of a sudden I saw a sweet older nurse, surprisingly calm, standing next to me. With a smile on her face and staring straight into my eyes, she picked up my hand ever so softly and leaned over, whispering

"Push." Two things immediately puzzled me: first, the expression on her face indicated she was oblivious to what was going on as everyone else was in severe panic mode, including me. Second, how can she tell me to push, probably risking her job, when the doctor had clearly screamed so everyone in the room could hear him? Now, I had a decision to make and once more I looked over at the doctor, who again yelled, "Don't push, Kent, do *not* push!" Again, this sweet, calm nurse smiled, gently patted my hand, and as before, looked straight into my eyes while whispering "Push." For some reason, I listened to her, pushed, and out came my son. Shocked, several in the room, including the doctor, ran over to assist. They quickly took my newborn son and cut the umbilical cord, rushing him off to ensure he could breathe. To this day, mother and baby are fine. Oddly, I never saw that nurse again to tell her thank you. And, in fact, I *may* have been the only one who did see her that day. So I thanked God that my little son, Matthew, was fine. He was definitely meant to be here, and evidently so was I. What a blessing to then take him home to meet his four-year-old brother, Christopher, and 17-month-old sister, Elizabeth, who didn't quite understand what this baby was doing, taking her place in their mother's arms.

Seven years later, in 1987, we left the Bible Belt, and sadly some dear friends, behind as my family moved just south of Houston, Texas, where we were closer to at least one set of grandparents. We knew it would be difficult to raise three children on my husband's teaching and coaching salary if we stayed in Kentucky. Also, I wanted a fulfilling job with an opportunity to advance as our children were now at a good age, early in their elementary school years. Moreover, my heart yearned to study spirituality with more like-minded people. The move was a challenge as it took a year for my husband to find a teaching job and six months for me to hear that my temporary aerospace job would become permanent. That day, coming home from work after hearing the good news, I was affected emotionally when I turned on the radio and heard the song "Turn, Turn, Turn" by the Byrds[1], mostly taken from the Bible (Ecclesiastes, Chapter 3, King James Version):

> To everything, turn, turn, turn
> There is a season, turn, turn, turn
> And a time to every purpose under heaven
> A time to be born, a time to die
> A time to plant, a time to reap
> A time to kill, a time to heal
> A time to laugh, a time to weep…

As I listened to the rest of this song, the message came. "There will always be changes and, see, everything is turning out okay." All was in divine order and everything we had gone through getting moved was just a part of life. After the transition, our family settled in to make this part of Texas our home. Wonderful opportunities lay ahead for our kids growing up, as well as good jobs for my husband and me. We had the closeness of family too. My husband, who had gravely hesitated over the change, later confessed that the move was really good for us all.

One Saturday afternoon, while alone in our new house, I lay down to take a nap and, unexpectedly, the vibration started up again. I had realized over the years that darkness had been associated with these experiences so maybe I could go with it this time and see what would happen. Slowly, I started to drift, though saying to myself, all is okay. I never left my bedroom but how funny that I floated to the ceiling and all over the room, ending up with my nose in the carpet and my body extended out diagonally, straight as an arrow. This didn't quite make sense and I was almost giggling to myself, but hearing the front door slam took me back in an instant. I was enthusiastic now, and instead of feeling afraid, my curiosity was piqued. Surprisingly, I later read in Robert Monroe's book *Journeys Out of Body* that he experienced the same straight diagonal angle and attributed it to the effect that the electromagnetic field of the Earth had on the astral body.

Sometimes I only remembered coming back, not knowing from where; not always was the landing smooth. It was like being a Ping-Pong ball bouncing back and forth in my physical body until finally settling in. Another time, while meditating to music at a friend's house during a Reiki class, I felt myself spinning *inside my body* as if I were on an amusement park ride. How strange, not getting that sick stomach like I normally would if being spun around. I had always envied my brothers and sisters, who could partake in *all* the rides.

The Silver Cord

Not long after these experiences in the early '90s, I began browsing the New Age section of the bookstores. My silent search to learn about OBEs led me down only a few avenues, as there were not many books written on the topic 40 years ago. During a trip to visit my brother and his family in Virginia, when I was in my teens, Dad took me to a bookstore at the Edgar Cayce Institute to help me find *something* that might provide insight into my experiences. But it wasn't until later that I purchased an amazing book that brought tears to my eyes: *The Silver Cord-Lifeline to the Unobstructed,* by Martha Barham, and James Greene. My quest for answers to some long-held questions had finally been satisfied. Unlike inspirational books, which were no doubt extraordinary, this one provided knowledge that rang true to my heart and helped me to understand that my experiences were, in fact, normal.

> Even though our body and soul are tightly intertwined and the curtain is drawn during our incarnation, the entity within us has out-of-body experiences (OBEs) all through our physical life....We are not usually aware of leaving our body, as this occurs most naturally in sleep, when the physical body is at rest and safe.
> (*Silver Cord—Lifeline to the Unobstructed*)

I immediately honed in on the words "not usually," and feeling relieved while wiping my tears, I was so eager to read more that I didn't put the book down until finishing it that same weekend. The authors go on to say that the OBE is very nurturing for us, as we actually go "home" into an unobstructed universe, and we usually don't have a clear memory since the experience is screened from our conscious mind upon returning. Furthermore, they say, "this is so designed in order to maximize the challenges during our search for individual destiny." As etheric beings, first and foremost, I learned we are attached ethereally to our physical body via a silver cord, much the same as a fetus is physically attached to the mother's womb. And I was relieved to read that "the Source" (God) "designed a fail-safe factor into the phenomenon of OBEs. It is *impossible* for a soul not to return to the body immediately if there is any significant physical threat to the body." The cord is only severed due to death of the physical body. Astonishingly, this silver cord is for real, and one that ties or connects us to our body always.

Another book, which belonged to my grandmother, is *In Tune with the Infinite* by Ralph Waldo Trine, first published in 1897. In the chapter on "Wisdom and Interior Illumination," this enlightening book states:

> There are some, having a deep insight into the soul's activities, who say we travel when we sleep. Some are able to recall and bring over into the conscious waking life the scenes visited, the information gained, and the events that have transpired. Most people are not able to do this and so much that might otherwise be gained is lost. They say, however, that it is in our power in proportion as we understand

the laws, to go where we will, and to bring over into the conscious waking life all the experiences thus gained. Be this, however, as it may, it certainly is true that while sleeping we have the power, in a perfectly normal and natural way, to get much of value by the way of light, instruction, and growth that the majority of people now miss.

Realizing just how natural this experience is supposed to be, I wanted even more to overcome my fear and understand OBEs. I remember wanting so badly to talk with my husband about my experiences but sensing that the subject somewhat frightened him. And once when I brought up the topic of reincarnation, he asked me to never mention the word again. Knowing he was brought up in the Catholic religion, I was not greatly surprised, though I had hopes that he might, over time, be more open to discussing metaphysics.

My information-gathering years continued, keeping me open to the possibility of another world as real as this, and soon I was led to hear authors speak at Whole Life Expos. I still recall seeing religious protesters outside the convention hall of one expo in Austin, Texas, because these topics were so controversial. Nonetheless, it was exciting for me to be around so many like-minded individuals with the same yearning to know more. Fortunately, I now lived near my sister Lee Ann, who was also spiritually driven, so we could exchange new books and talk about metaphysics, the subject about which we were both so passionate. Along with my mother, I heard Dr. Deepak Chopra, one of my parents' favorite authors as well as mine, speak in person at the University of Houston; I heard him later at many other places. What captivated me was hearing him talk, not just about life, but about death as well! He said we go to bed each night and dream, then awaken knowing it was just a dream. And, when our soul sheds the physical body for good, we look back on this world as if it was just a dream. I knew in my heart these words were true. Other than CT, the only education I had had was taking a class on death as an elective for my psychology minor in college. Our instructor told us that the only credible book written on this topic in the 1970s was by Elisabeth Kübler-Ross, although it was not allowed as a college textbook.

Letting Go of Dad

Little did I realize that my continued search for wanting to know more about this other, spiritual body was preparing me for letting go of my own

Love Promised: A Future Life Revealed

father, if you can ever be prepared to give up someone you look up to, love, and respect as much as I did him. Dad became ill and I knew he lingered because he didn't want to leave Mom. When she could no longer take care of him, he lived in a nursing home close by and since Mom lived with me, we visited Dad often. The nursing-home employees were surprised to see that he had so many family members—spouse, children, and grandchildren—come to see him.

Once, Dad told us that his sister, my aunt, had been there that day to visit him. We knew that she probably *had* even though she had passed away a few years before. Another time he told us she was standing in the corner of the room and we grinned, wishing that we could see her too. Mom had hardly left Dad's bedside in months so her cousin, Sylvia, came for a visit and convinced her to take a short trip and see some friends. For some reason, the second night Mom was gone, I didn't want to leave Dad's bedside either. He wouldn't speak and kept his eyes closed, but I talked to him anyway since he was awake but nervous, it seemed, lying still though he had bouts of shaking. As the evening progressed, I asked the nurse if she would mind taking his vital signs more often that night as I had promised Mom she would get the phone call in time for her to make the four-hour trip back home, if necessary. Also, I decided to stay with him through the night, as it occurred to me he might leave while Mom was gone. I had read before that dying patients in the hospitals or in hospice care would sometimes pass on when their loved one just stepped away to the bathroom. We may believe we are the ones who have the most difficulty losing someone who is dying, but I think it is just as hard on the one having to leave mourning souls behind. Keeping my promise, I called Mom at 4 a.m. since Dad's vital signs were declining every two hours. Another nurse, who noticed my Dad's shaking, said that he had Parkinson's disease; however, I knew that he had decided for himself it was time to go and he was just scared. Each time the bouts of shaking came over him, I held his hand and laid my body across his, hugging him tightly.

I remembered how, long ago, he had held me in bed at night when I was a frightened little girl after the OBEs. Now, it was time for me to hold him during his frightening time when he was about to leave his body for good. I whispered in his ear that all was in divine order and told him if death was anything like what I had experienced, then leaving the body would be as simple as letting go. Furthermore, I felt dying was not an ending, and as much as we would miss him, it was okay to leave. Though he did not say a word, it was obvious he was listening, and hearing my voice let him know he was not alone. On an intellectual level he knew what was being said, but I also know what fear can do to you.

A Beautiful Message

Knowing how frightened Dad was, and what it felt like to leave the body, I whispered how I wished I could take him halfway there to this place we call heaven. I also told him that Mom was on her way, if he could just hold on, as she would want to hold his hand one last time and tell him how much she loved him. Fortunately, my nephew Ryan, who is an early riser, walked into the room around 7 a.m. Always wanting to assist, he offered to stay with his Grandpa while I ran home for a quick shower. On the way back, when I was not more than five minutes away, the song "Somewhere"[2] by Barbara Streisand came on the radio and I knew my Dad, on a soul level, was trying to comfort me for what *I* was going through watching him leave. Not only that, this song was responding to the words I had just spoken to him during the night. Shockingly, the lyrics were overwhelming and my tears flowed.

> There's a place for us,
> Someday a place for us
> Peace and quiet and open air
> Wait for us somewhere.
> There's a time for us,
> Someday there'll be a time for us
> Time together with time to spare
> A time to learn
> A time to care
> Someday
> Somewhere
> We'll find a new way of living
> Well find there's a new way of forgiving
> Somewhere,
> There's a place for us
> A time and place for us
> Hold my hand and we're halfway there
> Just hold my hand and I'll take you there

Love Promised: A Future Life Revealed

Somehow
Someday
Somewhere

The moment was just too surreal. My sisters met me at the nursing home and shortly after that our mother showed up. It was then that I lost it emotionally because I knew how upsetting it would have been if she had not made it back in time. My mother, sisters, and I gathered around, holding Dad's hands, and they stood in amazement, hearing the story of the messages Dad and I gave to each other.

Saying Goodbye

Incredibly, Dad held on for a while, and we never left his side. Then, for the first time in over 24 hours, his eyes suddenly opened very wide but glazed over, it seemed. Mother quickly leaned over, hoping to look into his eyes one last time, but it was obvious he was looking at something majestic and not of this physical dimension. Dad then closed his eyes and drew his last breath of air. After they prepared his body, I visited his room once more, knowing he was still there both physically and ethereally, though the cord had been severed, much the same as when he first entered this world. I sat and talked to him as I had done several hours before and told him not to worry, that we would take care of his best friend and lover, his beautiful wife and soul mate, our mother.

Then, miraculously, we would all get in our cars to leave just in time to hear the song "Seasons in the Sun"[3] on our car radios. On this beautiful, sunny spring day in May, we listened to the lyrics:

Goodbye, Michelle, my little one,
You gave me love and helped me find the sun,
And every time that I was down
You would always come around
And get my feet back on the ground;
Goodbye, Michelle, it's hard to die
When all the birds are singing in the sky,
Now that the spring is in the air,
With the flowers everywhere,

I wish that we could both be there!
We had joy, we had fun, we had seasons in the sun…

I could hardly see through my tears to drive home but when I got there and realized all of us had heard this song on the radio, my tears and theirs quickly turned into laughter. Astonished, we stared at one another, saying, "Oh, my goodness, did you just hear that song?!" I'm certain Dad had help from his angels and guides as he knew what was needed to console us. It was not long before our brothers, who lived in Kentucky and Louisiana, showed up. The next night we sat for hours reminiscing outside my house. Mom enjoyed hearing us talk about all the fun times we had growing up with this wonderful soul we knew as our father. That same evening, our brother's wife, who had stayed behind with their young children in Kentucky, called to tell us a shocking story. "Remember the Presbyterian Church that you all used to attend?" she asked. "Well, it was struck by lightning last night during the middle of the night, *the night your Dad passed away*, and burned to the ground, no one hurt of course." Hearing the news, we all looked at one another wide-eyed, as if we could see the spinning wheels inside each of our heads.

Watching Over Us…

It wouldn't be long until my sister and I attended another Whole Life Expo in Austin, where we would meet Petrene Soames, a psychic medium who lived north of Houston. We decided it was time to see if our Dad would come through to talk…and he did!

Petrene Soames, a sweet British lady with a 300-year history of psychics in her lineage, would then become a favorite of ours. Through her, Dad let us know he was watching over us and was a *"force to be reckoned with."* We realized when talking with Dad through Petrene that just because we shed our physical bodies doesn't mean we leave our personalities behind. Not only did Dad's persona shine through, he also offered profound words of wisdom, as always. On Father's Day, we decided to visit again, so along with Mother and my daughter were my two sisters and their daughters. At the end of the session, Dad told us that he would be with us when we ate out afterward and that we should watch for white doilies and flowers. However, we were so engrossed in our conversation about some of the information that had come through that we had all but forgotten this particular message

Love Promised: A Future Life Revealed

until we went into an old Victorian house for lunch in an area called Old Town Spring, just north of Houston. The hostess and waitstaff must have thought we were extra-impressed with this unique place as, smiling broadly with excitement and speaking in high-pitched voices, we strolled past the tables with white doilies and flowers.

Dad's Surprise Visit

The day before Thanksgiving 1998, we visited with Dad once again via Petrene. This time he asked us to set a place for him at the dinner table and told us he would do something special. Dad always loved the Thanksgiving meal Mom prepared, and especially his favorite chocolate pie afterward, with a glass of milk. Before dinner, we listened again to the session on tape so others could enjoy it too as he had messages for everyone, even the skeptics in our family. And we did acknowledge his presence among our prayer of many thanks, hoping all the while we would notice something unusual happening. Nothing caught our attention, though, as we filled our tummies and enjoyed playing games later that night.

The next morning, however, my sister Lee Ann called. With a serious tone in her voice, she said, "Are you sitting down? You are not going to believe this." She went on to tell me how her husband, John, had a very startled look on his face when she awoke that morning. My brother-in-law, the self-claimed skeptic who liked to sarcastically tease us about "talking to the dead," went on to tell her of his experience during the night. He was awakened by a noise in the kitchen, which he suspected was their cat bumping into an appliance when jumping on the counter looking for leftovers. When he got up and walked into the kitchen, adequately lit by a light in the living room, he could see that there was a man standing with his back to him over in the corner where two pieces of chocolate pie had been left a few hours before. Astoundingly unafraid, John moved closer to the island, placing both his hands on the counter. He continued to look at this tall, slender man wearing dress slacks and a white undershirt, slightly bent over as if he was eating. As he slowly turned around, John was stunned. This man was his deceased father-in-law, who was now holding a piece of pie in his left hand and a fork in the other as he began to speak... "Tell Lannie all I wanted was a piece of pie and a glass of milk." He then smiled very big and there was a light coming from behind his bright, white teeth as though a flashlight in his mouth was pointing outward, John said.

Love Promised: A Future Life Revealed

This light continued across the counter toward him in what seemed to be slow motion. John never took his eyes off the light and when it reached his waist about three seconds later, he looked back up and no one was there. Flabbergasted, John immediately turned to the clock; it was 2:37 a.m. on November 26, 1998. He stood there for a moment dumbstruck but surprisingly felt very calm while taking out a sticky note and jotting down what had just happened, before he went back to bed. Knowing quite well that it was his father-in-law who had just appeared to him, he left the note on the counter so he would know the next morning it had not been a dream.

Having worked in the aerospace business himself, this experience that my brother-in-law felt blessed to have had opened his eyes to an area of faith and physics that previously had bordered on the "too strange to believe," he said. The experience left him wanting to know more—with questions such as why Dad came to him and not to his wife or someone in her family. And we had to confess, with a grin, we were all just a little jealous. Admittedly, if it had not happened to him, he probably would not have believed the story from any of us, and he later regretted thinking that way. "Was it a ghostly-type figure?" we immediately asked. "No," he said, "It was as if your father was standing in the room with me, flesh and blood, and then he vanished." Another puzzling question John had was why he did not freak out. And for goodness' sake, why had his father-in-law not said something more profound, he wondered, than talking about a piece of pie?

When hearing the story again, this time from John, while dining out with Lee Ann and him, I sensed the answers to these questions and knew that it had made a weak marriage stronger. Quite possibly, that was the whole purpose of Dad's visit. Needless to say, my brother-in-law never again teased my sister or me about talking to the dead!

Soon after this experience, I headed to Toys R Us and purchased a Parker Brothers Ouija board so that we could try talking with our Dad. What the heck, give it a try, I thought, as fun memories came flooding back of playing this "game" with my parents and some of their friends. However, after several attempts, the oracle planchette would not move with Lee Ann and me, so the box went straight into the closet. We were disappointed but figured that if it had worked, we would probably get addicted and depend on Dad for answers to life's questions that we knew deep down in our hearts we had come here to discover all on our own. It would be another five years before the Ouija board was tried again. Dad never stopped giving us words of wisdom, though, such as the day Lee Ann called, exhilarated, to tell us about the song she had just heard on her headset while jogging and thinking about Dad. It was a stressful time in her life and the amazing lyrics that Des'ree' wrote and sang offered her support when she needed it the most in the song "You Gotta Be."

Listen as your day unfolds,
Challenge what the future holds,
Try and keep your head up to the sky.
Lovers, they may cause you tears,
Go ahead release your fears

Stand up and be counted
Don't be afraid to cry

You gotta be bad, you gotta be bold
You gotta be wiser, you gotta be hard,
You gotta be tough, you gotta be stronger.

You gotta be cool, you gotta be calm
You gotta stay together
All I know, all I know, love will save the day

Herald what your mother said
Readin' the books your father read
Try to solve the puzzles in your own sweet time

Some may have more cash than you
Others take a different view
My, oh, my, Oh, heh, hey

More Challenges Ahead

It wouldn't be long until I would be hearing this popular song too, the words ringing true in my life as well. I was thoroughly enjoying my kids during their teenage years, and as a family we supported one another. As a wife, though, I was beginning to feel very alone in my marriage and time spent together as husband and wife was little to none. I also realized we just did not have much in common except for our kids, and over the course of

20 years, being busy working and rearing our children, we'd probably had less than five heart-to-heart conversations. A marriage is truly something you have to work at in order for both to be happy. And I'm convinced Earth is the school for relationships.

Now on the other side, our father would remain active in all our lives—Mom's, my siblings', and mine, and our children's—letting us know he was indeed watching over us. Dad left a teddy bear sitting on my sister Rebecca's nightstand though it had been packed away in a box the night before. Once, he left my brother Bill's car keys on an end table in plain sight the morning after three people, including me, had searched the apartment for over an hour. And our mother would always find little gifts in the oddest places, which played havoc with her head before we realized Dad could move things around. Two days after I'd stayed at Mom's she called me in a panic, wanting to know if I had come during the middle of the night and slept on the couch again. I said no and asked why, as her voice seemed a little shaken. She went on to say, "Please come over right away; I awoke this morning to find the couch that you had made into a bed and slept in two days ago is now made up into a bed again, the same sheets and blankets." I was immediately puzzled but quickly went over to find it was exactly as she had told me. I assured her I had put everything back in its place the day before. At times like this, one's rational mind will try every scenario possible to explain a situation that is simply unexplainable. This would not be the last time Dad let us know he was around.

Our children had dreams of their grandfather that brought emotional tears—visions while they were sleeping that seemed too vivid to be just a dream, they would say. Dad had loved his grandchildren and always wanted to be around them, taking them to the park, playing with them, and doting on them anytime he could. It was pure joy to watch because it reminded us of the fun years we had had growing up. Though our children were still young when their Grandpa passed away, every time we gathered for one of their events, whether it was baseball, football, tennis, theater or cheerleading, we would remind ourselves just how much Dad would have supported them in all their endeavors.

Overnight, it seemed, my three children had graduated from high school. I was saddened looking back at how quickly that seemed to have happened. I loved my children so and enjoyed spending time with them, watching them grow and supporting the activities that were important to them. As a mother, and like my mother before me, I had spent most of my life ensuring that my children were happy and now, very soon, I would be tearing their world apart. In this new millennium, I found myself facing more challenges than I had ever imagined.

The Numbers Begin

In the year 2000, repetitive numbers started popping up everywhere, such as the number 11:11 primarily and then 5:55. It seemed odd that these numbers kept reappearing everywhere. I'll never forget how shocked I was when glancing down to see 11:11:11 on a digital travel clock. Then the numbers 1:11, 2:22, 3:33, and 4:44 began. When mentioning the odd occurrences to a friend, she told me about a book Doreen Virtue had written that gave the meaning of these numbers, stating they are messages from our angels. After getting the book, I found it intriguing that occurrences in my life amazingly coincided with what the numbers meant.

The incidents continued to happen, and practically on a daily basis. In addition to digital devices—whether personal computers or laptops, stoves or microwaves—at work or at home, or in the car, I would also notice numbers on billboards, street signs, or the license plate on a vehicle in front of me. Additionally, I would see them on a purchase receipt showing the time of purchase or the amount of the purchase; the countdown on the radio of a song; the play clock stopped during a sporting event on TV or in real time. Or it was the length of time I spoke on my cell phone, my heart rate on the treadmill or the time itself, the length of a song; the number of e-mails in my inbox, or the time of flight on my itinerary. Amazingly, these numbers were everywhere and still are today, only now I also see them in combinations such as 11:22, 11:33, 11:44, and 11:55. It wasn't that I looked for the numbers to appear, for that would drive one crazy, and what a waste of time. The numbers were, and are, just there, in my line of sight, never one minute before or one minute after. They happen when I am looking over, glancing up, walking in or walking out, getting in or getting out, waking up during the middle of the night or going to sleep, and so on.

As an example, in one 24-hour period, I noticed these repetitive numbers: as I got in my car to go home for lunch, the digital clock on my dashboard showed 11:55 a.m. Arriving back at work, my desk clock showed 1:11 p.m. when I walked into my office. That evening on my home computer, I glanced down to see 11:11 p.m. After getting in bed, I realized the lights in my kitchen had not been turned off so I got up again, only to see 11:22 p.m. on my microwave. The next day I abruptly awoke at 5:55 a.m. and while at work that morning, I checked my son's flight itinerary, which showed he would fly out at 11:55 a.m. These synchronicities cannot be missed, especially when they occur on an average of three times per day.

With respect to seeing 555s in the early part of this decade, I learned that my angels were giving me the message to "hold on to your seat belt, big changes are coming your way," and Doreen compares the ongoing changes to being on a roller coaster. Within a year and a half of seeing these numbers repetitively, I had major back surgery; went through a divorce and dealt with the trauma that this caused my children; moved in with a girlfriend temporarily, then moved to a foreign country to live and work there for a short period of time. And, while there I received news that someone with whom I was in love had suffered a fatal concussion. So it came as no surprise to the NASA doctor in Russia that my thoughts of having a heart attack might be real when he asked me what my symptoms were and what I had been going through during the past year. "You have been through more major milestones in one year than some people go through their entire life," he said. I was in what seemed to be a 1940s hospital in Moscow, waiting for the results of my EKG and a barium x-ray. Calmly staring out the window, I listened when the doctor spoke to me but it was as though he was talking about someone else, someone I didn't even know, when he explained that I might have to be medically evacuated to Helsinki if I needed heart surgery. My only thought was that I wanted to stay there. I loved living in Russia and had made some dear friends, including Russian translators, with whom I worked every day on flight-crew procedures. Also, I had made plans to travel and see other parts of Europe with others who were working there on temporary assignment. And subconsciously, I was probably not ready to go back and face the loss and the life left behind. The EKG came back normal, but the doctor didn't totally trust their antiquated machine. I was also diagnosed with H. pylori, a stomach bacterium that, if left untreated for a long period of time, can cause cancer. A floating gallstone was a real possibility because it can cause symptoms mimicking a heart attack. Much to my dismay, it was recommended that I return home. Back in the U. S., I remember waiting for the cardiologist to give me the results of my tests when that sharp little stone passed through my body, causing me to bend over in pain. Ultimately, I missed out on the chance of going back to some dear friends in Russia and being in a neutral location that would help me forget about what I was going through at the time.

Love Promised: A Future Life Revealed

Wayne Dyer's Meditations for Manifesting ... Saved Me

My life was lethargic, it seemed, as I was still dealing with some health issues after coming back from Russia. Since I was not treated for the bacteria right away, eating anything became a major ordeal because it led to stomach cramps. It would take a second specialist to figure out that I should have been treated for the bacteria much earlier. Eventually I felt better and was glad to be home around family and my grown kids, but my continued heartache was one the medical field couldn't touch. For my kids and my now ex-husband, I would try once more to see if any of the pieces could be put back together again. My ex admitted that he didn't realize he loved me until I was ready to go, but by then, it was too late for me. And I was grateful that I was no longer in love with him when he confessed that he had thought all along his ex-girlfriend, the one before me, was his "angel." Oh my, all this time he thought he had married the wrong one... then I knew for certain what this space between us had been for so long. Yet, he did not want me to leave. Staying there naturally would have been the easier choice but my heart was pushing me to go, to go and find myself someplace else...but where I did not know.

It seemed, Wayne Dyer's *Meditations for Manifesting* might help, as they had done before; however, I did not really know at this point in my life what I wanted to manifest. Nevertheless, his profound words of wisdom greatly comforted me. The breathing exercises helped too and I desperately needed to hear these words, now more than ever before.

I know in each moment I am free to decide, no matter how much I protest I am totally responsible for everything that happens to me in my life. My past is nothing more than the trail I have left behind; what drives my life today is the energy that I generate in each of my present moments. I rid myself of my doubts by remembering that there is a valid reason for everything that happens. I realize that I am always free to let go and observe my life. The more I listen, the more profound the silence becomes. I know that my highest self is always ready to lift me up beyond the world I experience with my five senses. I know that I can connect my mind with the Divine mind and guarantee myself peace in any moment. I know I am strengthened as I seek to make truth my personal reality. I know that the very essence of my being and the way of transforming my life is love. My judgments prevent me from seeing the good that lies beyond appearances. I know that I am already whole and need not chase after anything to be complete. I am aware that I do not need to dominate anyone to be spiritually awake. I will work this day, at my purest intentions, for the highest good of all. I will radiate my sacred self outward, for the collective good of all.

Meditating to these words would put me in a relaxed frame of mind, ready to listen for that inner voice we all have within us. And, as odd as it may sound, it was easy getting to a point of relaxation where you didn't feel a need to even breathe. Dr. Dyer takes you through some "ah" and "ohm" sounds that you make with your vocal cords and which, according to yoga and metaphysics, tune the energy centers of the soul, called chakras. This word is derived from the Sanskrit *chakra*, meaning "wheel," and there are several points along the spine where this spiritual energy exists, spinning in the human body.

This meditation definitely helped while I was in the midst of making some important decisions. Not only was I confused, but also, as a mother, the tendency is to put your wants and needs last and the needs of your children first and foremost. But now, I found myself in a situation where following my heart would cause my grown children pain though I continued to pray and meditate for "the highest good for all." Subsequently, when asking for guidance as to what steps to take, I only heard one message: "Buy the condo."

Sometimes, we just have to listen and not judge or question whatever inspiration may come through, and simply go with what we get, no matter how trivial or irrelevant it may seem at the time. Also, there is a part of us that may not be able to handle the bigger picture just yet, so possibly we are given baby steps to take. My heart needed some space of its own to think and figure things out. And, fortunately, everything was falling into place financially for that to happen. As sad as it was during this difficult time, there was a part of me looking forward to living alone and just taking care of myself again. In the '70s, I went from my parents' home to a college dormitory to getting married, then rearing three children and even house-breaking puppies. Except for the short four months of apartment-living in Russia, I had never experienced this independence before. It was also during this time that I would very often hear on the radio a popular song, "Only Time,"[6] that spoke to my heart, by one of my favorite musical artists, Enya:

Love Promised: A Future Life Revealed

Who can say where the road goes, where day flows, only time,
And who can say if your love grows, as your heart chose only time,
Who can say why your heart sighs as your love flies, only time,
And who can say why your heart cries when your love dies, only time,
Who can say when the roads meet that there might be in your heart,
And who can say what the day holds if the night keeps all your heart.
Who can say if your love grows as your heart chose, only time,
And who can say where the road goes, where the day flows, only time.
Who knows, only time....Who knows, only time.

Chapter Two

A Moment in Time with Russell

The secret of health for both mind and body is not to mourn
for the past, worry about the future, or anticipate troubles,
but to live in the present moment wisely and earnestly.
—Gautama Buddha

Pebble Brook condominiums in Seabrook, Texas, was a place I had often visited since both my Mom and my nephew lived there. Soon I would hear that the original builders were selling some of the units they owned. The ending of my 25-year marriage was not bitter, only very sad. It was definitely a time for spiritual growth, a time of transitioning, understanding, accepting, and letting go. During this time that I was searching for answers, the very same songs on the radio would play over and over. Like the numbers, these songs came on over the TV, radio, or speaker system at the most unusual times and places, such as when I walked into the downtown McDonald's in Moscow and heard the song "I Hope You Dance" by Martina McBride. Every word spoke to me as I was about to make some very difficult, important choices in my life.

I also heard the song "Landslide"[1] not just by the original artist, Stevie Nicks, but by the Dixie Chicks, who made a remake:

> Oh, mirror in the sky, what is love?
> Can the child within my heart rise above?
> Can I sail through the changing ocean tides
> Can I handle the seasons of my life?
> I don't know…I've been afraid of changing
> Because I built my whole life around you,

But time makes you bolder and even children get older,
And I'm getting older too…

The people who wrote those songs knew me and what I was going through! Truthfully, it was comforting to know that there were probably many out there walking in the same footsteps. One has to admit that music and lyrics do have the power to change the world and, as a little girl, I had been taught to listen carefully for messages can come through songs. My decisions, however, were not just based on these songs or, as one might, say "on a whim," but the truth that lay behind those words could no longer be pushed aside. I was searching for direction in my life and wondering how my choices would impact others, yet struggling to not feel responsible for everyone's happiness, all at the same time. Using discernment, I followed my heart to walk the path alone and allow the universe to guide me, not certain what the future would hold.

My mantra was to start anew when moving into the Pebble Brook condominium in January 2003. The first night in my little place was somewhat frightening, as I awoke during the night feeling smothered and had difficulty breathing for three hours. It wasn't until my satisfactory evaluation at the doctor's office the next day when the thought came to me that someone on the other side might be trying to communicate with me…*or get rid of me.* Much later, I learned a spirit inhabited this property and had been seen by the previous tenants since it used to be his land. Furthermore, he didn't want me there, obviously. Okay, Dad, where are you, this is a force to be reckoned with! Asking for protection was all it took to never have that experience again. On another occasion, I awoke with an uncomfortable feeling after having a weird but vivid dream, one with an emotion so real that it sent chills all over my body…I'd dreamt of making love to someone in prison. This seemed really odd since no one I knew had ever been imprisoned. Upon waking, I quickly tried to put that thought out of my mind and got ready for work. But in less than six months, this dream would make perfect sense to me.

Meeting Russell

Shortly after I moved into the condominiums, Russell was introduced to me as the new maintenance man on the property. He did an outstanding job, as everything that needed to be worked on, at least at my place, was done very quickly. Wow, now that's service, I thought! Russell was a very handsome young man who, I later found out, was temporarily living with his single father at Pebble Brook. Russell's first thought was that I was a potential mate for his father, but the more he was around me, he said, the more he was attracted to me in spite of the 20-year age difference. One afternoon he stopped by to bring me a handle for my sliding glass door, which property management had promised to supply. I later learned he was disappointed at not being invited into my condo. Though he was handsome indeed, my mind did not look at Russell as a potential mate, *because* of the age difference. He was closer to my children's age so my mind never went there. Since he was new to the area, however, I told him about my nephew living close by, if he was looking for a friend.

One Saturday afternoon, Russell stopped by again and this time asked if he could come inside to talk. The day before he had helped to clean off my patio and replace an outside door lock that no longer had a key to open it. He wanted me to know what he had done on my patio and then asked if he could sit down because there was something he wanted to tell me that he was a little nervous about. He looked very serious, so I asked him if everything was okay. What he told me next caught me totally off guard. He started out by saying that he had not been with a woman in quite some time. My first thought was, "Why is he telling *me* this if he possibly means it in *that* way?" Nevertheless, I made no assumptions and waited for further explanation. After all, perhaps he had no one else to talk with and needed some guidance since this is not an easy subject to discuss with just anyone, *especially* your parents. Very cautiously, he went on to say that less than two months earlier he had been released from a seven-year prison sentence for inadvertently killing a man in a car accident. The details followed.

Hearing this story, my heart immediately sank and I could feel compassion start to well up inside me. Tears began to form in his eyes too, as he said, "Kent, I never wanted that man to die." My heart went out to Russell and for some reason I began to tell him some things that, by his reaction, I'm not sure he had ever heard before or could even believe. Other than family and a few friends, these were thoughts usually kept to myself.

Nevertheless, in my opinion there are events in our lives that we cannot begin to understand. I told Russell that if we look at our world only through human eyes, life seems very unfair. We are a soul, first and foremost, inhabiting a human body, and I went on to let him know of my belief in reincarnation, where one soul is reborn into subsequent human bodies over and over. Therefore, we can choose to experience life in many

Love Promised: A Future Life Revealed

different ways and advance to the point of not having to return. Furthermore, if our true self is the soul and not the body, then truly there is no such thing as death. On another level, as a soul we choose to experience all aspects of life in order to learn. I did not want to frighten him with stories of my OBEs but wanted him to know that we grow by making agreements with other souls who also come here to learn and grow. In other words, how do we learn forgiveness unless we have someone to forgive, as Neale Donald Walsch teaches us? Quite possibly, there is more truth than fiction to the statement made by Shakespeare when he said, "All the world is a stage, and all the men and women merely players." I did voice to Russell that I was still searching for more answers, especially when it came to the subjects of free will and destiny and how the two coexist. I told Russell that these were merely my beliefs, but maybe, *just maybe*, this man's time was up here on Earth and he was ready to go back home, and is now living peacefully on another level of existence. And *if* this were true, I said, "Why would you want to continue punishing yourself with guilt over something you didn't mean to do, especially now that you've served this time in prison, which must have been traumatic for you?"

I could tell Russell was somewhat taken aback by what was said. At the same time my words seemed to give him some liberation and also acceptance, because now someone besides his family felt he deserved to live in peace. I was so full of emotion at the time and so focused on him, it never clicked... I did not connect his story to my dream until later.

I had definitely found a new friend, and after hearing his story, I understood why this nice-looking young man who seemed so skilled, intelligent, and energetic was working as a maintenance man there at the condos. It was soon apparent that I was not the only one wanting and needing to start anew. He too needed to heal from the past and in some small way I was beginning to help him do that. I lent to him a cherished CT book called *Rays of the Dawn*, one that used to inspire and give me guidance.

One afternoon, Russell walked by my place and, seeing my nephew lifting a brand-new TV out of the back of my SUV, offered his assistance. Not only did I appreciate the help, it gave me the opportunity to introduce Russell to my nephew, who might be an avenue for more friends. (I later found out Russell was attending a local junior college, as he had done the last couple of years while in prison.) That afternoon, my nephew and I had plans to go see the middle school basketball team that my son coached, and I invited Russell, as he had just spent two hours helping my nephew with an entertainment center of mine. As it turned out, Russell loved basketball.

Having learned of my back surgery, Russell had told me I could call on him if ever needing help lifting anything. The next week, I took him up on his offer as neither my son nor my nephew was available to help me pick up some shelving from a store. After we had picked up the heavy box, we strolled through the music department, passing some Valentine cards. Russell looked over at me and asked, "Do you have a Valentine?" Looking away sheepishly, I smiled and said, "No, I don't." He very quickly responded, "Well, I'll be your Valentine." Oh my goodness! Did he just say that? I wondered. As we continued to walk along, my face felt very flushed when I stated, "Russell, I'm very flattered, but do you know how old I am?" The next thing he said surprised me even more. "I don't *care* how old you are." On the way home, I was still in shock and trying to figure out if he was serious. However, one thing was for certain—I was beginning to feel a little girlish around him and starting to enjoy the company of someone who had been a stranger just weeks before.

The next day, Russell stopped by before leaving for his evening class at the university. While visiting, we talked about school and his plans for the future. Each time we talked, I learned more about him and how fond he was of his extended family. Although single now, he had married and fathered a child at a young age. He told me of the despair he felt when he went to prison and had to leave his 2-year-old daughter. This pain of missing his daughter was worse than the brutal fighting in prison to protect others and defend himself.

Russell was such a good listener. He wanted to know about my children and, of course, the pain I'd dealt with in my life. Everyone has a story and, like many, ours were filled with somber memories. Our conversations seemed more like therapy after what each of us had been through over the last few years. The comfort we gave to each other helped tremendously in healing the past and we could talk openly for hours on any subject.

One week, Russell stopped by after work once again. As we sat on my couch talking, the look in his eyes made it obvious that the chemistry between us was building. We were becoming more than friends, which made me a little nervous. After the heartaches of the last several years, the probability of a happy outcome seemed slim to none, especially with a much younger man. I was concerned, too, about how upsetting this would be to my now grown children, still dealing with the divorce of their parents. That night, my nephew invited Russell out to a local bar to hang out with his sister (my

Love Promised: A Future Life Revealed

niece, Brooke) and listen to music and maybe meet some other friends. As Russell was new to the area, I encouraged him to go, thinking it might be good for him to meet some friends his own age. He definitely had some social life to catch up on.

Later in the evening, though, he came back to my place, quite excited, and asked if he could come inside. "Sure, why not," I said, thinking he wanted to tell me about the fun evening, long overdue after having been behind the other kind of bars for most of his twenties. "Did you have a good time?" I asked. "Yes, but all I saw were Kents everywhere." His response surprised me. And the way he said it, with a grin on his face, was so adorable, I couldn't help but laugh. His expression then became more serious as he looked deep into my eyes and said, "I sure would like to kiss you." At this point, it was obvious just how sincere he was; he also sensed my resistance was now gone. He gently took my hand, pulling me closer to him, then heard my whisper, "Okay, you can." It was a magical moment indeed. For me, a floodgate of emotions had finally been opened, after I'd given myself permission to honor these new feelings and not deny them any longer.

Falling in Love

Though the chemistry was undeniable, I was still very leery of a relationship that might eventually cause more pain, and I let Russell know that the 20 years might be too much to overcome. He asked me one night if I would consider him for a boyfriend if he were 10 years older or I, 10 years younger. My quick response, "In a heartbeat," left him somber for the rest of the evening, hardly speaking a word. The next day, when I told my mother about our conversation, she said to me very kindly, "Honey, of course he was upset." I was confused, but she went on to say, "If he really loves you, as he says he does, and wants you to feel the same, then he wanted to hear that you would be with him in spite of the age difference." Mom was so good at offering advice, so open-minded and objective. She never suggested what path to take; she simply put all the pros and cons into perspective, allowing me to make my own choices. Subconsciously, giving Russell this excuse was subtly pushing the problem away: I would not have to come to terms with a passionate love that I didn't feel I deserved but desperately wanted and needed.

It wouldn't be long before everyone knew we were in a romantic relationship and at first it was a hurdle for our families. Russell's parents asked him if he was out of his mind and I confess that I fully expected his Mom to pay me a visit any moment. I might have done that if it were my son. However, our relationship turned out to be more of a challenge for my grown children than for his parents, with whom I eventually became very close. No longer would I be known as "the lady in 107," and even his extended family welcomed me with open arms. Ultimately my children grew to accept him because they could see how happy their mother had become.

We eventually moved in together and were like kids making up for lost time, doing many things as a couple. He loved to be on the go as did I. Starting to live in the moment now, we finally put our pasts aside. Oddly enough, when we looked into each other's eyes, we truly never saw the age difference, though both of us had reservations from time to time, worrying that the other might eventually want to be with someone their own age.

When Russell and I lived together, occasionally some strange things would happen, such as the time we were getting ready for work one morning. Russell came out of the shower with just a towel wrapped around him and frantically wanted to know how come I had let a man into our condo. He went on to tell me that when he crossed the hall into our bedroom, he saw a man in a dark suit, vest, and hat standing directly inside the front door. I had never seen this angry look on Russell's face—it must have been the way he looked when getting ready to fight in prison. He hurried into the living room but was frustrated to find no one there and the front door still locked. I told him it was probably just my Dad, though the description really didn't match. Then I remembered the man who didn't want me on his land!

A month later, we moved into the nearby condo Russell had finished remodeling with his father, who by this time had moved into a new house. Though Russell was smart and artistically talented, getting a well-paying job was not easy for someone with a prison record and still on probation. The consequences of the past were starting to weigh heavily on his mind. As he had always been very skilled with his hands, he took a job as a welder but did not like the evening shift they switched him to in spite of his request to work the same daytime hours as I did.

Late one night after drifting off to sleep, I abruptly awoke, hearing the music on our stereo in the living room getting louder. I thought Russell had come home but what was he thinking, it was midnight. I quickly jumped out of bed, somewhat bewildered, and hurried to turn the music down as it continued to get even louder. As I approached the entertainment center, it occurred to me Russell was not even standing there. After turning the volume down, I realized he had not even come home yet. The front door was still locked, and our little schnauzer's paw had certainly not hit the remote control, which was sitting on the table. Heidi, in fact, was curled up in her little bed and my mind very quickly tried to rule out every possible logical explanation before it succumbed to realizing that something out of the normal or *paranormal* had just happened. Okay, who's here? I thought, knowing my Dad would not try to get my attention that way. After crawling back in bed, I went to sleep and told Russell about it the next day. He was less than impressed about it, until our invisible guest paid us another visit. Only this time it was not the land owner.

The Ouija Board

One October morning while I was home alone getting ready for work, a Houston radio station aired a special Halloween program. I was in the bathroom but stuck my head out to hear the conversation which, as before, surprisingly continued to get louder all on its own. This entity is really trying to get my attention, I thought, and at this very moment these DJs are talking about ghosts! When I shared what had happened with Russell, he again thought little about it until one night when we were both home and it happened once more. We had snuggled up together in front of the fireplace, admiring the decorations on our freshly cut Christmas tree. As we lay there not far from the stereo, we soon noticed the music getting louder. This time, by Russell's eyes, I could tell he was stunned. "That's what I've been trying to tell you," I said. He then jumped up and exclaimed, "We are going to get that damn Ouija board out of the closet and find out who this is!"

Russell knew that I had purchased the Parker Brothers game several years earlier. For some reason I had been inclined to take it out of storage, but had not anticipated using it. With what we were experiencing, though, I definitely wanted to try it again. We laid the board on a table between us and lit a candle. Russell and I slowly placed our hands on the oracle and surprisingly the thing started moving very quickly. He glanced up at me asking, "Are you moving this thing?" I said, "No, are you?" I tried to explain that this had happened one other time many years ago and that maybe we should just go with it. It didn't take long for words to form, and then sentences with messages that seemed applicable to our lives…Thus began the start of our nightly Ouija sessions throughout the holidays. We asked who was trying to communicate with us, and twice it spelled out "Wayildileujo," which, as we learned later, was the name of an American

Indian. We nicknamed him "Wavo" and for the next two weeks we couldn't wait to get on the board whenever we could. Russell had given up the welding job to be a salesperson at a local car dealership so fortunately he was home now in the evenings.

A few days later, Russell's dad, Ron, came over when Russell and I were on the board. To his and our amazement, a friend of Ron's who had passed away many years ago came through. Understanding Ron's skepticism, we told him to ask a question silently. The oracle started to move and we asked who was with us. When it spelled out "David," Ron told us that he once had a college roommate named David who was killed in a car accident. So Ron proceeded to ask out loud this time, "David, if this is you, what was the nickname we gave you in college?" knowing that neither Russell nor I would know the answer to this question. When the word "Marlboro" was spelled out, Ron's face turned from suspicion to awe.

As time passed, some information we received seemed valid and some did not. The lack of consistency left us in doubt and after a while the newness dwindled, the holidays were over, and life was busy with work again. Early that fall, however, my sister and I had joined a friend from Oklahoma named Judy and we attended a Hay House-sponsored *Mystical Connections* seminar where four psychic mediums spoke for several hours. It had been a while since we had enjoyed hearing Judy channel the other side herself, and we were all excited to hear Sonia Choquette, John Holland, Doreen Virtue, and Sylvia Brown at the Verizon Wireless auditorium. It was literally filled with those who had lost loved ones and wanted confirmation they were not dead. The long lines didn't surprise me and those who stood waiting shared their personal stories and the experiences which had brought them there. As with the Whole Life Expos in the '90s, it was great to walk away feeling so spiritually uplifted and ready to face the world again. These motivational speakers continue to delight in helping people fulfill their lives, and also connecting loved ones from both sides who desperately need to hear from one another in addition to hearing beautiful messages from angels.

Messages come in many ways. I still vividly remember awakening one morning in 1994 to hear my father-in-law say to me, "Tell them I'm not dead." In my mind's eye, I was looking down at a small, clear stream of water flowing over smooth rocks with a small amount of foliage. I then sensed my father-in-law next to me saying, "They called me Bugs Bunny; tell them I'm not dead." It hadn't been long since our return from the state of Washington where we had gone for his funeral, so I was timid to say anything to my husband, his son. But the excitement of what had just happened plus wanting badly to relay the message prompted me to do so anyway. My enthusiasm was soon shattered. My husband's weird look and speechless response left me doubtful that I would ever know whether they really called him Bugs Bunny. As my in-laws lived over 2000 miles away, I had not seen my father-in-law when he was very ill. However, knowing this man—who was kind beyond words, aside from the army-colonel mask he wore—I'd guess he would probably have asked the question, "What's up, Doc?" too many times, because he frequented the doctor over a five-year period before he was finally diagnosed with Lou Gehrig's disease.

After this inspirational day downtown with not one but four psychic mediums, my sister Lee Ann was prompted to select one particular psychic, Sonia Choquette, for a personal reading.

The Crossings in Austin, Texas

After the holidays, I learned that Sonia would be hosting a four-day *Psychic Pathway* class in January 2004 at the newly opened Omega Center called The Crossings in Austin, Texas. I even called to verify that one did not have to be psychic to sign up. I wanted to visit this place anyway after reading an article in the *Houston Chronicle* about how the Dell Corporation had donated land 15 miles northwest of Austin for the building of a progressive learning center. And this seemed like the perfect opportunity to kick back, unwind, and learn. Sonia teaches that we each have our own spirit guides gently helping us to navigate through life's challenges; if we can learn our own internal guidance system, our life will not only be easier, but also exciting and more gratifying. Sonia, author of many Hay House books, believes we are all psychic, but 90 percent of us are muted since we are vibrational beings primarily relying only on our five physical senses. Her goal is to teach everyone about tapping into our own sixth sense, where guidance flows freely. She is truly gifted in getting one's soul to move, not only through lectures but also through storytelling, music, dancing, and teaching the important message, "Trust your vibes." The musician who sang and accompanied her on the guitar was Mark Stanton Welch and, they make a great inspirational pair.

Sonia's conviction and inspiration reverberated through each of us, and before long, we were living in the moment and listening to our guides. We were each asked to take a quiet walk, silently asking our spirit guide for a message. It was a clear, cool, sunny day and the question looming in my mind was whether leaving my job to look for a more spiritually oriented position in life would be beneficial. I continued this beautiful walk yet nothing came to me until a few minutes later, when I was inclined to look up in the sky and noticed that way up high something was moving northwest to southeast at a quick, steady pace. Very quickly, I surmised it to be the ISS because there was no contrail indicating it was a plane and it seemed too high for one, anyway. I knew the ISS was visible approximately 225 miles above Earth, though I had yet to see it. The message from my guide was very clear…stay put. Another lady asked her guides why she was there at the class and was amazed to later see on the ground, side by side, a nickel and a penny. "Ah, my six cents," she said!

At the end of the class Sonia gave a brief reading to each person as she signed their book. Naturally, I was anxious to get a message, never having talked with her privately. "Are you out of your marriage yet?" she asked. Taken aback, I quickly responded, "Yes, but I'm dismayed with my grown children's emotional issues over the ordeal." She responded, "Oh, they will be fine; he was your father and oppressed you as a child so he is paying back some karmic debt." Totally missing the words "he was," I thought she was referring to my father. Seeing the confused look on my face, she said, "Your husband was your father in a previous life and oppressed you as a child. Your father in this lifetime was responsible for you being here this week." Okay, I thought, *that* makes more sense.

The last day, I was amazed when Sonia had each of the 50 attendees pair off with someone we did not know in the class. She asked us to turn our chairs and sit closely facing each other with our hands, one palm side up and the other palm side down, hovering over the other person's hands. She told us to relax and picture the person's spirit guide standing at their right shoulder, and had each of us take turns asking for information the other needed to know. The lady with whom I experimented was very kind, and we were both astonished at the specific information we were able to bring through for each other. This proved to us Sonia's point that with sincere, steady practice and patience one can learn to tune in to this other dimension. I went first, telling this lady she was one of four children and also that there was someone named Margie or Margaret who needed forgiveness. My partner proceeded to tell me that she was one of only three children, then very quickly a surprised look came over her and she stated, "Oh wait, I had another sibling, who died during childbirth!" With regard to the female name I had given her, she had to think for a minute before remembering a babysitter named Margaret who had bailed on her at the last minute. When it was my turn to receive a message, my partner told me she could see in her mind's eye a little blond-headed boy standing at my side, who was very sweet and affectionate with me. I knew right away she was referring to Russell and that she had sensed him as a little boy because of our age difference. And of course, Russell's hair was blonder when he was a little boy. She also told me my spirit guide said I was working too many long hours on the job and needed to take more vacations like this one. I gave her a high five on that note for it couldn't have been truer. Sonia says building that psychic muscle is like exercising any muscle in the body; at first it may be weak or you may not be able to get it right, but with practice it can be strengthened if one has a genuine desire to do so.

It was a little sad when this class came to an end, as I had gained new friendships with some beautiful souls just as passionate as I was over the material being presented. Little did I know, though, that a few exciting moments were coming up on my way home. As our teacher had instructed, we were to practice psychic sit-ups by remaining open after leaving the institute. I drove past what seemed to be a landscaping and gardening store with the compelling thought that I should pull over—there was some purchase I should make. Once inside, I moseyed around enjoying all the distinctive pieces, some obviously imported, but did not want to buy anything just because of my urge to pull over. I really wanted to practice my psychic sit-ups and let the item reveal itself. After I'd been walking around for some time, an employee asked if he could help. I told him no thanks and had just turned around to leave when I noticed at the checkout counter a 19-inch hand-carved wooden statue of a robed monk. When he told me this was a statue of St. Francis of Assisi, I immediately knew this would be my purchase. My dad's nickname was Wick, but his given name was Francis. If my dad, as Sonia had said, was responsible for me being there, I wanted a remembrance of his guidance.

Approximately five minutes after leaving the store, I was inclined to check my bag. There was no place to pull over on this curving, hilly road, but I kept looking in my rearview mirror to see my black suitcase in the back of my SUV. Mentally retracing my steps of packing, I continued down the road. This happened twice, and each time I turned my CD player back up, listening to the music and still feeling invigorated. The inclination then came to pull over and get gas. This message came twice but the gauge showed my tank was three-fourths full. Plenty to get me home so I continued to ignore the inclination. Next, an Exxon Mobile semitruck was passing me on the road. How strange—I don't consider myself a slow driver so this doesn't happen very often. Seeing the emblem on the truck, I had the thought yet again, this time as if to say, "Do I need to hit you over the head with a bat?" Out loud I said to myself, "Okay, okay, I'll pull over!" While holding the nozzle in my gas tank, I couldn't help but notice that the rear door on my SUV had been pushed down but not closed shut! How could I have missed that? Then I remembered not shutting it all the way because I had run back upstairs in case something had been left behind. Now, walking around to close the door, I saw that my suitcase had slid to the very back and was against the rear door. A big bump in the road or traveling at a faster pace might have led to my luggage being lost without notice or even causing an accident. What a lesson for me to trust my vibes, as Sonia says, and listen to those sometimes subtle messages. I thanked Dad again and talked to him as he sat in my front passenger seat all the way back to Houston, even if he was a carved wooden monk for the moment!

I had hoped Russell could go with me that week especially since he had not been able to attend the conference downtown, but his busy work schedule and the fact that he was a new employee kept him from it. My work schedule too had been hectic so getting away to the outskirts of Austin was a much-needed escape. And, I was doing something I loved.

In March, however, we would make a trip to northern Louisiana to see his grandmother, who was in hospice care. Around the same time, I had planned a surprise trip for us to California in celebration of Russell's milestone birthday. Grandma's passing was very timely, as we headed off one week later with the hope that she might come through one of the psychic mediums during the *Mystical Connections* seminar in San Francisco. Though disappointed, we realized that with 500 people present, there were just as many souls lined up on the other side trying to come through! This was my first time to hear Gordon Smith, known as the UK's most extraordinary psychic. He was absolutely fascinating as he called out specific and very detailed messages for audience members, leaving some in tears with messages and information that would have been impossible for him to know.

Since I had talked about Sonia from the class in Austin, Russell was anxious to meet her. Surprisingly, she immediately said, "You have an artist in you." While in prison, Russell had drawn some beautiful pictures with a

Love Promised: A Future Life Revealed

pencil on a drawing board. He later framed copies and sold a few at a local restaurant that displayed them on consignment. I'm not sure what else Sonia said to him, but he enjoyed the day, as I had hoped he would. Later that night, Grandma would blink the lights on and off several times in our hotel room to let us know she was there. The next day, Russell's birthday, we rode a Harley across the Golden Gate Bridge, then down beautiful Highway 1, with the mountains on one side and the ocean on the other.

The summer of 2004 began with us moving into a house but, soon after, we were faced with challenges. We began pulling away from each other, he more than I. I had always told him if he should ever feel the need or desire to be with someone his own age, I would accept that and move on; his happiness was foremost in my mind. Unbeknown to me at first, he had started using drugs occasionally. So for the next year, it was an on-again, off-again relationship, and I eventually moved back into my condo.

One time Ron and I were forced to put Russell and my daughter into the same rehab facility, a week apart. My daughter was not very happy about it and questioned how I could allow such a thing. Russell continued to struggle mentally with experiences he had dealt with while in prison, and my daughter was still trying to overcome the trauma of her parents' divorce while she was finishing college. The coping mechanisms Russell and my daughter had chosen were not in their best interests. My beautiful and talented theater student, who had been on the dean's list the year before and whose theatrical performances surpassed some of her older, more experienced, colleagues, was now escaping her life through alcohol. My decision to pull her out of school was difficult but I was scared of the consequences if I didn't. Addiction by itself can be debilitating, without the devastating, unwelcome, and abrupt changes one has to deal with in life. Though my daughter would now face her adversary, Russell, this healing environment would bring them both much closer. Sometimes, it's in such situations that one's soul is revealed to others who may only be strangers. The real healing is in the releasing and letting go, if that indeed can happen. In this setting, without me in the picture, my daughter saw Russell as someone like her who needed help so she befriended him, encouraging him to participate, since he had remained silent in his room. After hearing his story in a group setting, Beth spoke to Russell stating, "I'm sorry for being so unkind to you and I now realize that the only thing you are guilty of is loving my mother." Rehabilitation helped for a while, but eventually the addictions took control again.

The parting between Russell and me was difficult because we were still so much in love. Each time I tried to start anew without him, he would come back into my life again. He would text me to let me know he thought about us when watching the movie *Eternal Sunshine of the Spotless Mind,* where a couple's love survives a procedure they undergo to erase each other from their memories. And I remember sending him a text one day after hearing the new song "Collide"[2] on the radio because it made me think of him and—

> How even the best fall down sometimes
> Even the stars refuse to shine
> Out of the doubt that fills my mind
> You fall in time… I somehow find you and I collide.

Another time after he had started trying to date someone his own age, he sent me a text that said, "There will never be another love like ours." And truly, the love that had been so beautiful between us, and still was, never seemed to be equaled with anyone his own age Russell tried to date or have feelings for, he said. My own slight attempts to have another relationship were useless. I was open once to dating someone else, then realized talking about Russell had dominated the conversation—a definite no-no in the dating game.

When Russell wasn't in my day-to-day life, I would keep up with him through his father, as I was becoming concerned for his well-being. Ron and I had established a close connection because we both fought to help, yet not enable, our loved ones who struggled with addiction, a difficult challenge for all involved.

Chapter Three

Tragedy Strikes but He Is Still Here

When one does not understand death, life can be very confusing.
—Ajahn Chah
(1918-1992, Teacher of Buddhism in Thailand)

In December '05, it was becoming more obvious that Russell's drug use had worsened once again. His father had planned to call me one Sunday afternoon to talk about his situation though, when he did, I was not expecting to hear what had just happened. Ron was crying uncontrollably, his words only partially understandable, but I heard enough to learn Russell had just been in a car accident. My heart began to pound and I braced myself for more information. Clenching the phone and holding my breath, the next thing I knew, a female police officer was on the other end. Quickly I asked, "Is he okay, *is he okay*, did he survive?" After a brief moment of silence, she told me, "No, he didn't, I'm so very sorry; they are taking him away now." I felt myself weaken, slumping into the chair beside me, my stomach and head beginning to ache. Then, bursting into a screaming cry, I hung up the phone. What I couldn't see was that Ron had fallen to his knees, sobbing. Not more than ten minutes earlier, he and Russell had been talking on their cell phones. Russell's car had stalled and he was sitting in the emergency lane on Highway 225 in Houston, waiting for his father to assist him. Out of nowhere, a young girl high on methamphetamines and driving erratically decided to take her white truck into the emergency lane to get around traffic. What we did not know at the time, however, was that this had been her fourth traffic violation that day, and her second accident. Why she was still out on the road driving remains a mystery. The police report estimated she was traveling 79 miles an hour when she hit Russell's car, pushing it a quarter mile along the highway before it exploded with her truck on top of it. Before Ron fell to his knees, they had had to hold him back from running up to the car now ablaze with his son in it. The young girl escaped the accident with only minor injuries.

Wanting desperately to find Ron, I called my sister because the car she had lent me while mine was being repaired had a flat tire. I was too upset to even wonder how that could be; I had driven home in it just 15 minutes before Ron called. When Lee Ann arrived, she talked me out of leaving to try and find the scene of the accident, approximately 20 miles away, even though I cried hysterically, wanting to go.

It was hard enough for me to deal with the heartache and loss, but the kind of pain a parent must endure when they come upon the scene of an accident where their child has just been killed can only be understood by one who has had this same devastating experience. Not many are brave enough to even imagine what that must feel like; the mind simply won't go there.

I was waiting at Russell's mother's house that evening and when Ron arrived, he literally fell into my arms. We both sobbed. When there were no more tears left, we all talked about what had happened and the funeral plans that had to be made. Later, on the way home, I mustered up enough energy to go into a crowded BestBuy and purchase a memory stick to put pictures on for the funeral. I really dreaded going back home to this little place where our love had once blossomed. Standing in the checkout line, zoned out, my eyes and ears all of a sudden became focused on the James Blunt video and song "You're Beautiful"[1] that began to play. Numbed, and unemotionally mesmerized by the words, I stared at the TVs on the wall in the store—

> An angel thought I should be with you…You're beautiful, you're beautiful it's true, I saw your face in a crowed place, and I don't know what to do; cause I'll never be with you…and I don't think that I'll see her again, but we shared a moment that will last to the end…
> (Chorus)
>
> But it's time to face the truth; I will never be with you.

It was as if my mind was transported to another place in time because, gazing at the screen, I failed to recall where I was or how long I had been standing there. "Excuse me, may I help you?" the clerk said, as I checked out. With swollen eyes and holding back the tears, I left wondering, "Oh my, could that be Russell already?" I went home, crawled into bed, and cried myself to sleep.

When I awoke the next morning, the tears started to flow once again. I wanted so badly to go back to sleep and avoid facing reality, but could only bury my head in the pillow and cry some more. Listening to the message Russell had left on my cell phone a few weeks earlier that ended with "I love you" became a painful addiction. I finally got out of bed to fix myself a cup of coffee. Usually the quiet of morning is very peaceful but for some reason I was inclined to turn on the radio. Immediately, it seemed another song from Russell began to play. I sensed him standing next to me in the kitchen while bracing myself against the cupboard where we had once stood eating chocolate and vanilla pudding, our "cigarette" afterward. I think he was trying to tell me what he was dealing with at the moment, through the words "You and Me"[2] by Lifehouse—

> What day is it? And in what month?
> This clock never seemed so alive
> I can't keep up and I can't back down
> I've been losing so much time
> (Chorus)
>
> 'Cause it's you and me and all of the people with nothing to do
> Nothing to lose
> And it's you and me and all other people
> And I don't know why, I can't keep my eyes off of you
> One of the things that I want to say just aren't coming out right
> I'm tripping on words
> You've got my head spinning
> I don't know where to go from here
> (Chorus)
>
> There's something about you now
> I can't quite figure out
> Everything she does is beautiful
> Everything she does is right
>
> 'Cause it's you and me and all of the people with nothing to do
> Nothing to lose

And it's you and me and all other people
And I don't know why, I can't keep my eyes off of you and me and all
        other people with nothing to do
Nothing to prove
And it's you and me and all other people
And I don't know why, I can't keep my eyes off of you

What day is it?
And in what month?
This clock never seemed so alive.

All I could do was continue to cry, knowing he too was struggling with what had just happened.

Strange Things Begin to Happen

Walking back to the bedroom, I noticed that on my dresser my beautiful hand-painted egg from Russia portraying *The Kiss* was lying on its side on the thin pedestal for which it usually sits upright. Before my 2002 four-month stay working in Moscow, I had run across a picture of this beautiful painting in the images that faded in and out of my screen saver. Of the 20 or so images, this was my favorite. It depicts a woman being embraced by a man, obviously her lover, who is kissing her on the cheek. But you must look closely to see the image, described as "a veil of concentric circles." While in Moscow, I naturally was drawn to purchase this egg after finding the artist, Vladimir Stoupakov-Konev, whose expertise was hand-painting eggs by copying pictures that Gustav Klimt had painted in the early 1900s. Now, standing in my condo three years later, I stared in disbelief at this large egg lying sideways. Another day, it was turned sideways again after it had been set up straight. And, several times over the next few weeks, my screen saver actually froze on this picture.

As mentioned, this was not the first time I had experienced physical things being moved around by someone in spirit. My father, for the past few years, had continuously shocked our mother by taking things from one place to another. Still, one's mind always first tries to figure out a logical explanation. I never would have set the egg sideways, and accidentally hitting it would have knocked it off the pedestal completely. Instead, it was perfectly balanced on its side. "How *is it* they do that?" I wondered.

                                      Love Promised: A Future Life Revealed

Well, it is all energy and there was just so much more about life I wanted to understand.

I appreciated Russell letting me know he was around, mostly by the strong pressure in one ear in addition to unusual noises in my condo, and blinking lights. Each time I would try to quiet my mind and hear what he might be saying. Over the next three days, it became even more apparent that he was trying desperately to make contact. Russell's Aunt Vickey and her daughter Tye, Russell's cousin to whom he had been very close, drove down from Tyler, Texas, to comfort Ron and help in any way. They too were devastated by what had happened, as was their whole family. I did not feel comfortable, however, saying anything about my experiences until I heard about some *they* were having. During the middle of the night, Russell's dogs started barking feverishly for no apparent reason. Late another night, Ron awoke to hear a loud crash in his computer room. When he raced to see what had happened, his printer had been knocked off the desk onto the floor; no one was in the room.

The next day Vickey freaked out when she caught a glimpse of Russell from the waist up—a shadowy figure wearing the sweatshirt he was killed in, as he whisked around the corner in the hallway of his father's house. And, Ron would feel his left ear ringing as he stood in front of his bathroom mirror. We later met at Russell's house and, each taking a different room, started packing up his belongings. Mine was the art room upstairs. As I carefully packed things away, all of a sudden Russell's air compressor, plugged into the wall, turned on all by itself. In shock, I just stared at it, then it shut off after 30 seconds. Minutes later, it happened again and I finally got up the courage to call the others into the room. We all stared in amazement when it turned on again. I knew it had to be Russell, knowing how those in spirit can manipulate electricity. Tye was very skeptical until she exclaimed aloud to Russell, asking him to turn on the compressor once again if it was indeed him. Within a minute, it turned on for 30 seconds, as it had done before. Tye's eyes opened wide as she stood there bewildered. We also noticed a colder spot in the room, and I sensed strong pressure in one of my ears, something that was now happening quite often. We left that day feeling somewhat mystified.

The next morning I awoke to yet another uncanny song on the radio, "Angel,"[3] this one by Aerosmith. It was as though I was hearing the lyrics for the first time:

i'm alone, yeah, I don't know if I can face the night
I'm in tears and the cryin' that I do is for you
I want your love
Let's break the walls between us
Don't make it tough
I'll put away my pride
Enough's enough
I've suffered and I've seen the light
(Chorus)

Bayayby, you're my angel
Come and save me tonight
You're my angel
Come and make it alright

Don't know what I'm gonna do about this feeling inside
Yes it's true, loneliness took me for a ride
Without your love I'm nothing but a beggar
Without your love a dog without a bone
What can I do? I'm sleepin' in this bed alone
(Chorus)

Come and save me tonight
You're the reason I live
You're the reason I die
You're the reason I give when I break down and cry
Don't need no reason why
Baby, baby, bayayby
You're my angel
Come and save me tonight

Ron's brother in Kilgore, Texas, called to say the *Houston Chronicle* with his nephew's obituary had been thrown into his yard that morning. Strangely enough, he had never subscribed to the paper, nor had it ever been thrown in his yard. I had once told Ron about the psychic some in our family would often visit to communicate with our father. I confessed to taking Russell there once, hoping his grandmother on the other side might help him deal with his drug use. Hesitating to suggest it so soon, but feeling that Russell needed to talk, I asked Ron if he would be interested. He gave

Love Promised: A Future Life Revealed

me a definite yes so I called and made an appointment with the psychic for Friday, the day after Russell's funeral.

December 15 was a beautiful, cool, sunny day in Shreveport, Louisiana. Russell's artwork had been displayed and the program planned. Ron asked me to read at the service a beautiful love poem Russell had written to me. Though I was extremely honored, it was truly one of the hardest things to do. Still, it gave me the opportunity to tell Russell's family how much they had all meant to him, and how special the father-son relationship had been. Standing at the podium, I had to pause for a moment as emotions started to well up inside me. Here I was getting ready to read aloud to a group of people, some strangers, these intimate words of love from Russell...while he lay in a covered casket next to me. Will I get through it? Can I do it? My heart began to pound as I took a sip of water, then slowly looked into the audience, where my sister and niece sat. The compassion on their faces was obvious, their eyes glowed with concern. Time seemed to stand still as everyone waited patiently. I glanced quickly into space, then murmured to myself, "Please, Russell, help me," hoping no one had heard. Suddenly, warmth came over my whole body and my voice quavered only once.

Ron, too, spoke during the ceremony, braving the same experience of reading poetry Russell had written. His cousins shared stories of growing up together and along with Ron, they recognized me as the love of Russell's life. My few words after the ceremony could not express my heartfelt appreciation. In addition to the song "You Raise Me Up" another was played during the ceremony, one that Russell had recorded in a sound booth for fun when we had taken a family trip with his mom, dad, and daughter, Chelsea, to Fiesta World in San Antonio. Listening to the lyrics of "I Swear" was more poignant now than ever before as we sat staring at the casket... "I swear by the moon and the stars in the skies, Like the shadow that's by your side, I'll be there."

A military graveside service followed, as Russell had served in the Air Force. Walking past the row of flowers, I hoped to find the condolences my company had sent though a funeral attendant standing close by stated, "Ma'am, the cards are removed before the flowers are brought outside." As I was disappointedly walking away, the last funeral spray toppled over on me. The attendant quickly ran over, apologizing as he pulled it off me. When he did, I turned and noticed that this particular spray still had the card left on it. It read "United Space Alliance." I looked at him and said, "Please, no apology necessary; instead, *thank you.*" The Morris family was indeed in mourning and still engulfed in shock. Along with Russell's Mom, I held on to Chelsea as we watched Ron lean over to kiss the casket that cradled his only child before it was lowered into the ground.

If Your Deceased Loved One Could Talk, What Would They Say?

For the loved ones left behind, grief can seem unbearable at a time like this…minds are traumatized and hearts are ripped apart, especially if the crossing was abrupt, with no preparation for the unimaginable event. What we found, however, is that this shock can be experienced by all, including the one who just left. And we learned, too, just how important spirit communication is for the healing of deep sorrow; otherwise despair, blame, despondency, or frustration and anxiety can remain or even build.

Ron's and Vickey's lives would soon be changed forever when we went to visit Petrene, the psychic medium through whom I had spoken to my dad many times. The only thing she knew was that Russell had been killed in a car accident. Tissues in our hands, we sat waiting patiently. I prayed for a good connection while Ron and Vickey had no choice but to be open-minded, desperately seeking answers for any sign of Russell and the strange occurrences leading up to this day. Petrene immediately tuned in to his energy and the following conversation ensued. Petrene's words are in *italics.*

It is really good that you all came because he is all right, but he has been completely freaking out. First of all, was he hit from behind? We nod our heads yes and continue to listen. *Good thing to know is…he absolutely did not suffer nor was he in any pain; he is in major shock, as in "What the hell happened?" And then I get "What the hell hit me?" I get this really bright, huge flash of white light; warm feeling like being completely surrounded by marshmallows and it's like zooming out of body at an incredibly fast speed. Again, you have to know he did not suffer. He's freaking out because he has been trying to get in touch with everybody ever since and he has been doing all kinds of crazy things. Have you had things being knocked over? It's almost like a blundering, blustering, not just cute little things happening, but chaotic because he has been trying to communicate, "I'm here, I'm here, and I'm still here."*

Love Promised: A Future Life Revealed

We nod yes, not wanting to stop the session and tell her all the things that were happening, but very much listening for more information. *Okay, he's really relieved and glad you are here because he's happy to know that you can communicate with him.* Petrene pointed to Ron and his left ear. *With you, with this ear, have you had someone like shouting, tickling, because he is standing up close and shouting at you trying to catch your attention. I know it's difficult to know.* Ron nods, "Yes, my left side." *His energy is like this...* Petrene slumps down in her chair with both arms hanging by her side. *You have a serious extended family, a lot of you because he has so many people around him, and they are trying to help him calm down and let him know it's okay, but until he could get in touch with you and have this conversation, he can't calm down. Because he wanted to let everyone know he was alive.* Petrene then turns to me. *To you, he is telling you, like I told you, I told you all that kind of stuff, like in some way he told you something was going to happen, like you knew, you knew. Did you have that kind of feeling? Even though you didn't want to recognize it or admit it in some way.*

For a moment I feel puzzled, then it soon makes sense. A year before Russell was killed we agreed to no longer have an exclusive relationship. We knew how much we loved each other in spite of the significant age difference; yet because of it we were intellectually struggling with what direction our lives should take. We sat in his truck one night lamenting the strong bond and feelings of love we had for each other, but also understanding on another level, I now know, that we wouldn't be together much longer. As we sat in his truck and cried, Russell turned the radio up louder and asked me to listen. The song, "I Will Remember You" by Sarah McLachlan began..."

I will remember you
Will you remember me?
Don't let your life pass you by
Weep not for the memories

Remember the good times that we had?
I let them slip away from us when things got bad
How clearly I first saw you smilin' in the sun
Wanna feel your warmth upon me, I wanna be the one
(Chorus)

I'm so tired but I can't sleep
Standin' on the edge of something much too deep

It's funny how we feel so much but we cannot say a word
We are screaming inside, but we can't be heard
(Chorus)

I'm so afraid to love you, but more afraid to lose
Clinging to a past that doesn't let me choose
Once there was a darkness, deep and endless night
You gave me everything you had, oh you gave me light
(Chorus)

All we could do was look at one other with tears in our eyes. After all, it would have been too difficult to imagine…And I sensed "death" but thought it was me, not him, or was it? It seemed like a self-inflicted Romeo and Juliet moment and my logical mind was trying to interfere and rationalize, since I was the older of the two, that it would be me leaving or crossing over. Along with my tears, everyone else started to cry. *Everybody cry and he's saying, yeah you knew, you weren't listening, like it was all so far and I can't believe it. Neither of us was being awake enough and here it is to know.*

Was there another car involved? Because he is upset, saying it was somebody else's fault, reckless driving and they can't get away with that…he is swearing a lot, like, "That bastard's got to pay." Did he have a child? Is that a girl? We acknowledge the truth with a nod. *Yes, because he is telling me about her, is she all right? And what's going to happen, will she be okay? He is so glad that you are all here, thank God you knew what to do and he is saying Kent has been absolutely amazing, holding it all together like she knew what to do helping everyone along. Excuse me, he is just really crying and sobbing and relieved in some way, you can imagine anyone going through that would be incredibly shocked.* We all start to cry, knowing that Russell is so relieved we are there. Petrene hands us more tissue and says, *"It's really good to cry."*

He is asking, what's going to happen? What are the police doing? Because he really wants everything to be followed through and he feels like it's not happening fast enough, papers have been moved. Keep your heads calm but don't give them a minute's peace because they need to do their job. He is annoyed; there is something not okay about the accident scene. Something has been changed and is not as it should be, ask lots of questions, he says. When you hear more about it in the future, he wants you to come back and really get that clear, something is not being presented right. Was there any kind of white car involved? It was a white truck that hit him. *It had to do with the angle of the hit or where the truck actually was and everybody is confused because something is missing, and it was not intentional that it happened. He keeps giving me the impression that the person was not paying attention. As well, he wants everyone to know that on some level he knew he was going, on an everyday level, he was trying very hard to be here because he knew that everyone was worried about him…was he going to make it, was he going to grow old. And in some ways, he is pissed off that this was taken away from him. It's not that he wants this person to be punished but at the very least he's saying they should make things right. There was more than one person in this truck unless they were on a cell phone or there was some other distraction. He is telling me the truck was full, there was a turned-up radio, cell phone, or there was more than one person. They were not in a calm situation; a lot was going on in the truck.*

[An investigation later ensued to determine how the accident had happened but it would be six months before the girl driving the truck was arrested. We felt it might have had to do with her being the stepdaughter of a police officer, as ongoing inquiry never revealed why she was still on the streets.]

We then ask, "Did he see the vehicle coming in the rearview mirror?" *No, it seems like an incredible fast accident that came out of nowhere, the hit was so hard and he was out of his body immediately.* Petrene stops to listen for a moment to what Russell is telling her…*He is so, so sorry for everyone and even though he said things to you and yet he knew at the same time, he's saying, I can't believe and I would have said so much more and like with you, Kent, he wishes that he would have expressed recently how he felt (he's sighing) a lot more often and a lot more clearly and he feels like he was playing cat and mouse and he didn't mean to and he wishes he had said he loved you more and did love you, and you are the best thing that ever happened to him and he is so sorry. And to his father, you, he says that at times he made it difficult for you, blaming you more than he should and he is really sorry about that.*

Petrene looks at Vickey. *To you, he is being really playful; you two had a serious rapport, a sense of humor together, he's saying "Can you believe this?" and he is pulling your hair a little bit and, in fact, he is asking what are you doing with your hair? Did he have some kind of joke with you?* Vickey is shocked and her cry breaks into a laugh as she wipes her tears. "Russell used to call me Big Hair when teasing me about my 1980s hairdo." *Exactly, he is kind of doing the same.*

He has so much energy, I'm exhausted, and he's like bouncing around and going so much faster than I can speak. We look at one another, nodding our heads and chuckling, but with tears in our eyes, as we all knew Russell's hyper side when he was here in body. This is even more confirmation he is in the room, trying hard to get through as much information as possible. We are also relieved for his sake, knowing how difficult it must be to be here one moment and there the next, not being able to get anyone's attention—a real chore when you were used to getting everyone's attention pretty easily in body. And there is so much left unsaid when leaving so abruptly.

Russell is saying... "I can tell you, I'm going to get this sorted out" and on another level, he says, "I'm going to be able to communicate with you like nobody has ever communicated before" and there is a part of him, Petrene says, *that he is so excited about... even though he is so distressed and shocked at what happened and because of how you all are, he is assuring you, I'm going to get this right, he's like I'm going to be on TV.* (We chuckle.) *He's serious, "I'm going to be the guy on TV that the medium sits down with and I'm going to make things happen, he is dedicated, and you will know it's me," he says.*

And that's just what Russell would say...He was determined; we all knew he could do whatever he was passionate about or focused on. *Did he have serious injuries to the middle part of his body; did you see any of that or know anything about that?* "They wouldn't let me get close," Ron said. *Okay...he is just showing me it was pretty bad, but he didn't feel any of that, as he was out of his body instantly. Did the watch stop? It **has** stopped.* Ron confirmed that it had. *He's calming down a little bit now, he wants you to talk to me now; he wants you to ask questions. Did you have the funeral yesterday or the day before?* "Yesterday," we said. *Yes, okay he is just asking about that. Who got seriously tongue-tied in what they were saying, or trying to say in doing the right thing? Not one of you, somebody else.* Ron spoke up. "Tammy did, his oldest cousin." *Yes, and how did the preacher mess up, because he messed up a couple of times?* "He stumbled and mispronounced a couple of names." *Ah, yes, he's telling me about that, the funeral in general, and he is saying it was a beautiful thing, and you all did wonderful with the amount of time you had, everybody worked overtime. He's saying there were some beautiful pictures.* We acknowledge that copies of Russell's artwork were displayed in the foyer of the funeral home in addition to the personal photos chosen to display in a movie format on a screen before the service. *And that made him really happy.*

He is saying black onyx...Are you going to have a stone, or are you going to put some stones, or some jewelry... What's the thing with black onyx, because he is talking to me about that? "He had a black onyx pyramid," Ron says, "like a small marble paperweight, he had it in his house and now I have it in my house, in fact I had it this morning. *"Good, because he is talking to me about*

Love Promised: A Future Life Revealed

*that…he is sending shivers up and down my spine and telling me this is your little way to communicate with him. He wants you to really sit down and feel that, hold it close to your heart. He is saying don't feel stupid because you can talk to me, like I'm here, because I **am** here even though you can't see me. The only problem is that you have to be careful about the chair you sit in there because you misjudged it; you nearly fell out of it earlier. Do you remember doing that?* "Oh my gosh!" exclaims Ron, "yes, that desk chair turns over all the time."

Kent, what do you want to say? "Well, I'm thinking my Dad was there to greet him…they didn't know each other but were so much alike and Dad knows how much I love Russell." *Yes, he says about your Dad…he sees him from a distance, his light, and there are so many people around him, lots of extended family. And since it has happened, he is aware of all these presences and can feel their love and support, but he hasn't let anyone get near him. He was freaking out and wanted to talk with you guys first and let everyone know he's all right. And now that you have had this session, when we are finished here, even now, he is calming down and he will be able to look around, get help and see how things work.* Feeling protective, I say, "Okay, good, my father can help him understand what it's like over there." *Absolutely, yes, when you talk to him, he is such a little boy and he is laying his head on your shoulder, he is saying I'm so sorry, I wished that I had listened more carefully and took you a lot more seriously and all the things that people told me about how life can be. Just like that, how he could find himself there…He did listen, but he did not do enough to be ready for now and he wishes that he had explored the subject more…he is just having a wise smile, and telling me, I guess I have a lot to learn.* Often I would share my philosophical thoughts and books with Russell about life in general and the afterlife, so this made perfect sense.

Our Session Continues…

He wants you all to know very, very clearly, one, that he is there, he is with you and he is going to communicate but, secondly, he wants you to know, it's almost ironic how ridiculous time is, that time and space has no distance. He is saying don't be afraid of time like it goes on forever, there and here, it's all the same. It's not even there and here, there are millions of places and basically we are all a part of it, there isn't a separation, and it's just so, so simple, so much more simple than he could have ever imagined. There really aren't any divisions; he just wishes that you could know, that you could see what he is seeing and experiencing now, and when he relaxes and let's go, there is so much peace, it's amazing. It thrills us to hear Russell talking about the other side and letting us know that he is beginning to adjust.

What's this dog that's driving him absolutely mad? Ron starts to laugh out loud and we just smile. *The dog can see him, okay, I don't know if you are aware of that, it's as if the dogs are saying, "What! You're here and now you are there, what are you doing there?"* How do you know his dogs are behaving so *differently?* "They will start frantically barking in the middle of the night and when I get up there is no one there." *That's what I'm saying, the dogs' reality is no separation, and they see no separation. The dogs can see him physically... Touch me, pet me, what are you doing just standing there.* Russell did love animals and especially his little schnauzers...he played with them often and showered them with attention and affection. We know they are missing him.

Okay, what about his daughter, he really wants to talk about his daughter. "Chelsea is her name." *Okay, thank you.* Petrene pauses as Russell communicates with her. *He is very, very sweet, and very respectful. I only met him once but he is saying thank you so much. Okay, about Chelsea. Is she with her mom?* We nod yes. *Her mom doesn't appear to be handling it too well with Chelsea; she is making her fearful about the whole thing. You know that?* Chelsea had mentioned at the funeral that her Dad had planned to get her the Sunday he was killed and this might not have happened otherwise. But we all let her know this was clearly not the case. *Russell is very upset about his daughter being afraid and it may be not so much about what the mom is saying as what she is not saying. Maybe she isn't saying "It's not your fault" and he doesn't want his daughter to feel that way. Come talk with me and sort things out, he is saying. He is very, very concerned about finances in the future for his daughter. Is there not anything left?* "They don't have too much," Ron says.

He is now going back to the accident and saying it was not his fault. Do you have any idea...? I mean he is saying what's happening with this case, the *police need to... (Pause)...Do you know what happened to the other people and was there insurance?* "I'm going by there this afternoon," Ron says, "and my insurance company called me 20 minutes ago, just before I got here, we are working on it."

Okay, good, because he is saying, Dad, I'm counting on you, I can't do it, you need to do this for me and I need you, I'm trusting you and I'm going to be with you all the way. He is going to do everything he can to make sure that happens. There is plenty of money there so that his daughter is okay; he really needs to make that happen. Keep talking...anyone.

Ron speaks up and asks, "Is he upset with me for doing anything at the funeral?" *He is basically smiling; but he is a little bit embarrassed. And he's saying, don't tell her, don't tell her, as in, don't tell me. Okay, so keep it to yourself as he's just a little bit embarrassed for me to know. He is smiling; can you see that he might be embarrassed?* "Yes," Ron says. *He's smiling and he definitely thinks that's amusing and that's you, and that's okay, he is not at all mad at you.* We start to grin, knowing that Russell is talking about the song he recorded that we played at the funeral. Russell was a great artist with his hands, but he sang like the rest of us, a little off-key!

Vickey says, as she breaks into a cry… "Can I just ask him if he knows how much my girls and I love him and my granddaughters, because the five-year-old cut off her hair at school so she could put it in his casket." *He's very solemn when you say that and he is hugging you tightly, saying I know, I know, comfort them and comfort yourself and, of course, the shock and suddenness and every bit of it is extremely hard to deal with, but…when you do and see how amazing it is, the communication and that life goes on. It isn't like you think… all of that is going to be so amazing for you, for them, for all of you.*

He's saying it's a real tough way to do this but he is actually telling me that he has been chosen, was chosen, to basically bring this lesson, that he could be physically not here but you would all not only grieve, grieve, grieve, and accept the world here and there, but that you would all learn something much, much greater. It is all the same place and you would understand if you could put away loads of your own limitations. It's fascinating because he is showing me this big group of people who are telling him, job well done for making that difficult choice. Okay, so even though on a conscious level this was all an accident, on another level it was a choice that was made about a year ago. And, yes, I don't know who can remember a year ago, but then, he very much accepted and made peace with his spiritual or higher self and agreed to do things this way. So even though it appears such a shock, on another level, it's about a much bigger thing, but of course he feels all of your love.

Vickey asks, "Does he know when all of us will leave this Earth? I had a dream about 15 years ago that I had cancer and the doctors told me it was too late. I don't care, I just wondered if he knows."

First of all, I couldn't help looking myself, I just want to assure you that you are not going that way, and despite what anybody says, if you smoke, eat bad things, people get cancer for one simple reason…they hold things in whether it's pain, anger, fear, trauma, and they don't get it out and express it, so eventually it turns on itself and activates the cancer, which we've all got it in us. It's much better to be swearing your head off than keeping it all in, get it out and you don't get cancer.

Crying, I say to Petrene, "Does he know how much I love him? I think he does but I just want to know." *He says, absolutely, of course he does, like a fresh spring day and he just brings like an absolute open field filled with light and bright yellow…he is laughing right now because he says his dad is not used to him talking like that.* Ron quickly speaks up, "I was just thinking that same thing…I guess we all ask ourselves this—things I could have done better, if I could have been a better dad?" *He says…Come on, Petrene, tell him…He shows you being this lovable adorable thing, and your only failing, which wasn't your fault, was that in your past and your background, you didn't have enough love and he says because of that you gave all that you could. How could you possibly know how to express it any more than you did?* "Does he know how much I love him?" *Ron too asks with a weakened voice. He says that you will always be close, as in standing together, you are him, he is you, like always, and be happy for that…no amount of time, space, different dimensions, different lifetimes, nothing can separate or part that. He tells me you have the same smile, I don't know why he is saying this, and he is saying you have the same heartbeat, so you are the same person, exactly.*

We just sit there amazed at some of Russell's remarks. Ron then says, "Has he been trying to let us know something?" *As you say that, the first thing he's been telling me initially is that he's been causing all kinds of chaos ever since he went; he's been trying to get in touch very strongly. The first thing that I got, I saw something being physically pushed, knocked over, something you would totally say, "Wow."* "Oh, that would be the funeral spray at his graveside service, for one," I say. "And the computer printer," Ron adds. *Exactly, so that's the being pushed over part but with you all, I feel, you've had all kinds of chaotic, crazy things, maybe a noise here or telephone or a TV or lights or maybe something wrong with the stove, little things too, it's kind of somebody causing chaos around you that didn't make sense but if you add them all up, they make up a lot of sense.* Knowing how spirits communicate with mental images, signs, and symbols, I know when Petrene says "stove" it might have been the knob on the heater of the truck that Russell had sold my son, as it turned on full blast the night he died. When that happened, because he never turns his heater on, Matthew immediately thought of Russell.

Where is the poem? He wrote some kind of poem. We all gasp and start to cry again. *It might not have been something he always did, and yet he wrote a poem and he wishes that it were here so it could be read out loud because he meant it with all his heart. You all know what he is talking about, I don't, so please be quiet for a minute and think about the words and this is his way of*

Love Promised: A Future Life Revealed

being with you right now, he is very somber as he talks about that. He tells me poetry really wasn't his thing, but the time that he did write, it came very easy to him, meaningful, and pouring out of himself. Ron and I both talk about the poems Russell wrote. *He's just telling me that you all are such good people.* Toward the end of our session, we share some of our experiences with Petrene to validate the information she was given.

Healing Hearts

The hour-and-a-half long session seemed to take only minutes and we were not only amazed but also relieved that we were finally able to communicate with Russell. I was glad that my father and so many others were around him to help in his transition. We told Russell how much we loved him and that we would try to be more open to his communication. Sharing hugs and goodbyes, we let Petrene know how very grateful we were for having such an outstanding conduit.

Communicating with Russell the day after his funeral had been a wonderful and necessary experience. It was pure therapy, allowing each of us a chance to ask questions, obtain answers, express our thoughts, and confirm our feelings…but most important, to listen to what Russell needed to say. Not only that, we knew Petrene had no way of knowing the incidents and facts surrounding Russell's death, which helped us believe even more that, indeed, Russell *was* still alive and there with us. Naturally, it didn't take away all the pain and suffering but the connection was very healing on both sides. And it was just one more confirmation that death is definitely not an ending; love lives on, and very possibly this other side *is* more tangible to an individual crossing over than our human, conscious minds can even fathom.

As we headed home, I told Ron we could always pull out the Ouija board and try communicating ourselves. What the heck, we thought, it was worth giving it a whirl. For one, it was the same board that Russell and I had used. It still carried his energy, which was very important, so what better tool to use.

Before we had that chance, however, on December 18, a really odd experience occurred. It would leave me wanting, and needing, more answers. That afternoon, I picked up my PalmPilot to tell my sister about the details of a TV program, *Angels Among Us*, which I had noted in my calendar to watch that night. I wasn't prepared, though for what was staring me in the face. Shocked, I said to Lee Ann, "You are not going to believe…what *is* this…and how did it get here?!" "What?" she said. I went on to tell her that there had been a recurring appointment set on this day with the information *Anup K. Patel, November 18, 1983—December 18, 2004, R. I. P.* My sister sounded dumbfounded, as expected, so I told her she would just have to see it. After hanging up the phone I sat alone, baffled. No one had been in possession of my PalmPilot but me. And why and how was this stranger's name added to my calendar, with what appeared to be his birth and death dates?

Our First Session

Two days later we had our first Ouija board session, at the condo where Russell and I had lived. Ron's friend JR was there to take notes and my sister Lee Ann was anxiously awaiting whatever might come through. We set a picture of Russell on the table along with some of his personal belongings, and lit a candle. After a moment of silence and prayer, Ron and I carefully placed our hands on the oracle. Everyone, including Ron and me, waited in anticipation of what would happen. It took only a couple of seconds and, astonishingly, it started moving. [*Note:* communication from the other side will be shown in italics]

"Who is here with us?" I asked. *Baby Girl.* My heart started to pound, these first words were an affectionate name Russell used to call me, and the tears naturally flowed, as I knew in my heart it was him. The oracle continued to move...*Anup.* OMG! This is the name that showed up on my PalmPilot. How did he cross over, Russell? *Killed.* How? *LP.* Ron then said, "You mean by gas?" *Yes...*After this, our curiosity and questions continued...Suicide? *No.* Who murdered him? *Gopa.* What is his last name? *Patel.* Is he a relative? *Yes.* What should we do? *Talk to Petrene.* Why was he murdered? *Enemy, drugs.* Did you know Anup here? *No.* Do you know him from that side? *Yes...California.* Is "R.I.P." what we think? *So Anup can Rest in Peace.* Almost dumbfounded, we stopped for a moment and just stared at one another, our minds and hearts swirling. We quickly started up again...How old is Gopa Patel? *26.* Birthdate? *1,5,81 ...Happy, stay with me...*We will, babe, we will. Lee Ann and I then asked, "Have you talked with Dad over there?" *Yes.* What did he say to you? *Gave advice, calmed me down. Surreal, you can create whatever you want.* We looked at one another, a thousand questions stirred in our minds. *Wow, babe.* Gosh, Russell, when are you coming back? *2023.* Lee Ann then asked, "Is Baby Girl coming back with you?" *Same time, Eva.* Shivers went up my spine. Lee Ann then asked, "Do you have a message for Ron?" *Love u.* Ron then asked, "Do you have a message for Kent?" *Wow, Baby Girl.* We assumed he was talking about what it is like over there. In fact, we were still somewhat in shock that this was happening and the hour somehow flew by. Russell closed out the session saying, *Love Kent…Time to go 2 bed…there is a season.* And then the oracle moved across the bottom of the board, "*Goodbye.*" I knew immediately what he was talking about when he said, "There is a season." It was the consoling song "Turn, Turn, Turn" by the Byrds from many years earlier. And I knew that was just what he was trying to do.

It was impossible not to cry, wanting so badly to reach out and touch him. I needed a hug and so did his dad. Putting up the board after everyone had left, I sat alone, excited and mesmerized, though my heart was sinking at the same time. Gosh, it was just yesterday, it seemed, that we had been playing this so-called game ourselves. Russell and I would talk about it afterward, smile, and put the board up…then we snuggled in bed and fell asleep. This time the game didn't seem as much fun as before. My tears started to flow once again. How can this be, now you are the one who is over there? Life is just not fair, it seems. Why, oh why?

We could not wait to get back on the following week and continued to communicate weekly. If I broke down and cried, Russell would tell me to be strong, as the emotional tears weaken the connection. *Don't cry all of the time, just sometimes, you are closed then…breathe, baby, breathe.* So I tried to be strong, especially during the sessions, as did his father. Also, many times he would tell us, *Remember, I'm in a much better place.* Knowing this made us feel better.

Looking back at our first session, it was like kindergarten compared to the ones we would have in the future. They usually lasted approximately two hours, then Russell would tell us he was being called. "Who is calling?" we'd ask. *Angels.* Continually, we were told they stay very busy in service, helping other souls to cross over. We asked once, "How do you feel?" *I feel the same only with no weight.* Other times when ending a session, Russell would tell us to get some rest…*I don't have to sleep, but you do.*

On a subsequent session we had with Petrene, I was surprised to hear her tell me that the information showing up on my PalmPilot with the name Anup K. Patel was about me. When I asked her to explain, she told me it was my energy that brought the information through. It was a test and had nothing to do with Russell…so it naturally left me with wonder and curiosity. I searched the Internet for this name and was shocked to find a blog written by a young girl in San Antonio, Texas, on the very day this young man had died. She was disheartened about just losing her friend Anup Patel… and how "sick to her stomach she was from being so upset." What was worse, she went on to say, is that she didn't know whether or not it was suicide. Was it the same person? It had to be…but how futile to try to resolve the matter; after all, how could I?

The holiday season just around the corner was sure to be difficult and somber. In addition to struggling with Russell's death, my sentiments went out to his family, who had just begun to enjoy this time with him again. And I very much appreciated still having my children, and would cherish time spent with them.

Seeing Russell through the Eyes of His Family

I was very fortunate that Russell's mom and dad had accepted me with open arms, after the initial shock of our age difference. Though his parents had been divorced since he was a teenager, they came together as a family for outings and even vacations, especially since they had been deprived of him for so long due to the prison sentence. And as Russell wanted me right beside him I got to know his family well, and relished hearing stories about him from their perspective.

As an only child, Russell had parents who adored him from the day he was born. He grew up in a stable, upper-middle-class family as both his parents were educated at universities in East Texas and Louisiana, and had good jobs wherever they went. When they noticed their little blond-haired boy was a quick learner, they had him tested and found an IQ of 140. Russell attended a private school early on, then transferred to the public school system. He was full of life and never did anything halfway, most times pushing the envelope to see how far, how high, or how fast he could go. He loved the water from the time his Dad started teaching him to swim, at the age of one. As he grew older, his house became the hangout of the neighborhood, especially with the new pool and slide that were a surprise for his tenth birthday. He was very fond of his schnauzers, named Colby and Sable. Russell developed a love of art, drawing and taking things apart to see how they worked.

When he was 16, Russell's parents divorced. This had a major impact on his life. The continuing disagreements and outbursts of anger, Ron said, were not healthy for a child. Reflecting on the past one day he told me that if he had realized the impact this would have on Russell, he would have tried everything to stay married, and hold his family together. Russell seemed to lose his direction because, Ron said, he felt they did not provide enough comfort or guidance during this time. Russell began struggling in school and running with the wrong crowd, eventually getting involved with drugs at the age of 17. However, joining the Air Force soon after gave him the grounding he needed. He married young and had a daughter at the age of 19. Now, Ron says that Russell just seemed to always try to cram as much living as possible into what turned out to be a relatively short lifetime, almost as if he knew his days were numbered.

Unlike my family, Russell's had never talked much about death, the spirit world, what some call ghosts, or the "other side" until we met. Ron *now* believes the story that was handed down in his family about his great-grandmother who spoke of angels dancing around the grave of her sister. Even though Grandma had sworn it to be true, the family was always skeptical. And now that the subject of reincarnation was becoming more than just a passing thought, Ron understands why he had such a vivid dream years ago of being shot in a Western bar back in the 1800s. As a child, he literally fell out of his bunk bed, he said, feeling the pain where he remembered the bullet hitting him.

Though Russell struggled with addiction, he was a beautiful soul to many during his brief lifetime here on Earth. His prison buddy, Chris, would later tell us that Russell did not deserve to be there, that "he was an inspiration to us all." Another friend who grew up with him wrote on his memorial Web site:

> *Russell...*
> *You changed my life and today I'm more of a man due to having you as my friend. I don't let people inside, you know that. You were one of the few that got to me...You have no idea how much you meant to me. I used to tell you then, but because we are guys it kind of went without saying...You were the brother I always wanted. I've always spoken of you through the years...as my only real friend. Please know that what I am now is due to the kindness and gentleness of your heart. You are and always will be my best friend. Nobody can take that from me...You meant so much to this world and you will always be remembered...*

> *Michael*

A New Place to Heal

It was difficult living in the little condo where Russell and I had shared many memories, so it came as no surprise when the opportunity to move came. Friends of Lee Ann's had just listed their home and the brochure in her hand quickly caught my eye when she happened to bring it with her to a session on January 6, because she wanted to show Ron an example of how she planned to market one of his homes.

Everything happened very fast. The next day, my mortgage loan was approved online and Ron offered to loan me the closing costs until I could get my money out of savings. Lee Ann and I hastily took Ron over to see the house before leaving town, and I grabbed the board to get Russell's advice when we got there. When we started to talk with Russell, he told me what price to offer and said, *This house is for you, babe, make a spot for me in the corner.* I told him my concerns about whether or not I would get the house since offers were already coming in, and I would have to sell my condo to make the deal. What he spelled out next brought tears of laughter to our eyes. *No worries, Dad and Lee Ann can make it work. Lee is like me, she can sell sand to a nomad.* We then quickly picked up the board and left.

Two days later my offer was presented to the owners and my sister cut her commission to make the deal. And my home, already remodeled, was listed right away. As it turned out, a cash buyer not needing a home inspection came along, and the closing on my Pebble Brook condo came one week before the closing on the house. Packing up and leaving the memories behind was bittersweet, without a doubt. On February 14, two days before moving, my place was a wreck, with boxes everywhere. The pain was still fresh in my heart and I felt overwhelmed. Stopping to take a break, I wondered why the radio was off, as music was my company and helped me to relax. Turning it on, I sighed as the song "Valentine" by Martina McBride began to play. At first it didn't even occur to me what day it was, as I had been cooped up packing for hours. Then, it hit me like a ton of bricks and I sat down on the floor, crying. At the same time, I realized that these tears were not just out of sadness, but also out of appreciation for Russell thinking of me that day. Listening to the words helped me to refocus and keep going, knowing he had just nudged me to push the button and hear the song. It was hard saying goodbye to the little condo we had once shared, but the new place that would be home had a beautiful backyard, gorgeous landscaping, and a pool with a waterfall—just what was needed to meditate and heal. We later laughed when Russell told us he accidentally spooked the new owner at the condo one day by making the lights flicker, as he sometimes frequented the little place that he said was worth a fortune.

Off to Dallas

Russell told us on Dec. 29 that the New Year would bring us much closer. Soon after, I found online that Gordon Smith, the amazing British psychic Russell and I had heard the year before, was scheduled to be in Dallas the first week in February. I correctly assumed that Ron and Vickey would want to go.

Russell thought it was a great idea and said he would do his best to come through. However, he also told us we couldn't imagine how many souls on his side wanted to speak with their loved ones in body. Sitting at work late one Friday, I was looking at the calendar on my PalmPilot when weird things started to happen. This electronic device was going absolutely haywire. I watched in shock as all applications opened, closed, and then ran on top of one another. The calendar jumped from one day to the next, then one month to the next, then all appointments and meetings were deleted! I started to panic and everything appeared back on it again. All of a sudden it froze on Feb. 4, 2006, the day logged to attend the conference in Dallas with Gordon Smith. With a big grin, I exclaimed Russell's name out loud. Nothing, however, would make it move off this date, nor could I turn it off using the stylus. "I'm leaving work now, babe, *that* was too funny, but you'd better fix this thing before Monday!" I said. He obviously was excited about the trip and confirmed it on the board Sunday... *Yes that was me, LOL, it will be fine tomorrow.* He assured me no data was lost and powering it completely off would reset it. And the pressure in my right ear the night before while reading in bed? *That was me too, I was telling you to move over, luv u.*

There must have been over 500 people at the downtown convention center in Dallas that day. Before the session ended, Ron bought Gordon's book so he could get in line and speak with him, if only briefly. Ron let him know how very much we had enjoyed his presentation and demonstration of the spirit world, and then told him about Russell. Gordon looked slightly away with a glazed look in his eyes, saying, "He is standing right next to you." With that large a crowd, it was okay that Russell did not come through, we just felt fortunate that we could communicate with him ourselves, even if it was just on a Parker Brothers game board! And hearing Gordon was just more confirmation for Ron and Vickey who, along with me, witnessed the tears of several family members in the audience who were shocked to hear stories from their loved ones on the other side. These stories not only confirmed their loved one was alive and well, but also brought comfort, wisdom, and direction regarding the future lives of those still on Earth.

Far Away

It would not be long before I noticed hearing the same song over and over again. It would come on just when I was getting up in the morning and turning on the radio, or when getting in my car. Or, it would start playing when I switched from one station to another or as I walked into a store. Once there was no sound coming from any radio station other than the one playing this song. Russell had said the veil between us is very thin and that he was very close to me, yet in many respects he was so far away. Without even asking, I knew he had sent me this song. The music video, officially released February 13, 2006 was about a dying fireman on the job talking ethereally to his lover. It was uncanny.

"Far Away" is by a now famous Canadian band called Nickelback. The lead singer, Chad Kroeger, claims this is the only love song they've recorded about actually being in love; their other songs only talk about it. When first hearing it on the radio, I burst into tears as I could feel the passion of Russell's heart with the same intensity Chad sang his song...

This time, This place
Misused, Mistakes
Too long, Too late
Who was I to make you wait
Just one chance
Just one breath
Just in case there's just one left
'Cause you know,
you know, you know
(Chorus)

That I love you
I have loved you all along
And I miss you

Been far away for far too long
I keep dreaming you'll be with me
and you'll never go
Stop breathing if
I don't see you anymore

On my knees, I'll ask
Last chance for one last dance
'Cause with you, I'd withstand
All of hell to hold your hand
I'd give it all
I'd give for us
Give anything but I won't give up
'Cause you know,
you know, you know
(Chorus)

So far away
Been far away for far too long
So far away
Been far away for far too long
But you know, you know, you know

I wanted
I wanted you to stay
'Cause I needed
I need to hear you say
That I love you
I have loved you all along
And I forgive you
For being away for far too long
So keep breathing
'Cause I'm not leaving you anymore
Believe it
Hold on to me and, never let me go
Keep breathing
'Cause I'm not leaving you anymore
Believe it
Hold on to me and, never let me go

Keep breathing
Hold on to me and, never let me go...

This song continued to pop up often, and at the most unexpected places and times. I lost my train of thought whenever it came on, and when alone I shed enough tears to fill an ocean.

The Weird Stuff Was Becoming Commonplace

Not only did I start documenting our sessions, the numbers, and the songs, but I also started to log all the odd occurrences we were having, such as Ron's and my computers at work shutting down on their own within two hours of each other. Other times each of our televisions would turn off right in the middle of a program. We started finding pennies, and yes, there are pennies from heaven! Russell says, *I do arrange for coins to be found...*and find them we did, in the oddest places. Ron noticed the pillows on his couch had been moved around. After he put them back in place, he would notice they had been moved again that same day. My smoke alarm was triggered without their being any smoke. I constantly had to synchronize the time on the microwave, stove, and CD player in my kitchen, as one would be changed by an eight-hour difference. One day Russell's picture that hung on my wall was on the floor. It must have fallen, I thought, but the glass had not broken. Another time, I came home from work to find it slanted 45 degrees on the wall, the particular night I was invited out to dinner... hmmm. Our next conversation started with...*I want u to know that I want u 2 be happy 4 rest of this current life. Whatever you do I will be looking out 4 u.* Were you with me the other night, babe? *At a distance, about five light years away, ha, ha.* Ah, so you *were* there? *Close, but not that close, babe, just your space.* What do you think about him? *Nice guy but u have yet to meet next one...don't rush baby, mine always.*

And he was right; the attraction had no real chemistry. What was good, however, is that it strengthened the great friendship this guy and I had when we'd worked together. Thinking back, I couldn't help but be curious about the picture and how it had really become slanted. So, I tried banging the wall hard with my hand but it was so sturdy, the picture wouldn't budge and no one had been in the house but me.

One night while sitting at my computer, I heard a strange noise coming from the speakers, a "cha, cha" sound every few minutes. I made sure the

Love Promised: A Future Life Revealed

noise wasn't coming from any place else; neither the TV nor the radio was on. Russell later confirmed he was trying to talk but couldn't get his vibration low enough. Another day when relaxing in my new backyard, I noticed my dog staring at something in midair. I carefully watched her sniff whatever it was, and knew it had to have been Russell *or* my Dad!

Every now and then when we got on the board, Vickey would call with questions. It always intrigued her to ask something we didn't know. I think the continued validation helped her to believe, plus there was always the exciting "wow" factor that never seemed to get old with any of us. One day she said, "What colors did I buy for you today?" Knowing he was being tested, Russell teased and said, *Blue is my favorite color.* "But what color of flowers did I put on your grave?" *Red.* "Oh my goodness!" she exclaimed, "I bought those red carnations just today and no one knew but me!"

One day, a picture that showed up on Ron's PDA displayed the back window of a truck with the name "Baby girl" in large white letters. He called to ask me about it, thinking I had sent it to him, but I had never seen it. Another time, on the long drive from Houston to his hometown in East Texas, Ron came up on a semi-flatbed truck carrying steel pipes. He started to pass the truck when suddenly a voice in the car shouted "Speed Up!" so he did. Quickly switching lanes, he turned to see one of the large pipes slide off the bed of the trailer. It would have hit his vehicle if he had not moved when he did. Russell confirmed the voice was his. Another day, while driving to visit his mother in East Texas, Ron heard a very deep voice coming from the backseat of his SUV. He quickly turned down the radio and listened, when all of a sudden he heard the voice again. This time it didn't sound like Russell's. The voice then spoke again, very clearly stating, "A woman up the road is in need of help." Ron watched carefully as he drove but never saw a woman by the side of the road. Puzzled, we asked Russell about the experience on the board and he spelled out *Michael.* We then said, "Michael who, you don't mean Archangel Michael?" The next thing he said shocked us, *Yes and someday Kent will hear him too.* I think we were so stunned at the time that we forgot to ask more about the woman who needed help. Russell later told us though, that Archangel Michael was referencing Ron's mother who, on a soul level, was asking for help to cross over. To confirm, we asked, "You mean to the other side? *Yes.* Ron remembered that it actually made sense. At that time, his mother was physically beginning to suffer and was having trouble speaking, though some in the family felt overly protective and did not want to see her die. Ron would later whisper in her ear that it was okay to leave and we wondered how many souls must hang on for the benefit of those they are leaving behind.

Another morning I abruptly awoke to hear the words "Hey, Kent," which seemed to come from right above my face. Looking over at the alarm clock, I saw it was 6 a.m. and wondered why it had not gone off, then realizing it had never been set. An important business meeting requiring my attendance had been scheduled for 8 o'clock, so this wake-up call from heaven came just in time. And though the voice sounded like a female's, Russell later told me it was Archangel Michael, who can speak in many voices.

One day when Ron was at work, he and a co-worker turned around and saw a desk chair moving backward all by itself. It then bumped up so hard against a shelf that it shook some things. They were both in shock. Ron turned and said, "Did you see that!?" and wide-eyed, his colleague said, "Yes, how did that happen?!" The next time we communicated with Russell, he confirmed... *Yes, moved chair trying to get out of your way, was proud of myself...took a lot of effort. I do know how much stronger I can get before going to different level soon.* What level? *Fast learner, I want to share my experiences with some on Earth.*

Once, Russell's cousin Tammy called her mother exclaiming about her experience. She and her husband had just been in an argument when she walked into one of her kids' rooms to pick up their toys. Suddenly, all the electronic toys came on at the same time. It frightened her at first, but when she acknowledged Russell out loud by name, they all went back off together. She then looked up in the corner of the room to see Russell from the shoulder up, smiling at her.

With many such incidents happening on a weekly—sometimes daily—basis, it was becoming obvious to us that Russell was indeed still present in our daily lives and wanted us to know it. *I love you all and am watching over you.* How is it you know if we are in need of help, we would ask? *I just know, energy is so easy to tell changes. We can sense things changing when the brain and consciousness split. U can sense energy of the soul.* He once told us... *At the moment of crossing, u feel the energy that makes up your consciousness.*

For me, the repetitive numbers continued every day. Also, street lights would go out at night just when I was approaching them, passing under them, or sitting at a stop light. These incidents began to remind me of all the past experiences my family had had with our father. Sitting at the kitchen table many years ago, my family was getting ready to sing "Happy Birthday" to me when the telephone rang, but no one was on the other end. It continued to ring four more times. I hung up each time because there was no response, yet there was a pause as though someone was there. I finally realized that it was my Dad on the other side, calling to wish me a happy birthday! Grinning, I said, "Thank you, Dad" and the phone stopped ringing, though the odd looks from my kids began. Another time my sister's cell phone rang my brother's cell phone. That wouldn't have been so odd had they not been sitting near each other in the kitchen and dining areas, where their phones were on different tables. They just stared at each other trying to figure out what happened, before acknowledging it had to have been our father.

What's It Like?

"Russell, when we first started communicating, you said, *Wow, baby girl.* We assumed you were talking about what it is like over there but would you confirm?" *The awe, if u could just imagine the beauty here and it is only a breath away. I am looking out the window and can see way more than you, many dimensions. Freaked myself when crossing, it was like looking through a one-way mirror. I was pounding on the veil at scene, did not want contact with other side. Now helping new souls. We are on a plane here, another level learning and teaching, your Dad teaches. We are so close, so close 2 you.* My daughter asked, "What do you mean "on another level," does it have anything to do with how someone dies?" *No, it represents the soul's level of development.* Are there babies in heaven? *Yes, but no crying.* Another time we were told the other side is like school and he had an angel with one wing for a teacher. What do you study? *God...you see his light all over. The presence to a soul is unbelievable. God is neither male nor female.* Have you seen God take on a human form? *No, but could. God can be anything.* He also let us know about his one-on-one classes, which had to do with learning patience because he didn't have too much of it when he was here. We then laughed, because his father and I could certainly vouch for that! Russell thanked his dad for keeping his two schnauzers and said, *Think I scared Boots the other night, he followed me outside.* Ron immediately remembered finding the dog shaking and scared, sitting in the dark next to the air conditioning unit. Russell went on to say, *I'm taking care of Sable for you, Dad.*

On this side, he would say, *we communicate with only thought and sight,* and *it is almost unbelievable how simple God's world is.* When we wondered early on what he did for fun, he mentioned playing with his other pets that had crossed over before him, and a continuation of the artwork he did here on Earth, such as drawing and painting. He said he also likes to *see the world.* Beyond Earth, you mean? *You cannot imagine what it is like, it goes on forever.* Are there extraterrestrials? *You are it.* Funny, Russell…Okay, what about other species? *There is plenty of life out there.* Is there really a hell? *You are closer to it than you know. There are lower levels of spiritual growth and when crossing over, they perceive the opposite of heaven. It's like buying a car with no AC; you are glad to drive it but are miserable.* We then asked about the movie, *What Dreams May Come. Generally, a soul that commits suicide has not lived enough experiences to know how 2 cope.* Oh, and the movie *Always* with Richard Dreyfuss, I have always felt that most of it was probably true. *Yes, about 85 percent.*

What do we look like to you? *Actors, that life is so short. We choose to come back to Earth to learn life's lessons.* Do you have feelings of regret? *It isn't the same feeling of regret. Just a wish that you could have done more and experienced more with those left behind.* So short, you say, what about time? *Four months to you is like a second over here…just an analogy. Time doesn't matter here.* Vickey called once and asked Russell what language they spoke on the other side. *We use thought, in rare cases inaudible sounds can be heard.* Like when you tried to speak through my computer speakers? *Yes, it's like trying 2 talk thru water.*

The fun part about our sessions with Russell, as bittersweet and even difficult as it could be early on, was that he made us laugh with every conversation. One time, when getting emotional, he lightened the mood as the oracle started circling the moon in the upper right corner of the board. We then asked, "What's that supposed to mean?" and he spelled out *mooning you all.*

Some questions he could not answer, nor could he have answered them when he was here, as he would tell us…*I'm not a doctor but sometimes I act like one* and *Crossing over doesn't make you all-knowing. Every soul has an aura. Colors can change. As an example, green usually represents a soul that needs to be 1 with Earth and needs love and peace.* Also, early on, if he couldn't answer a question, he would say, *There are times when spirits, like me, new here, aren't able to access everything.* But once he told someone that their problem was due to a small stomach ulcer and they asked, "How do you know?" *Because I can see it,* he told them. On another occasion my extended family went out to dinner on Mother's Day, and there must have been 20 eating together at the table. He would later tell me how neat it was that he could hear everyone's conversation all at the same time. *It's so amazing 2 be able 2 see everything I see, more than one event at one time.* Can you be at more than one place at the same time? *I see more than one thing, but can only be at one place at a time though I can hear everything and your thoughts too.*

Once we asked him whether or not someone's theory of the way humanity began on Earth was true. Instead of spelling out the *Yes* or *No*, or going to the words on the board as we expected, he spelled out...*What was my least favorite lunchmeat...Bologna.* We laughed hysterically. Then there were the more sentimental responses to personal questions about the space that now separated us. Someone asked if he experienced emotions and could feel over there. *Yes, there are emotions here too but just not the same. I do feel joy and sorrow at the same time, my tears aren't wet but they are heartfelt.*

Russell would go on to compare crossing over and being out of the body to taking off a heavy coat and then getting out on the interstate, going 70 miles an hour when you have just learned to drive. In body, Russell was a fast driver, so it didn't surprise us when he said, *I just thought I could move fast, that was nothing compared to now. I still have a body; you just can't see it with your physical eyes.* He would go on to tell us. *As a soul we are free to create whatever we want; it is so surreal; you would be excited to be here, a real paradise. The colors are so vivid here, almost blinding. Colors are the music of life.* I told him that I had dreamt of looking up to see a cluster of other planets very close to Earth and how strange it had seemed. *It is so close, you don't know the view from here, great view; the world is so small, if you could only see.* You don't have darkness there, do you? *Always light. Mirror image of what you experience. Not like what you experience but yes.* Confused, we looked at one another. *I know it is difficult for you to understand. Here is like a duplicate of Earth, only there is no pain, pollution, hunger, killing, or disease.* "Will communication be better someday, as in our next life?" *Not always. You all will develop senses better, thought reception.*

"Where are you right now?" *Lying on the couch, smell my feet, no shoes needed here.* "Which couch?" *Small 1... feet hanging.* Laughing out loud, someone jokingly said, "Can you see us since the back of the couch faces us." *I can c u, can you see through things, hmmm.* "Do you walk on the ground?" *Tell Vickey, feet on the ground, not same as Earth.* She asked to have him elaborate on what he said. *Above you, plane is 3 feet up, walk softly.*

He would go on to tell us, if they wanted a vehicle for transportation, they could create one with thought. Or they can just think about where they want to be and are there instantly. There is no waste, he says...*if there is something you don't need any more, it just dissipates.* "If you do have a body that we can't see, Russell, what do you wear?" *Long white robe.* All spirits? *No, u can have any clothing, yes. I have my blue boxers.* We all laughed and I immediately imagined them underneath that robe and said, "Well, I guess they can make you wear a long white robe, but they can't take away your boxers, huh, babe!" *You got that straight.* What is it like where you actually live? *Mine is like a dormitory style of life, part of a mansion, share with others, many floors but no steps, bright lights. It's comforting, nice, and peaceful and joy 2. Not same as you experience as a house.* Is it hard to communicate with us? *Sometimes.* I know you have to slow your vibration, so I guess it would help you if we could relax and meditate in order to speed our vibration up. Would this make it easier on you? *Absolutely.*

When I asked Russell if he had a girlfriend in heaven, he said, *No, on Earth. Relationships do exist over here, but all souls have their own space. Although both of us have lived before, the soul connection was Russ and Kent...the love that you and I had was and is the deepest we have ever had. Your love made me a better soul by you, but just didn't always know how to love me.* I couldn't help but get emotional and he went on to say, speaking of the relationship that I'd had with the person who died before him, named Glenn...*He is a good soul, he has been around some and wants u 2 be happy...heart of gold. Baby, I know this has almost been 2 much for you but you made his and my life. Without you we would never have had unconditional love.*

Russell, we believe in angels but we want to hear what you have to say about them. Also, we've heard they do not incarnate on Earth? *True, they are of the purest light and full of God's love, they are teachers.* And what about Archangel Michael? *Have mostly seen him from afar, they are very occupied, closest to God.* Tell us about Jesus? *He is at top level; you can feel his presence but not always see.* Russell, are we holding you back, as one person implied? *You keep on, baby girl, makes me forever.* When will we get to see you? *When God allows it, sometimes u will see us, corner of eye passing fast. And u get that feeling that u are not alone, because you are not alone. Ask for what you want, if you don't see it then it won't come.*

Love Promised: A Future Life Revealed

The hard part during the earlier board sessions was the wound that was slow to heal; the memories and emotions of the tragic accident that lay fresh in our minds; and then the constant dealings with the police and court system that Russell's parents endured. Missing Russell in the flesh was difficult during the first year of communication, knowing he was with us but not being able to reach out and touch, feel, and see him physically was painful. Sentimental moments these sessions became indeed, times we wouldn't give up for anything, and we anxiously awaited our next get-together. Surprisingly, I loved it when Russell would remind me of intimate moments we used to have by using only certain words that let me know, while keeping everyone else wondering. Then usually he would end with the words *Don't tell* and make everyone else laugh. We were teased if the conversation between us got mushy, like when he said, *My God, I wish I could wrap my arms around you and pick you up again...*these words brought back so many memories of when he used to walk through the front door of our little condo. *I hug and kiss you but you don't always know it.* Our moments together with this Parker Brothers board game, however, were like being on a date and having a chaperon between you. Once I heard the song "Woman" by John Lennon while in the shower and asked Russell if he had sent me that song. *Yes...*and before we could finish our comments, we made the others nervous that we were getting ready to have an X-rated Ouija session!

What's the Purpose?

Eventually, we started asking questions about how and why this was happening. Russell, just how does this work—is it one or both of us whose hands need to be on the oracle? *Both energies, electrons, energy and heat moving very fast.* Ron and I did talk about how warm we seem to get when we communicate. *Put your hands on your forehead, feel the heat.* And truthfully, most times we had to lower the AC or the heat. Once someone mentioned blindfolding ourselves as a test and Russell told us that our eyes needed to see what our minds were spelling out, once he impinged the thoughts onto our brain. And truthfully, the oracle would move so fast that we needed someone writing down the letters that were sounded out to be clear on what we were being told. If the sentence was long, we had to put slashes between the letters to figure out the words as the oracle didn't pause between them. With reference to the high pitches Ron and I sometimes hear in our ears, including the warmth, while on the board, Russell said *Yes, telepathically, you are fast but my subatomic vibration makes it hard for you to hear me.* Later, we started digitally recording the sessions when it was just Ron and me, as Russell said he wanted to have some private sessions too. He said he could focus his energy better. Sometimes he would go so fast, we couldn't keep up and he would apologize and start over. Other times the words would come to us before he finished spelling them out. If we ever tried it with a different combination of people, Ron and I were told to get back on. We also asked if he had to filter information he gives to us through the personal guides we had heard we all have. He then told us…*Yes, and I can tell you anything as long as it does not change your destiny.* And whereas he had told us before that he couldn't access some information in the beginning, he later told us he had moved up a level and his IQ had doubled. *Still, there are some things I am not allowed to say.*

As our communication continued, Lee Ann asked what I thought was a joking question, "Will Ron and Kent write a book?" We were both shocked at Russell's response, *Best seller.* Joking or not, we began to wonder if there was a higher purpose to our sessions. He later told us that his goal was to… *make us at peace till our next life…*and further stated…*Write a book that tells about my life, b4 and after I met Kent and how I learned to love…how love lives on, tell our story.* These words landed in the deepest part of my soul. I sighed, now realizing his seriousness. Hesitantly, we asked again…*You have it within you to do this, do it for me.* Will you assist us? *As much as I can, I need more training.* Do you want us to include the truth about your drug use? *Yes, tell it all, it might help someone else, the demons are now gone.* Tears ran down my face. Long before this, Russell had used the analogy of the little creature in *Lord of the Rings*, who constantly enticed Fyodor to get "the pretty" or the ring that carried power to describe addiction. My heart sank, as I know how disturbing this affliction was to Russell and to all those who deal with addiction of any kind. To know he was at peace now meant so much to his father and me. And writing was something I knew we had to do… for him if for nothing else but.

We asked Russell, "How it is that you are here with us and we can communicate so easily?" *You are so open to here, not all can do this, I am so lucky to have this group. Can you feel my presence?* Most times Ron and I could, by the pressure I felt in one of my ears—like the feeling one might have with the altitude in an airplane, only there is no pain. Ron's neck and arm muscles would twinge when we started the sessions and our body temperature would escalate. Afterward, when everyone had left, I felt subtle static electricity all over my lips, and Russell would later verify he had kissed me goodnight. And to this day, he pops the lights in my bathroom every morning and every night, letting me know his loving presence, often when the lights are turned out. A compliment for sure—Ron had told Russell and me long ago that he envied the love we shared; it was extremely rare. Another time when we asked Russell how this is happening, he said... *We all think this is real; you are in a trance to fulfill your destiny, blink of an eye.*

Our Curiosity to Know More Kicked In

In March of 2006, Russell told us he was different from when he first crossed over, much calmer now. *I'm a teacher.* What do you teach? *Acceptance that they are here and no suffering crossing over, I am learning much about life, what I could have done different, will make up 4 it next time with baby girl.*

Talking again about the differences between here and there... *One thing that makes you separate is vibration, can u feel it, u are much slower than here.* Once Russell commented on an interesting NASA TV show I had watched about the Earth, other planets, and infrared light. *Rock like atoms, Earth is like a rock. Our energy is retained by what and who we touch; yes, everything is constantly changing. We are here too but with a much higher vibration. Know that you are loved and a part of the light of God's love and spirit.*

Thinking about NASA made me contemplate the *Columbia* crew that perished in February 2003, just after Russell and I met. Without question, he had heard me talk about this with the group before our session started, and made the comment... *planned to cross over at the same time... a lesson.* For whom? *They were in agreement. Finally at peace, one no longer here, went back already, Ilan.* Oh! That's the astronaut from... *Israel, he's on a mission, he will fly again.* Where to? *Moon.* Oh wow! and what about... *The others are going to oversee future flights... many talents.* Are they going to help out in going back to the moon and then Mars? *Big way, will point out problems.* China is going to lead the space race. *Yes, babe, some do wonder. They will have problems too... Very interesting things to come.*

Sometimes, we just asked questions about life in general, and we were told... *Souls have free will but u are destined 2 do certain things b4 you choose this life. On crossing (back) over, your experiences are shown 2 u, flashed before u; you realize the things u could do better.* Why is it we get to choose one life path over another? *For a learning experience, u must experience them all; you*

are a spark of God itself, a spark of the Creator. Did God create the world? *Yes, but we made it the world it is. God allows us to create. You select 2 experience the things that life has 2 offer; 2 rejoin God, you must experience good and bad and share and learn from them.* Though God must have a preference about which decision one will make? *She wants u to make decisions, take the road to your highest self.* Ah, you are making the point that God is not necessarily a "he." *Right.* It was asked, "Why did God give us Ten Commandments?" *He didn't, he does have commitments. Why would God command people who could not live up to it? He gave us free will but laid out the goals.* So then, why did God give us ten commitments? *To define the path for living a spiritual life; to find our higher self, he wants us to make a choice and follow it but he does not command. God has a sense of humor, it is heaven after all. And I can't tell you how peaceful it is here. Again, you would be surprised at how simple God made all of this.*

Once when we were talking about humans eating meat, we were told, *Vegetarian increases energy. Humans started as vegetarians and will eventually go back to being vegetarians. Animals sick; will carry disease. Energy levels of fear after slaughtered. The energy stays for a while like ours does; can't you sense my energy on shirts?* A medium can often sense energy on objects. Sometimes we asked questions about things we already knew to see what he would say, but then also about things we wanted to know more about. What is gravity? *The opposite of magnetism.* What are black holes? *Planets create a dip in magnetic plane and are held there by gravity.* Who is responsible for global warming? *We are creating our destiny. Humans could make a difference but won't. In one hundred years, oceans will be three feet higher and you would have beach front property.* Interesting, I live 25 miles inland. Why do we age? *The body slows down as it ages because the subatomic vibrations are slow here on Earth. We are at a much greater level of vibration.*

It wouldn't be long before Dad joined the conversations. Russell had told us...*He is a very good scholar to us new spirits, everyone likes him.* It later became obvious these two were becoming best friends. I had always told Russell that he reminded me a lot of my dad, i.e., he was handsome, open to new ideas, loved to be on the go, had never met a stranger, and enjoyed life immensely.

Here Comes Dad!

Hello, my girl. Russell, is this you? *No.* Who is it? *Wi..* Before my dad could finish spelling his nickname, Wick, I excitedly asked, "Dad, is that you?!" *Yes, barged in on sonny boy. He and I get along.* I was very surprised for this was the first time Dad had come through. As we started to speak, my cell phone rang but I just ignored it, so excited was I to hear from Dad. It stopped but started ringing again and whoever it was just left a message. I went on to ask, "Is there anyone else with you?" *Others in and about, just us talking to you.* My phone received a text message and then Dad spelled out...*Tell Lee Ann to cool her jets.* Curiosity overcame me, so I took my hands off the oracle to see—the message indeed was from Lee Ann. We continued to visit, then he needed to leave. By the way, I'm sure Mom would love a message from you, Dad...*Love of my Life, Bye Bye.*

I could not wait to tell Lee Ann, remembering that contacting Dad was the very reason for buying this board although we had not been successful the few times we tried. She was thrilled and as Dad joined our conversations often, we included a picture of him on the table too. With both of them, we were guaranteed an entertaining conversation. Russell would start out by saying, *Wick wants the mike* or *Wick wants the floor.* Or we would guess it was Dad, sensing the energy change in the oracle, which reversed its direction, moving faster in large circles before spelling anything out.

Over the next few months other family members who joined the sessions would sometimes ask questions, the answers to which neither or only one of us knew, which made their skepticism go away. It was not only validation for them, it was also fun and many times amazing. At times, however, some information given, involving personal situations, did not come to pass. Having learned about the numerous potential paths one can take due to our own free will, I was not surprised at the explanation given. We come here with much guidance from our guardian angels and spirit guides, though noninterference on their part is crucial for a soul's growth on this plane of existence. Yet, divine intervention can happen, we were told, and the opportunities for personal choices are boundless. From this other side, they can see all potential paths. *The most likely to be traveled has the brightest ending...brightest as it appears like the gold at the end of the rainbow. Like a prism of light each color is a path. You can change the path you are on but not the destiny.* Therefore, it was understood, that when a prediction was given the probability or path could end up differently from what was previously told, due to free will. *The Silver Cord* states that there are no mistakes only missed opportunities. But one always gets a chance to balance the energy, whether in this lifetime or another. Russell did tell us, *When you get it right, you don't have to come back anymore. Wish I had known how special I was, didn't appreciate, now I do.* From what I understand, prior to each incarnation we have certain agreed-upon milestones in our life that will come to pass but there are many, many paths between those markers.

Furthermore, according to Russell, when asking questions pertaining to certain individuals, *it is much easier to find their information if they are in your lifeline.* An analogy was given—*it's like picking up a book or folder sitting on your desk and looking at it.* Information for those outside our lifeline may be difficult to access, if at all, they say. *A lifeline consists of many lifetimes we have interacting with souls we continue to reincarnate with, as necessary.*

Russell usually told us where he was standing or hovering and what he was wearing, and who was passing by. Sometimes it became crowded on his side. *The plane where we go to communicate has many others wanting to watch and learn.* Russell says that on their side, words are not used. Communication is with thought alone and there is no need to tell a white lie. *It is only in human form that we wear masks and may find a need to alter the truth. God speaks to all through a universal language.*

Once Russell told his Aunt Vickey…*Be there for Tammy.* We knew that he was referring to her daughter's husband, Anthony, who had been diagnosed with stage four brain cancer. Sensing Vickey's helplessness, Russell reassured her…*I will be in the crowd to greet him. Life goes on, it is really simple. It was like waking up. I really am beside you, big hug.*

One thing we confirmed time and time again when communicating is that the personality remains even when the body is shed. We looked forward to our sessions each time, never quite knowing who would show up first from our lifeline. *Ready, gang, Russell will be here in a minute.* Yes, we are; who is this? *Guess… White dress, big eyes, long hair.* "That's the way Perky described herself one time," I said. Perky was the nickname of our grandmother, our father's mother. *Smile baby it's story time.* Who's "baby?" *U 2 girls…* Just to be sure, who's this? *Pearl.* Ah, we thought it was you, we love you, Perky! *How are my favorite girls?* Good. Beth, who was at this session, spoke up and said, "How old was Perky when she died?" Very quickly the oracle began to move…*I didn't die only changed form.* We sure wish the veil was thinner so we could see and be with you. *Me 2 honey… OK, the big Kahuna wants on.* We all laughed out loud, knowing who she was talking about. *Your stubborn Daddy…what a pair of clowns, and Rusty is just like him.*

Can This Be Evil?

Another important message came when Vickey was concerned about our communication, especially using this board. She asked, "Russell, is this evil?" *You are a part of God and me too. How can this be evil? It just helps* get through what you already know about life and love…live on, love always. But Vickey wasn't the only one concerned at the beginning. Another night when Russell had said goodbye, the oracle started moving again. It spelled out a name that we had not heard in past communication. The oracle's movement was different and before we asked a question, it stopped. JR was a little nervous about lesser-evolved spirits working through us and Russell later told us, *I would not let any negative spirits in…one did try to join us, I cut the connection. JR was right and tell Vickey not to do the board alone anymore.* Vickey admitted to buying a board for herself since she lives four hours away and can't always join in our sessions. And, oddly enough, the oracle moved quickly with just her hands on it. But negative information would come through that tended to frighten her, and Russell would later confirm the messages were not true. *It moved by her own fears, moving while spirit guides were not there. There was negativity from another spirit; Abe not a happy soul.* Dad and Russell went on to say in another session…*it is not to be taken lightly and should always be done with two people; there are souls at lower levels who have not had many lifetimes, are not as evolved, and may try 2 trick u when asking. Like God says, ask and receive. Ask for protection.* Can spirits invade our privacy here? *No, u must want them around you. There r souls with desires 2 connect a willing one. Yes, some can get closer than you want but not into your soul.* He would go on to remind us of our unique link, and also that there was nothing to worry about. *This is okay for now.*

Russell often gave me messages from my spirit guide, whose name is Thomas, he said. Is Thomas, my spirit guide, here with us now? *Looking… he guides others sometimes 2…His spirit here, Saint Thomas.* Did you say Saint Thomas? *Yes, the part of his spirit from Saint Thomas, the guide, is a part of Thomas's soul. A part of his light is your guide.* Wow…hmmm, I've always felt so very protected and guided but, I'm curious, did he live a lifetime here on Earth? *Yes.* Well then, whoa, wait a minute…you aren't talking about the Saint Thomas of Aquinas, are you? *Yes.* What, are you serious!? You were not using the word "saint" loosely, then. Goodness, I'm worthy of having a declared saint to guide me? I stared in amazement. Was this his last lifetime on Earth? *They say yes…* "Who are they"? *Elders, teachers.*

My Little Corner of Heaven … Not Forget Our Deep Love

I loved being reminded that Russell was around and knowing he existed on this other plane or level of consciousness. *Been waiting—God I love doing this, smells good.* Interesting! You can smell the candle burning? *We smell with our mind. Kent, you will see me in a dream soon.* Excitedly, I wondered why there had not been more dreams of him. Ron then spoke about a dream he had. "It was so real, Russell, you were standing in a doorway and there was light around you. You had on a purple sweatshirt and yellow shorts. Is there some significance to the doorway?" *Entrance to my house, bright, my little corner of Heaven.* Wow, it seemed so real. *It was. Ask.* OK, babe, I do have a question. I was on the treadmill the other day when all of a sudden it started speeding up on its own….then it would slow back down. This happened several times though I never touched the controls. But I do remember how you used to stand on it behind me and put your arms around me, tickling and kissing me on the back of the neck. *Oops…there are no coincidences. I am the sound you hear and the shadow by your side.*

One day on the board, we just weren't getting the message, it seemed, and I could practically feel Russell's somber mood. Is there something you can't tell us, babe? It was obvious he was having trouble spitting it out, so to speak. *OK* (pause) *babe, you will meet someone again…not for a while; your heart will need to heal but not forget our deep love.* I was so overcome with emotion; I arose quickly and ran to my bathroom, shutting the door. The tears would not stop flowing. I knew, deep down, that as much as I never want this communication to end, it's not what our life here is supposed to be about. It's about living in the physical…and if I'm here and he is there, there must be a reason. I went back to the session, where Ron and Lee Ann were waiting. As hard as it was for Russell to tell me, it was because of his deep love that he went on to say…*Your life is a journey, and I don't want to see you in so much pain forever. Always know that I am there beside you.* Solemnly, I said, "Really, you can see another person?" *Just know it will be, so don't worry about it. For sure he will not be as handsome as me, bow wow.* Now wiping my tears while laughing, I said, "Thanks, Russell, are you saying he's a dog?" *Have a sense of humor…Of course you will know that I will be jealous like I was sometimes. Ours was a love not many have, next time u will be mine."*

Was It Karma?

From time to time, Russell would mention his accident and the girl responsible for his death, giving his dad suggestions on what to do next, or for his daughter. Ron told him that the girl who was responsible for his death was finally arrested. *Yes, so sad for her family…please know this is her choice. It is good she is off the streets, she has not stopped using.* Anything else we can do for you? *Visualize me in healing light.* With tears in our eyes, we told Russell again how much we missed him. *I know but I can't come back. It was my destiny to leave, every outcome is chosen before you enter; the paths vary due 2 free will. Yes, accidents just don't happen. They appear to u like accidents but trust me, there are no such events.* Russell, this brings to light another subject, somewhat sensitive. It seems you died in the same manner that you caused another to die. Though you'd had alcohol in your system, your attorney was able to prove that you were not over the legal limit. Also, the man you hit on this pitch-dark interstate during the middle of the night was traveling 45 miles an hour, without any taillights on his trailer. His truck then crossed the median, as you know, and hit an oncoming vehicle and it was this driver who died. However, the courts still convicted you of intoxicated manslaughter and you served several years in prison. Now you have crossed over essentially in the same manner. One cannot help but wonder if this is karma—not the concept of being punished but on a soul level, choosing this experience to grow spiritually, is that right? *Was best to exit, he chose to leave also. Thomas says a life experience for a life experience is an even trade.*

One other time, the subject came up again. In our hearts we knew that no grudges could be held against the girl responsible for Russell's death, any more than one could harbor ill will against Russell for the young man he accidently killed. Sensing my need to further understand, my guide was there to assist. *My sweet soul, blessed are you… Thomas here, what do you wish to ask?* Oh, thank you for coming; I am so humbled by your presence. Can you help us understand how karma works? *On a soul level, all are in agreement. One in ten chooses to resolve pain and exit in a manner that resolves it, to their soul. Some choose not to resolve until next lifetime… my thoughts with you, dear.*

As our time on the board continued, Russell began to speak often of a future life that he and I would have together. At first it just seemed entertaining and, still mourning his loss considerably, I was comforted to learn we would be together again. However, as the sessions continued and I began to gather all the fascinating details which had come through about this next life, our story became much more intriguing. Soon we would travel with great excitement to the hometown where Russell and I would supposedly live, and verify the places referred to and the information given.

Chapter Four

Spiritual Scavenger Hunts Reveal a Future Life

Just as a man discards worn-out clothes and
puts on new clothes, the soul discards
worn-out bodies and wears new ones.
—The Bhagavad-Gita, the Yoga of Knowledge, Part 1

It was not long before Russell started giving us clues about Toronto, Canada, and our next life. He said we needed to think about a trip there soon. So we did! We planned it in conjunction with the 2006 Hay House I Can Do It Conference. Attending these seminars had always left me with more wisdom and inspiration than when I arrived. Before we left, Russell would say, *Go to Washington Avenue and look between 8 and 12. It will change by the time we buy there.* Using Google Map, we found the street, but it was right in town and didn't seem like a residential area. We live downtown? *Yes, because of you, government…elected official.* You're kidding! What will our names be? *Mr. and Mrs. Right.* "Cute," I said, grinning. Now, what are our real names and can you tell me a little bit about our future life?" *Mark and Eva, we will be close, yes sweetheart, the perfect couple. We will have the life everyone dreams of.* Goodness, you said we would come back in the same time frame, around 2023. When exactly are we coming back? *2023 me, and you, 2028…We will be childhood friends.* Will we know each other from this lifetime? *We will know each other at sight.* Will we really remember each other, though? *Like a favorite smell, stop us in our tracks, magical, next life.* Is that where we grow up? *No, Little Oak, meet there, a suburb of Toronto, way from downtown. On trip, you will be walking to the street that we will walk holding hands.* Will I remember this place in my future? *There will be someplace that your spirit will recognize, yes. Look for that special place on*

Love Promised: A Future Life Revealed

this trip. What age will we be when we live on Washington Avenue? *You or me?* Both of us... *Me 36, you 31, we will be head over heels.* Who's going to go first in that lifetime? *Not gonna tell, like a thief in the night, in our sleep, Notebook.* That was our favorite movie! In fact, Russell, do you remember we saw it together and it affected us so much, we went home, laid on the floor and cried. It was about the time we were going our separate ways, and the movie was about a couple, madly in love, who lived in the little town of Seabrook, just like how we lived here in Seabrook, Texas. *Yep, babe.* Will we die together too? *Same day, yes, minutes apart, old age.* Wow!

How old will our children be when we live on Washington Avenue? *8, 8, and 3.* What?! We have twins? *Be afraid, be afraid, ha ha.* Well, if I'm going to work for our government, will we have a nanny? *Yes, of course. I love this time together, our bond is very strong. I still think I can do this better... communicating. I am going to get much better. Get much-needed rest.* The oracle slowly moves to "goodbye." Are we done? *Only for now, Ontario.* I love you. *Love you more.* You leaving? *No, am spending the night. Hugs and kisses...Hey, babe, take board on trip.* Yes, of course.

Off to Canada We Go!

Thanks to Ron and his frequent flyer miles, very soon he, JR, Vickey, and I were on a Southwest flight to Buffalo, New York, with our clues in hand. After landing, we rented an SUV and headed north across the Canadian border. I had once been on a work-related trip to the beautiful city of Montreal to attend a meeting at the Canadian Space Agency and wondered if Toronto might be the same. As we headed north on the wide-open, four-lane road, we saw one fairly large town that was spread out on both sides of the freeway. Noticing the town's name was Oakville, I wondered if this was where Little Oak Street would be built someday.

Driving into the largest city in Canada, which is also the provincial capital of Ontario, was exciting. Toronto, today, is considered a major financial center in the world, and is one of the top ten global cities. The closer we got, I thought to myself...And I'm to be an elected official here, in the middle of this century, really now?

Hearing Hay House author and speaker Wayne Dyer that night was relaxing and we decided to have coffee and dessert afterward at one of the many Second Cup coffee shops downtown. Straining to see out the window through the darkness, I saw an old, oddly shaped building across the street, with taller ones towering over it. How uncanny that I felt so drawn to it. Two couples sitting next to us began talking about this unique building and the lawyers' offices in it. We knew it would be one place to see up close, and were excited to finally be here.

It had been a busy day but when we were back at the hotel we pulled out the board before going to sleep. *Welcome, long day.* As usual, we exchanged "I love you's," then asked Russell what he had been doing. *Following you around.* Vickey then asked, "Are you happy?" *Missing the physical, but yes. Can't wait for you to see Washington Avenue...* Ditto, think we'll be going Sunday as tomorrow is another Hay House day, then Vickey's birthday celebration afterward. Russell, is that historic building we saw tonight by any chance the one you said my spirit would recognize one day and we would be holding hands walking down that street? *You don't think you got that parking spot by accident, do you? Yes, next life.* We've scored already! "And come to think of it, I circled the street twice and was just about to give up and go back to the hotel," Ron said. He continued, "Hey, I've been meaning to ask you about the light on the wall at home that moved up the ceiling very quickly, then went away. I waved my hand, attempting to cover it, but no, so strange." *Spirit Flash, concentrated energy on my part.* Vickey then asked Russell what she had left him at the cemetery. *Yellow flowers and tears, remember, I'm not there, tombs are for the living.*

Russell, what is your or our last name in this next life? *Wexford.* Oddly enough, Ron had this thought earlier when seeing a Wexford Park on the map of Toronto. Will the park be named after a relative? *No.* What will be my maiden name? *Stone.* Are our parents alive now as children or babies? *Yes.* Wow...that's freaky! Is the town of Oakville where Little Oak will be? *Yes.* During the conference tomorrow, we will see medium John Holland. *Lots of spirits will be trying, me too... Get to bed.* Night, babe, love you...*Ditto.*

The next day, we first heard the very humorous Loretta LaRoche. Then we enjoyed John Holland, a great speaker and medium. But with the great number there, hence many spirits, we didn't hear from Russell. After lunch, we shopped and bought Sonia Choquette's

Sonia Choquette and Russell Morris

Love Promised: A Future Life Revealed

new book, entitled *Ask Your Guides,* and took a minute to visit after her uplifting talk.

Looking at the picture taken of them in San Francisco, she remembered Russell and offered her condolences. She then looked at Ron, who had tears in his eyes, and said, "He was your teacher and he was ready to leave." I told her of our communication and Russell's desire for us to write a book, then asked for her permission to use the picture. "Yes," she emphatically responded. Furthermore, we were in awe when she told us, "More than that, I will also endorse the book."

Signs and Synchronicities

We decided to skip the evening talk as we were anxious to find Washington Avenue and look for any other significant signs. Much to our surprise, though downtown, Washington Avenue was a small, older residential area and the street was much shorter in distance than imagined. I had pictured a busy street with concrete townhomes and small yards. However, this avenue turned out to be a quaint little street with older, two-story brick and wood-framed homes with typical yard space and trees. Though they were slightly run-down, we figured they might have been built in the mid-1900s. We quickly found the houses, which were indeed numbered between 8 and 12, and stood in the street to snap pictures, not knowing for sure which house would belong to the Wexfords.

Saint Thomas's Church at the end of Washington Avenue

Facing Washington Avenue, at the end of the street was a delightful surprise—a beautiful, old red brick Anglican Church named St. Thomas, the name of my guide.

Street parallel to Washington Avenue

Another street parallel to Washington Avenue with significant names

We then drove around the corner and found something that truly shocked us … a street parallel to Washington Avenue, named Russell. This was an incredible sign in more ways than one. Mouths open, we stared in disbelief at this street sign and then at one another. Around the corner, we found the other parallel street and another street sign that would again stop us in our tracks. This street's name was Glen Morris. Glenn was this special person in my life, who had died eight months before I met Russell, and Morris was Russell's last name.

I think it was then that we were almost immobilized by what we were experiencing. As we snapped pictures, we understood just why Russell was anxious for us to see Washington Avenue. Driving two blocks away from this residential area, we found a quaint little shop that bore the name of Russell's daughter, Chelsea.

Chelsea Shop in Toronto, Canada

Clearly, the synchronicities could not be ignored; we were amazed. As we continued our self-guided tour of downtown, we found the beautiful University of Toronto and what seemed to be their parliament building; historic structures we thought for certain would still exist 50 years from now. We took pictures of both buildings, thinking they might be significant in our next life, since Russell had stated he would be a writer and I would be involved with politics. The intriguing building we had noticed from the coffee shop our first night in town would definitely draw us back. A unique edifice called Flatiron, it seemed one of the oldest in town. The name was fitting, because the building was in the shape of an iron, being narrowly curved in front and flat at the back. Russell had said this building would be very important to me in my next life.

Gooderham "Flatiron" Building, 1892, Toronto Historical Board

The thought of leaving the next day was depressing, now that we were developing a special affinity for this area we were visiting for the first time. That evening, we ate at a place called The Keg which also happened to be the name of a popular restaurant in my little hometown. While at the bar waiting for our table, we reminisced how perfect our day had been and made a toast to Russell, one another, and the wonderful trip. We relaxed during dinner as we celebrated Vickey's birthday and enjoyed a delicious dessert. Having accomplished everything and more on our agenda, we looked forward to ending the night with Russell, knowing he was anxious to talk.

*Hey, Gang, I know u r so glad you all came. Told you about Washington Ave…*I became emotional as this all started to seem real, and I also realized why he had only given us the clue, Washington Avenue. One, he wanted to surprise us and two, we might have had trouble believing it if he had simply told us on the board. As healthy skeptics, sometimes, we have to see to believe when it does not involve something that requires faith or trust. Russell went on to say…*Almost too much, next time we get it right, babe. Time will fly.* It was dreamlike to think about the future life that was beginning to unfold. Being more convinced of it now, Vickey had a string of questions. What will you look like in your next life and will you be as good-looking as before? *Are you kidding, better-looking, ha, ha.* What will Kent look like? *She will be blonde, hot, I am a boob guy, got it all.* My face turned red but then again, that was my uninhibited Russell speaking, for sure. What color hair will you have? *Blond, tan, we have good features.* What will be our nationality? *Scandinavian…*Will we be born in Canada? *Yes, my dad is alive.* Really! Ron laughed and told Russell he was now jealous. *Four years older than his wife.* This scavenger hunt excited us and the questions poured out more quickly.

What will be your parents' profession? *Parents will be in healthcare, physician…as before; I will be a little spoiled.* Will you have any siblings? *Sister, older.* Vickey says, "Can we be in your family physically down the road?" *Yvonne, my sister…* "You mean me?" *Vickey, yes, older.* "Oh my, I thought you told me one time I was going to be Rachel, 11 years old in my next life and that I would die with my mother in a plane crash?" *The plans and agreements have changed. Souls can change.* How did mine get changed? *Others changed them.* Others? *You, higher self.* What changed it? *Mostly you…The experience you need will present itself.* Vickey then asked, "What year will I be born and is your Dad, Ron, going to be in your next lifetime?" *2020…She will be as cute as me. His soul wants to come back as my grandson…those are his agreements.* Wow, I've always felt 2020 was a significant number for me.

It was natural to wonder about our life, so I had to ask some questions. Can our agreement to be with each other in this next life change? *We are in total agreement.* And you can see what we look like? *I can see our images.* What about my parents' professions? *Mr. Stone is…* (Russell pauses as the oracle goes in circles) *my God, he is a lawyer.* The big half-circle building we saw in downtown Toronto that appears to be a government building, will I work there? *Until you move up to State House...I will never have to pay for another ticket again.* We all laughed and his dad remembered how Russell had accumulated many speeding tickets. Russell, since we will grow up childhood friends and be head over heels for each other as you say, will there be another in our life? Will it only be each other? *We will always know that we are one, yes.*

Who will be our kids, Russell, anyone we know in this lifetime? *Dutch wants to be but plans are not agreed yet.* Dutch was Russell's great-grandfather; Ron and Vickey's grandfather. *I told you about Washington Street.* Wow, yes you did, babe! Russell was so proud of himself. Just to be sure, is there any significance to that church being St. Thomas? *Of course, yes.* Then Ron asked, "Do you still see me living to be 82 years old, as you once told me?" *But once again, you agreed.* "Russell," I asked, "Is this my last life, as one psychic told me recently?" *It is your choice. There are some things yet to be agreed upon in Toronto. Our life is agreed on; who will assume some roles, yet to be decided.* I love you...*U more.*

Everyone Has a Mission in Life

Were you with us today when we were talking to Sonia? Did you try to come through with any information? *Not really, she was busy on her mission. Get busy, you two.* Did you hear Sonia tell us she would endorse the book? *Will help sell my story, people will find this hard to believe, communicating.* I began to think out loud, trying to figure everything out. If we write a book that can connect the two lives, will this be proof of reincarnation? *Don't you think all of this will have a big impact on people.* Are you asking? *No, I am stating, of course it will, there definitely will be a connection between the two lives...An event will open that door.* Will someone in our future life be interviewed about the book, if this all becomes public one day? *U got it, will make news.* Who will be interviewed? *We will face the revelation together...* I was dumbfounded as it started to hit me that possibly Mark and Eva will find this book written about their life 40 years before it all happened and the information, depending on accuracy, would be indisputable. And it did seem Russell was giving us just enough information, in slow doses, to help us come to this conclusion. But who were we to bring this to light? Did I really sign up for this before coming here? I thought. Remarkably, it took making this trip to open our eyes. If Russell had offered this information up front, would we have believed him as we do now? We talked a few minutes, a little mesmerized to say the least, then got up from the table. In less than a minute, we sat back down, realizing we had not even given Russell a chance to say goodnight. *Thanks a lot.* We knew he was saying this jokingly, of course. *I love you all… it will never die, I love you, baby girl.*

Clearly, the curiosity about our future lives picked up after that day. Furthermore, what started out as comforting or entertaining words on the board were starting to take on a more serious tone. And yes, as I imagined earlier that day, it was turning out to be a mission for us as well. Would anyone believe it, I asked myself. Then the thought came to me…that is not for me to determine and, as the old saying goes, don't shoot the messenger!

On Sunday, though we had hoped to see inside some of the significant public buildings Russell had mentioned, we had to be content driving around. But that was okay, for we had plenty to sightsee in a day in this exceptional city. Before we left, we drove once more by the Flatiron and also down Washington Avenue. To complete our trip, we stopped at Niagara Falls on the way back to Buffalo. This scenic view was stunning and the sound of the rushing falls, a gift from nature. Our trip home was quiet and reflective.

We Have Orbs?!

Our next time on the board Russell said, *Don't you all know there are great times ahead for you all? Didn't I surprise you all with Washington Avenue?* Yes, babe, only those were more like revelations than surprises. I also figured out which house will be ours, since you and others decided to pose for us in the picture. It has to be the grey house with all the orbs. And is that you in front of the red house? *Good, babe…* Who are the others? *Souls of relatives from your next life who came to see you while you were there.* Huh?

The word "orb" was first coined in fifteenth-century French and English as a term used in astronomy to refer to a spherical celestial object. Russell tells us also that an orb is the energy center of the soul, the heart of the being. He says they view themselves and each other as unique patterns of energy. If appearing to us, he said, they would take the form of how we last knew them in the human life we shared. As far as an orb is concerned, I tend to also believe that this is the same energy body discussed and pictured in Ken Wilber's *The Integral Vision* when he refers to this energy as the "causal body." Ken states that we have three bodies, i.e., gross, subtle, and casual. These correspond to three states of consciousness, i.e., waking, dreaming, and formless sleep. More commonly, these bodies have been referred to as the physical or corporeal, astral, and ethereal bodies.

Russell said to me, *Yes the grey house will be ours...same character, only very updated for us, pure luxury. You will have the inside all painted in yellow with family pictures all over the house and we will put a large stained glass window on the front of the house.* You can see that?

The future home of Mark and Eva Wexford

In May of '06, just after our trip in April, Russell begins, *You will make another trip to Canada...there is a lot yet to discover.* We were elated to hear about another scavenger hunt. When do you want us to go? *February 2007.* Wow, that's quick! It will be pretty cold then for us Southerners, don't you think? *I want you to get a taste of Toronto winter...I think your spirit will love it. Winters there are special. One day we will walk through the snow, holding each other to stay warm.* Sounds romantic, babe, where are you right now? *On your right side nibbling your ear.* I just felt a twinge! *And I do see a trip to Ireland.* Are you kidding? *No, we've lived there before.* I've always wanted to go there... amazing; now I know why.

You Said What Again?

Can we talk about the book again, babe? I just need to confirm something you mentioned when we were in Toronto? *Sure…Again, my mind was still questioning.* I had believed in reincarnation for some time and I wanted to tell our story mostly for Russell. But, wouldn't someone from India be better qualified? I thought. Okay, honestly, is this book supposed to *prove* the theory of reincarnation? *To the masses who read and see u both. The story of this communication will be hard for some 2 believe until next time.* As Mark and Eva, right? *Yes…I* do know that polls in the U. S. have shown this belief is rapidly becoming more widespread. And you say we are both supposed to write the book? *Will be a collaborative effort, both of you will contribute. Will show u something very startling on our next trip. As I said, like a shadow, will be by your side.* Oh, that's right… *"I Swear!" My song, hello…*

"Well then, whoa, wait a minute," I said, getting just a little nervous. "My guide is Saint Thomas of Aquinas whose works, called Thomism, are highly regarded in the Catholic Church. But this orthodox religion most assuredly does not adhere to reincarnation. And you want me to tell the public that I'm being guided by this famous saint to write a book which may someday prove reincarnation? *Yes.* Oh, my God…I *will* get shot. People will think I am crazy! *People thought Jesus was crazy.* Okay, yes, good company but even he was crucified! Can someone get me… not a glass, but a bottle, of wine, please?

Russell Greets Grandma

On June 9, Vickey called Ron to the hospital as their mother, Ann, had only a short time left on Earth. Russell once told us, *No one knows the day or time they should leave…your higher self is a part of God, stays with God. Spirit guides help you make choices on Earth and other levels; in fact they help you make your decisions all the time.* When the time came, Russell later told us, *I was there 4 Grandma…the sight of her face when she saw us was a real blessing. New body feels strange at first.* "Have you and Mom been around us some?" Ron asked, "I sure have been replacing a lot of light bulbs lately." *She did make power surge…does not know how to control it. She was frightened at first; can you imagine me being the calm one?* How is she doing? I thought she might have popped in on the conversation by now. Is she here with us? *No, she is kind of like in orientation, very organized when you pass that way. Know*

Love Promised: A Future Life Revealed

she is fine. She won't be able 2 come thru this board for a while. Her angels have her busy. Tell Vickey she liked the dress but not the pink, it wasn't her color. Vickey was glad to hear that their mom had liked the dress she had picked for the funeral, but obviously not the pink lipstick. Ron and Vickey were very glad to hear their mom was doing well, as her last days in the hospital had been difficult. It also made them think about how their dad would do without her because they had been married 59 years. Vickey asked, "When will Dad pass?" *Angels won't allow special date before next birthday.*

Russell reminded us of his own power surges, including the time my bedside lamp popped so hard, it quit working altogether. *Sorry, babe, I have a problem controlling the strength sometimes.* And, while pet-sitting at a friend's house, I awoke one morning hearing the slow-moving ceiling fan above me make a clicking sound as though someone had yanked the chain. I looked up to see that the fan was slowing down, and then it came to a stop, gradually reversing its direction. *Don't you like the electrical tricks? Momentary interruption.* You never cease to amaze me, babe.

Talking earlier about Ron and Vickey's mother passing made me think about the movie *Defending Your Life* with Albert Brooks and Meryl Streep, where Brooks's character gets killed in an accident. Streep's character is already there and they become friends, discussing what they went through getting to Heaven. "Is this what it is like when you cross over?" we asked. *Some parts are correct, the ending not so much.* Russell, did you choose to die in an automobile accident? *I had 2 leave to prepare my soul 4 Canada. I have said b4 a soul does not know or understand all when they pass over…which is part of the reason Ann has been slow 2 talk.*

A Much-Needed Conversation

It wouldn't be long before Russell's mother, Dianna, wanted to join the conversation. She had heard us speak of our communication but was very leery. Still in pain over losing her only child and then both parents, all within an 18-month period, Dianna wasn't sure she was interested. That was okay with us, who were we to judge how she or anyone else should feel about it. Russell told us…*Be gentle with her…expectations, she will be skeptical at first.* That day, she sat curiously at the table, then Russell spelled out…*Hi Mom, I love you and I am sorry for the things I put you through.* We could tell by the numerous questions she asked, some even telepathically, as we told her to do, that she was indeed trying to figure out if it was really her son.

It didn't take long, however, for the skepticism to wane as Russell answered question after question about things of which we had no knowledge. He even brought up a recent incident of her falling down, and gave her messages from relatives on the other side that made sense to her. *CRS is here.* Dianna spoke up right away and said, "Those are my dad's initials—Charles Ray Story," and he went on to give her a message. When she asked Russell what he himself had been doing, he told her, *School... There is so much that earthly minds do not understand. The colors are so vivid here and the separation is so thin, there is heaven so beautiful Mom, I am by your side now.* I didn't know if she knew, however, that he did not mean that in a philosophical sense, so I asked Russell where he was in the room...*between u and Mom, tell her about the propeller.* Many years ago, CT offered a simple analogy when explaining energy, its vibration, seen and unseen: when an airplane propeller moves at its highest speed, you can't see it anymore with your physical eyes but it is still there. Russell went on to tell us all...*there is much more to my spirit than you all saw here this life.*

For entertainment, before Dianna left, Russell asked permission from her spirit guides to tell about her most recent past life. He also said that on a soul level, she had negotiated in the future to be the father of his grandchildren in our next life. Her hometown would be Montreal but she would later move to Toronto. *Since you are in my lifeline, Mom, these things are easy for me to see if they've been agreed on. Mom, I love you and I am still around you and by the way, there will be a new car sitting in your driveway soon.* "Well, I don't know about that, I just paid the taxes on my other car and I'm not planning on getting another," she said. *Just wait, you'll see.* After the session was over, Ron and I felt this communication was healing for them both, especially since they were not on speaking terms when Russell crossed. Dianna would eventually plan a trip to Toronto with her husband and take Chelsea along to see for herself all the exciting places we had found. And within three months, a brand-new H2 Hummer was sitting in her driveway.

The topic of past lives came up again and I asked a question about a past life of my own. *An experience in a past life can make u more aware of what makes u who u are. All u are is all that u have been.* Why do I keep thinking about the name Mary? *Lifetime, England, Wexford, early 1900s.* Wow! And Wexford will be our last name next time, is that a coincidence? *There are no coincidences.* Ah, right. What was my last name then? *Smith.* Interesting, that is my maiden name in this life. *Have to go, babe, being called, hugs and kisses. Don't forget to see if you notice me tonight.* OK, 'night, love you too.

Love Promised: A Future Life Revealed

More Clues for Our Next trip to Toronto

Late spring and summer of 2006 were filled with many sessions as we got more clues for our next trip to Canada. *Hi, Gang. Hey, babe...Would you trust my answer?* Huh? *Give me a bit, finishing a project...*Ron and I waited while the oracle slowly went around in small circles. After about ten seconds, we asked if he was with us. *Above you.* Is there something wrong? *No, sorry, good to talk on board. I was with newbie...*Oh, someone who just crossed? *Yes, California person. I have had that experience so I got 2 counsel him.* What happened? *Truck hit bridge.* How old? *27.* Male or female? *Him...* Sadly enough, sounds familiar. *Yes, looking back, it felt a bit like a dog being chased by a dogcatcher. I wouldn't let them get close to me at first. I didn't want to be there, and seeing you all on the other side, well, it was like watching ten movies at once.*

*BTW, there is another site for you all to find in Toronto, like Flatiron. It will jump out at you next trip. I am anxious for u to go back...*You mean in February 2007, when you told us to go again? *Yep.* Will you tell us some more about Toronto? We need some more information for the book if we are supposed to write one. *If you are a good girl, ha, ha, there is more I can share.* Laughing out loud, I anxiously awaited more data. *We have gone through many experiences already...our souls will live a near-perfect life on Earth, next we will get it right.* And when we don't reincarnate anymore? *At that point one can become a spirit guide...*Oh, you don't become a spirit guide until you've completed the karmic cycles? *Not a true guide yet.*

Russell, with all this talk about reincarnation, did our life together as Russell and Kent play out the way it was supposed to? *Eve, not the way we would have preferred but the way they were agreed. You entered my life to show me love. I entered your life to show u that u deserve a truly special passion, u are worthy.* Do you mean person instead of passion? *No, passion, passion...in your life u didn't think u were worthy. Didn't we awaken feelings not experienced B4?* I knew in my heart he was right. Even with my "Pollyanna attitude," (as my daughter frequently described me), I had grown to think of myself as being unworthy. "Yes, indeed, you did give me passion and it was wonderful." I went on to ask Russell if we always choose more than one lifetime before we have finished our current one. *Not every time b4 we chose to be together, now, you, me our time. We chose this ahead of it and will choose Canada together. Remember when u cross over, I will be at your level.* And you said once, we will know each other from this lifetime? *On a soul level.* I went on to ask him what our challenges will be next time...*We will have all we need, each other.* Sometimes, we didn't get the detailed answer we wanted, though; it was usually only what we needed to hear or what they were allowed to say. Lee Ann reminded me that Russell had said the two of us would be together till we are old and grey...*Till we are bald too...*We cackled.

Russell, I know you told me our ages when married and living on Washington Avenue, but how old are we when we start dating? *U 19, me 24...Toronto.* So, I'm an elected official, and you are a writer? *Yes...some 1 has to finish the book.* I see you took your humor with you! Where will you work or who will you write for? *Magazine and part-time 2 for BBC.* At work I've seen several news articles from the *Toronto Star*, will you write for them? *No, but will write guest column.* Well, it sounds as though you will have an important job too. *Moderate...U will be the well-known 1...you will be written about in papers.* Interestingly, I also read that Canada wanted to someday build, at Cape Breton, a space center equivalent to the Kennedy Space Center in Florida. Will we be involved with Canada's space program or a spaceport there? *Politics, u will be big supporter of Space Center.* This is fun...now, where will we go to school? The oracle circled slowly in the center of the board as it usually does when Russell is checking on something or accessing information. *U Brigham, me Un of Quebec.* Wow! Are you talking about Brigham Young in Utah? *U go to college 1 year in US then u decide 2 join me, hand in hand, u won't be able 2 stay away, me either.* For what reason do I leave for Utah? *Wild hair...U have best girlfriend who goes there.* "And, when you say join hand in hand, you mean we get married," I said, grinning. When is that? *20 and 25.* Will we live in something like married housing? *Parents have money...*Which ones? *Both...Rent.* This is just way too cool, so, what will our degrees be in? *Mine is in literature, minor in journalism; U corporate finance and public relations.* Wow, guess that makes sense, with the careers we choose...What extracurricular activities will we have? *Skiing.* Good times...can you tell me our kids' names? *Only 1...ok... Cambell Jane.* I do love that name, so this name will be one of our twin girls? *Yes, C J Wexford.*

That next weekend, I attended a girlfriend's wedding with family and friends. It was followed by dinner and dancing at the Galvez, a beautifully remodeled hotel in Galveston. At times like this, I missed Russell even more. Later in the evening, there was a free-for-all on the dance floor and we girls enjoyed ourselves. On Sunday, we were talking about our weekend just before putting our hands on the oracle and Russell obviously wanted in on the conversation. *Hey, I'm here.* Hi, babe, are you busy? *I'm not busy, it's God's day. Glad 2 see you having a good time, babe. You should have seen me out there on the floor last night…you know I can get down.* Everyone giggled and I couldn't help but grin, remembering Russell had rhythm. Wish I could have seen you! *U have seen it, babe.* Everyone laughed while I shared some of our fun times together…Yes, you could dance, Russell. *Dang right… others watched me make a fool out of myself.* Laughing still, I confirmed, "You mean those on the other side?" *Yep, was dancing right next to you.* JR wrote down what he thought Russell had spelled out next…*My soul buddy Shere got a laugh out of that.* JR quizzically looked at me saying, "Who's Shere?" Quickly the oracle moved…*Don't even know a Shere, I swear…My song.* We chuckled when we looked at the letters on the paper and realized Russell was saying…*My soul buddies here got a laugh out of that.* This was just another reminder that our personalities remain even after crossing because that's Russell, dancing with me from across the veil, not worrying what someone would think. Also, when Russell is spelling out long sentences very quickly, he often doesn't pause between words. If someone is taking notes as either JR or Lee Ann would do, we sometimes had to go back and figure out exactly what was being said by putting a slash between the words. If it went too fast, a letter might be left out at times, or we would have Russell spell out the word or sentence again. He would jokingly say, "Lord, can't you keep up?" At other times, he knew it was just going too fast for us. *Your wedding will be just as grand.* My wedding, what about you? *Me 2 silly.* Can you see it? *Can see vision of it, it is agreed upon…can't see things that won't occur. Have I told u how good u look, love u.* How sweet, I love you.

Have an agreement to tell u… What's that? *Cammie's sis and brother.* Cute nickname! You mean their names or anyone we know who will be reincarnated? *Names only, there are some things yet to be agreed for Toronto. Again, who will assume some roles is yet to be decided.* That's right…so what are the names? *Derrick Julian.* You mean Julia? *No, DJW…* Oh, you mean Derrick Julian Wexford? *You got it.* Sorry, I'll be more patient while you spell them out…*Derrick Julian, Rachel Hanna, and Cambell Jane.* How exciting, and what beautiful names. *Dogs in Toronto.* You can even see our pets? *Cocker spaniels… two, Winnie and Mack.* The picture of our future life is really fascinating…the fact that you have so many finite details, what a wonderful lifetime. *We will have everything we need… Toronto, we are almost there.* Russell, I remember when seeing the Flatiron building downtown, we heard someone say in that coffee shop that there were lawyers' offices there. You've told me before that my dad would be a lawyer…by any chance, will he have an office in this building? *As a child u will visit him at work there…at first u will be afraid of the place but later u will remember it right from this current life.* You know, I did feel very connected to that unique building.

Will I have a sibling? *Hold on…one; a brother Karl 2 yrs. older. He and I will be buds.* Interesting, can you tell me what our parents' names will be? *Your parents are Ben and Heather Stone; mine, Andrew and Olivia Wexford.* Unbelievable, what will my brother Karl do for a living? Will we be close as brother and sister? *College counselor, very close…we will all be childhood friends, had a vision of us ice-skating as teens, 3 of us.* Darn, I'm good…Well, you seem to have all the answers; so how tall is Eva—hopefully more than my height of five feet two? *7 ft.* What! *Kidding, you, fair skin, blonde, 5 feet 9 inches…me, good-looking, 6 feet 2 inches.* How cool it would be to see what we will look like.

Can you tell me more? *I see u dancing in snow on a street downtown with me….hmm…so cool.* Sounds wonderful…and what month or astrological sign will we be born in? *Aquarius and Gemini…*Which one? *You are Gemini. Feel me near you?* Is that your energy I feel next to me almost every morning lying in the bed? *Yep—mmm. U will be 10 years old when visiting your dad at Flatiron.* I was so drawn to that building and want to go inside next trip. *She is taller.* Who? *Your mother taller than father, couple of inches…*Guess that's where my height will come from. What will be your sister Yvonne's profession? The oracle circled for a few seconds…*Wow; she is an attorney and a bad ass 1.* Vickey will laugh. *You will be astonished on next trip; will tell you more as u get closer to trip.* Okay, can't wait, love you, Russell. *U more… do not be so long…I love you still and forever.* He could see the tears in my eyes…*Nothing is ever wasted, every emotion is worth it. I can see some things but can't always predict how it will happen.* It was time to close the session… *Come back next weekend, for me that is a blink…I really love you, Eva.* Gosh, it would seem odd to call you Mark since that is my ex's name! *Have a sense of humor, but call me Russell!* 'Night.

Love Promised: A Future Life Revealed

Let's Talk Canada!

Russell begins conversing about Toronto, telling us to go inside their city hall and other government buildings plus Flatiron next time we are there. *U never know what you will find.* What's that? *Just go...I can't tell you everything, sorry.* Russell would tell us this many times. I guess we just wanted it all spelled out for us, no pun intended. So, can you give us any clues about what to look for when we are in there, is it a person? Or is it a picture with the name of a relative who will be in our next life, such as the name Stone or Wexford? *Sort of...u will see.* Weird-sounding or not, Russell went on to tell us there was a picture for us to see in Toronto that he had painted in 1948 when he briefly *walked in* and used the hands of another to paint a picture of the Eiffel Tower. What's stranger, still, he said...*u will be drawn at the bottom of the tower around several others, no one u know, and some flowers.* What do you mean "will be"? *It's already done.* Did you indeed paint it; I'm confused as to how that can be...Oh, were you working through someone else? *Bingo...*And it's hanging in a government building? *Look at initials on it 4 a hint...MT...so big.* Who were you then? *East of Wexford...*Russell! *Babe, I have the same devious behavior.* Really now, you mean as Eva looks in our future life? *I drew u as u are now.* You can see my face? *Yes.* Gosh, how could you have painted in a past life what I look like today? *Hard to comprehend 4 u...darn, I'm good.*

I told Russell that this sounded pretty odd, though I had heard and read before about the subject of walk-ins, especially in a book written by Ruth Montgomery, a former White House correspondent. Against her mother's wishes and afraid her career would be ruined, Ruth wrote story after story about people who didn't feel they were the same person anymore, because ultimately, they weren't. They figured this out after a period of time, frustration, and self-reflection. As it turns out, and according to many who believe in this concept, two souls can agree to exchange places. The soul leaving has completed his or her karma in life, and the other soul steps in to fulfill a purpose that didn't include the need to be born or even grow up. They just had a specific later-in-life mission to accomplish. Walk-ins eventually rearranged their life, such as moving on to other friends and different jobs. Many divorced because they no longer loved the person whom they had married. Sometimes other people would notice the changes in this person before they noticed it about themselves.

We were told the walk-in experience is real, but the thought of Russell painting a picture in 1948 of the way I look today was challenging. And, it was the first I had heard of someone entering another's body just to use their hands. I wanted to explore and find whatever it was that Russell had told us about.

The concept of no time, as I had often heard, is difficult to understand...the fact that we live in a linear universe with a past, present, and future is my human perception. What about the nonlinear universe, however? We need experts capable of looking beyond our current scientific facts or theories to understand the possibilities not yet discovered. Watching *What the Bleep*, where scientists, doctors, physicists, and philosophers explore this subatomic world is fascinating, because it deals with an area where the current laws of physics don't apply. So, could it be possible? Could it be that the world I'm in when out of my body is not obstructed by time? Maybe it *is* plausible that Russell drew me in 1948.

I do have a very strong desire to know the truth, whatever it may be, and to separate fact from fiction. Being open-minded and having OBEs kept me from automatically discarding another's theory. However, to me, there are some crazy ideas in the world, it seems, so it is wise to be discerning. Being a healthy skeptic doesn't mean you can't or won't believe, you just may want or need more time and possibly research to help make that decision or take that leap of faith. One thing that would help me, then, is finding that picture in Toronto, or at least that is what my left brain tells me.

U will be amazed, more clues to follow, wear a heavy coat in Feb...About Toronto, u will see our future favorite spot. Different than Flatiron? *Downtown but close by, you will know it. One more thing about the trip, go looking for Pine and Little Oak Streets.* You mean in Oakville? *Yes, Pine and Little Oak intersection. The separation between you at this moment is very thin and at this veil, I know I am only a blink away from you.*

On our second trip, we definitely wanted to explore this much smaller suburb where we would supposedly grow up. *Eva will have long blonde hair...I just got a glimpse of the next life...just came to me. One day we will have a bicycle accident and run into each other. You will scrape your leg. I see us there sometimes.* Wow, how many life plans on Earth are defined before coming here? *Most plan one because many agreements are needed. I love you and have you in my destiny.* I just thought one chooses their next life once you cross back over. *Just meant to be, we have the same energy and lifeline, kindred souls.* From what I had read and heard, and then from communicating with Russell, I believed that souls incarnate into different groups and how we choose to come back into a different physical body within that lifeline. Souls work within a group, playing different roles in one another's lives in order to have varied experiences and learn life lessons, moving into higher levels of consciousness. How many souls are in our lifeline? *Between both of us, 1245... we go way back.* Wow, that is a lot! *Lifelines come back, we each have some connection. Souls can be connected to more than one lifeline.* Is this the same as soul mates? *Three soul mates but not always. No more than 3 in one lifeline.* How does a lifeline relate to a plane? *Many planes per level...* How does a lifeline relate to that? *Like a clan...to move up.* Are we at the same level? *No, but we will be when I see you again here...* What is my last big test in life, Russell? *Letting go of connections to the world...u will let go of these things by writing.* What things, babe? *You are so close; you are so very spiritual... Will tell you later.* Okay, thanks, Russell, sure wish I could see you with my physical eyes. *I am working on spiritual abilities; at some point, yes, u will see me. More on Toronto another time...* It seemed my inquisitive mind was wearing him out, almost like a child does their parent!

That first Father's Day was emotional for Ron. Russell said, *Dad I wish I could be there in body to hug u.* And I told Russell to be sure and tell my Dad hello on this special day... *He knows you wish that for him.* After a pause, with the oracle moving in circles, he starts up again... *Hey, Wick says "Hey, baby"...He's over at the next house visiting. He's a hoot. Everyone enjoys his spirit and intellect. Love you girl, see if you can sense me tonight hugging your neck.* Dad, give Grandpa a big hug for me too.

The next time we got on the board, Russell said... *It's about time, gang. How is everyone?* Well, you most likely know, so, what have *you* been doing? *Busy, learning more about the universe, observing...the secret to it all is so simple; art and school, teaching too.* What are you teaching? *Art of Love...* I couldn't help but laugh and say, ooh, ah! *Ha, ha, not in the physical, spiritual love, girl, you are silly.* I remembered that soon after Russell had died, a psychic casually mentioned, "Russell wants you to have sex with someone else." This seemed shocking because it didn't sound like him. In fact, he was the jealous type. Plus, I knew it was way too soon for me to share my heart with another and casual sex wasn't my thing. So I disregarded the comment. The next time we got on the board, Russell quickly told me, *that was not what I said at all...I am missing having sex with you. No human can get it 100 percent correct.*

Energy, It's All Energy

Russell, a psychic once said that I should ask my spirit guides to let me rest more. She said they don't let me rest. *Sometimes you leave body. Don't rest your body enough.* Can you explain more? *Body doesn't rest when you are out. You counsel troubled souls.* Interesting…don't we all leave our bodies at night? *Very often but most people don't remember.*

I've been seeing what seems to be clear energy patterns vibrating… patches, sometimes small but also large. It usually happens when looking at horizontal lines or plaid patterns such as on curtains, window blinds or on paper—sometimes just staring into space. No pain associated, but is this a blood spasm in the back of my neck? *U are okay, u are seeing veil, thin spots. There are times 2 u see them out of corner of eye…like ripples on pond.* Yes, that's right. Lee Ann, who was with us this time, asked if these were migraines. *No, gifts 2 develop.* Then she said, "Is this something spiritual?" *Yep, seeing thru veil, spirit guides, not always someone there.* Well, babe, sometimes, I wake up around 3 or 4 a.m. with this feeling on the left side of my body… it's like a slow, subtle wave of fast-vibrating energy moving up and down my face, neck, and upper torso. *Vibrations in sync can feel like a wave of sensation. Somewhat like the feeling a person gets when channeling. Get some of the stones…special stones.* What kinds exactly, or what colors? I have a couple in light pink and dark purple. *I know you have some…energy stones.* Yes, I've heard stones carry certain kinds of energy. *Remember, nothing is as it appears to be 2 humans. Stones, white and red carry highest energy.* Which stones and why? *Ruby and diamonds…the way it interprets light.*

The other day at work my radio went off by itself. I felt your presence so strong and the pressure in my left ear was intense, lasting for almost 15 minutes as opposed to seconds. *When you feel sensations so strong it means we are in same space like u walk thru me, sharing spaces.* Wow, did you get that close? *U got it…arms around you. Didn't it feel like a chill or like that feeling you get when your hair tingles?* Yes, that too. Every so often, strong chills go up my spine, making me shake, and I can't control it. It's almost embarrassing when around a group of people. Is this what I heard might be kundalini energy? *Yes, release of energy, spiritual from the soul.* Your cologne is starting to fade on your shirt I sleep with…*Spray my cologne on it please.* JR starts teasing us and Russell chimes in…*Lighten up Erwin, it could be worse, I could spook you, ha ha.* He went on to say on a more serious note…*If u could only see what I see, the dreams that u are living are not the real thing, a*

Love Promised: A Future Life Revealed

test and growth experience. There are many things I am beginning to understand and master...like God said we could do.

Once we recorded Russell saying *there are many whore wishing that they could talk thru board.* After the outburst of laughter dwindled, we said, "What?" *Ha ha... Who are, but God loves the whore too. None are without sins, no one better, only living out their chosen life. One person does not cross your path by mistake, by accident. By destiny, everything planned...Many roads to same destination.* We have so much to learn. *I am very grateful 4 the experiences of you sharing your life with me. I have not said tonight how much love I have for you. I am so glad to talk to you again.* Me too, Russell, it's fun to laugh with you again even if on this so-called game board. I love you, babe. *You more, baby girl...Kisses for you; hugs for the rest of you. Behind u blowing you kisses.*

Off to the Monroe Institute

Off and on over the next several months, Russell would gradually give us more clues about our next trip to Toronto. But there were also two other trips I was preparing to take. Because of the experiences I'd had moving out of my body and back in again, a class at the Monroe Institute looked intriguing. In the early '90s, I had read a book by Robert (Bob) Monroe on OBEs, called *Journeys Out of Body.* Bob Monroe had been a successful sound production artist in New York City, eventually owning several radio stations in the 1950s. However, starting in 1958, he had experiences of spontaneously separating from his physical body that changed his life. Later he would start an institute near Charlottesville, Virginia, and use techniques he created with sound to induce these altered states of consciousness, and also as an aid in healing with sound therapy. Monroe's patented binaural beats or audio tones are called hemispheric synchronization or Hemi-sync, and the sound was developed to "simulate more coherent brain wave patterns, which are shown to enhance whole-brain activity." Without Hemi-sync, tests have shown incoherent brain wave patterns that can limit thought processes. This technology is used not only to induce OBEs but also for relaxation, sleep induction, and learning and memory aids to help those with physical and mental difficulties.

I decided that taking the first "Gateway Voyage" class would be an investment. After all, wanting to understand what I had experienced was a lifelong desire. I asked Russell for advice on whether or not to go, as I had now become accustomed to doing that for almost everything. Even though we are here to make decisions ourselves, I trusted him. Russell says those in spirit are not all-knowing but do have a larger perspective on life, especially when it comes to the soul; they can see beyond the illusion of time and they don't have the ego-mind or brain getting in the way of the heart as it tries to guide us along the path to our highest good. If there is something he doesn't know or is not allowed to tell us, he will say so, all the while stating…*it's your choice, free will, many paths.* For me, just getting confirmation I was on the right path could keep my mind from worrying, which we humans have a tendency to do. Those dreadful emotions can truly block the flow of information coming directly from our higher self and our guides. I think from that side, we all look like drama students, or so I've heard!

Russell, I was thinking about signing up for a class at the Monroe Institute, what do you think? *U will enjoy.* Yes, just going to a remote area for a week in the mountains of Virginia in the fall when the leaves are turning colors sounds so refreshing, doesn't it? *U are going 2 have a unique experience.* Cool, you coming too, babe? *U will get a lot from the class…of course, will be with u there.* Is there anything you can say that I need to know before going? *Let spirit soar out of body.* After signing up, I couldn't wait for the class in October, a much-needed break from work.

That week in Virginia, I met like-minded individuals in an extremely relaxing atmosphere. I had never felt so comfortable sharing stories and was happy to be at a place to experience what had been kept hidden for most my life from people I knew, even some family. It was good to hear others' stories as well. Anxious to try Bob Monroe's techniques, I hoped to move past the fear experienced as a child, when I didn't understand what was happening.

Our introduction to one another was to get to know the new person next to you and then introduce them to the group. For six days, we had what are called focus sessions in our Controlled Holistic Environmental Chamber, or CHEC, units. At first, I was expecting OBEs, which caused apprehension, and thus a block. Finally, after 24 hours of getting there and winding down, I was able to relax. And during some of the sessions, I could feel the subtle but intense vibration and part of my body lifting out. Also, it took a day or two getting past some unexpected emotions as there was a guy in the class named John who surprisingly reminded me very much of Russell. I avoided him at first because of the painful memories…then realized I needed to know him as John in order to focus on the class. John had studied Zen Buddhism and Ken Wilber's Integral Therapy so he was

Love Promised: A Future Life Revealed

an enlightening person to learn from in the class, besides our own great facilitators, Paul Elder and Karen Malik. The workshop consisted of sessions throughout the day, each in our CHEC units, which provided isolation from light and sound. In each unit was a speaker system with headphones, and we heard Bob Monroe's voice take us through the focus sessions using the binaural-beats technology and guided imagery. Several sessions were held daily, and when each was over, we joined together as a group to discuss our experiences. I was hoping to have some magnificent OBE experience but most times my mind was filled with anticipation, expectation, and a little apprehension which still blocked the total experience. Karen told me that expecting it put me in the thinking mode so I was not experiencing the now, and I realized just how true that was…Seldom had I ever tried on my own at home, but if I did, the experience never happened. It was always when I least expected it that the spontaneous OBE would occur.

I did have some unique experiences, as Russell had told me. At different times, I saw pinpoints of stars; whirling violet colors; a small circle within a larger one; and my name being called out by a male's voice. But more unusual than anything, aside from the vibration and sometimes floating or weightless sensation, I heard the sound of music—a base guitar during several sessions, at what seemed to be various tempos and speeds. First it was heard from a distance and then much closer, it seemed. In subsequent sessions, the sound of a harp started playing along with the guitar. When I asked in our group session what music was being played through our headphones, I was told there wasn't any. Russell would later tell me…*Angels play music here and u got a hint of it.*

One evening, we watched a previously recorded *60 Minutes* television program about a man named Joseph McMoneagle. His expertise in remote viewing made him the number one psychic associated with the U. S. Army program called STARGATE, an intelligence gathering-operation that was created in the 1990s for national security purposes. Afterward, we had a surprise visit by Mr. McMoneagle and were able to ask him many questions. I took this as an opportunity to ask if, in his opinion, Russell could have painted in 1948 a picture of the way I look today, and he said yes. His further presentation on timelines and how we can exist on other levels at different times helped to explain this apparent anomaly that I would learn more about when communicating with my father.

It was hard to say goodbye after that exceptional October week in the mountains, with gorgeous fall weather; delicious, healthy food; and new friends from all over the U. S. and Japan. On the last day Laurie Monroe, Bob's daughter, handed each of us our certificate for completion of the class. Sadly, we heard she made her own transition to the other side two months later.

Hi, babe, that was a pretty neat class! Were you there the night Joseph McMoneagle spoke to us as a group and we tried remote viewing? *Remote viewing is a special gift. Not all can do it...Takes linking mind with your spirit guide's.* Was Dad there too? He would have been fascinated. *Hold on...He said we're sharing duty watching over you.* Guess we all keep you pretty busy, huh? *Some more than others...*And this guy named John who had a striking resemblance to you? *Just to let u know that I was there, he has a good soul.* How did you like the class? *Boy, very cool.* There were some very interesting people there too. *Except one, kind of snippy...*Oh, my, you are right! *She has many lives left to get it right. I didn't care too much 4 her, everyone else was there 4 right reasons.* During the sessions, I sensed you were there during Focus Level 21... but was having a difficult time with some programmed fear from past OBEs. Someone called my name...was that for real? *Yes, there...takes much practice. Patrick called 4 u.* Patrick? *Yes, ur angel.* Cool, were you there? *Background... kept u from falling down.* What? *I kept u from falling over rug there...u going over the rug corners.* Wow! I did almost trip a couple of times over the corner of the rug in that room where we all gathered. Guess my feet were not floating on air like my head seemed be doing, coming out of those sessions.

Before getting off the subject, I had to ask Russell if Bob Monroe was still around this institute he founded, even though he had crossed over in 1995. *Yes, but he lets others direct it now.* At the end of one of our last sessions, we were told to ask for five messages from our spirit guides. As I sat quietly in my CHEC unit, the messages came very clearly: 1) Love oneself unconditionally, 2) See the beauty in all things, 3) Seek understanding, 4) Fly Free, and 5) Trust. On the way home, after that week of serenity, my mind was already resisting the rat race. As trained to do, I compared it to other things in life that were worse things and felt much better.

Celebrate Your Life!

In November 2006, Ron, JR, Lee Ann, and I met at the airport for our trip to the *Celebrate Your Life* conference sponsored by Mishka Productions.

Russell had said… *You will enjoy Arizona, call on Friday.* "Call who?" I said, thinking he was telling us to call someone after we got there…and he was! *Me, silly, on board, my cellphone.* We checked in and made our way through security, which had become quite a hassle since the 9/11 tragedy. It didn't occur to me while going through this checkpoint that I didn't have to put my cherished silver ring through the x-ray machine, since it was not metal. But I did, and when I reached the gate and looked down at my hands, it was no longer there. This ring, which I had purchased on a cruise ship many years before, was handmade by a spiritual maker in Indonesia and had three beautiful energy stones. As the others waited, I rushed back to the security gate to see if it was there, but no such luck. Though excited about the trip, losing this ring made my plane ride to Phoenix somewhat sad.

Calling Russell was first on the agenda once we settled into our hotel rooms. Hey, babe, do you know what happened to my ring? Did they eventually find it at the airport? *Guy picked it up, was in front of u…*Are you serious?! I can't believe that. What is his name? *Refugio…*Will I get it back? *No, will talk to his spirit guide.* Was he from Houston? *Phoenix…*So you will talk with his guides and see if he will return it? *I will, babe.* Lee Ann then asked why the ring was lost, thinking there might have been an underlying reason. *Only a thief to be a thief; a guilty conscience…Don't sweat it, it is just a thing.* Yes, but you know how important your things were when you were here! *Hmmm, got a point, babe, get out and see what u can find. Well, get going babe…I'm going with you.* Let me see if anything can be done. *We'll see.*

It had been a long day so we treated ourselves to dinner at P.F. Chang's restaurant in Scottsdale before retiring for the night. The next day we thoroughly enjoyed listening to James Van Praagh, and Christiane Northrup's keynote speech was hilarious, especially for us women. How excited we were. Russell had told us, *you will enjoy tomorrow; don't any of you spend a lot of money. There is nothing here to buy that can improve our communication.*

The following day, standing in line, I met a delightful lady named Sally, who said she was inclined to give me a CD by Peter Sterling called *Harp Magic.* Though having just met, we definitely felt a soul connection and the music was unbelievably similar to the harp-like music I'd heard while at the Monroe Institute. Russell told me that night in Scottsdale… *This CD is for you to sit on patio writing.* Will it help me write the book? *Yes, angel therapy. By the way, babe, like the ring.* Uh, oh, sorry, Russell, couldn't resist. Isn't it uncanny, though, I found this booth selling the same handmade jewelry as the ring taken from me? *Bad girl, u didn't listen to me but I forgive u, ha, ha. The green stone in the ring reflects your aura.* I am glad to find another because these rings are unique. But I still love my other one and wish there was a way to get it back, since no two are made alike. *Refugio's guides have not given…Check the airport.* Okay, babe, will do.

The conference was exciting, and I felt like a kid in a candy store, waiting to hear so many good metaphysical speakers who had authored books I'd enjoyed reading. Meeting new people who had the same spiritual passion we did, left us feeling open and free with our conversation.

Miracles Do Happen

When I got home, the loss of the ring was still a disappointment and it meant forgiving the person who took it from me. My mentor, Dad, had always taught us to put things in perspective. If something unfortunate happened that we had no control over, he would tell us to look for the good and turn it around. So, I decided to meditate, still in the mood of gratitude for our trip. Listening to the *Harp Magic* CD, I sat cross-legged on the couch with my eyes closed, picturing the universe bringing the ring back to me if possible. But if not, I hoped that whoever was wearing it could appreciate its beauty and take care of it. Then I sat for a while in silence. My feeling became one of indifference and no longer did I feel saddened. After all, my guides had led me to find another special ring, which I never would have purchased had it not been for losing the other.

Soon afterward, I was getting ready to go out to dinner. As I was putting on a pair of jeans I had not worn in six months, I was stunned to see my lost ring in the left front pocket. I made sure these were not the jeans I had worn at the airport, and even wondered if I had not had the ring on that day. However, I definitely remembered taking it off at the airport. There seemed to be no logical explanation. Bewildered but elated, I put the ring on and left the house. I thanked God, my spirit guides, Russell, my angels, my dad, *and* the universe, for bringing my ring back, but who would believe me? Then it occurred to me that was none of my concern.

It was the weekend after Thanksgiving when we talked on the board with a group. My son, who was living in Missouri with his older brother and girlfriend, had flown home for the holiday and wanted to join in the session, which was at Ron's house. Along with Mom, Lee Ann's husband, John, joined the session. Russell started out by saying *Boy, it's been a while. Howdy, Matt…Believe in miracles.* Matthew had his own miracle story to tell. On the way to the airport in St. Louis, he had hit a large rock on the side of the road when he was blinded by the sun coming over a hill. The right front and back tires blew out and he was surprised at his ability to maintain control of the vehicle, despite being frightened. There had been nothing but open fields, and now he was in the middle of nowhere, about to miss his flight, or so he thought. Through the sun's glare, he looked up to his right and miraculously saw a gas station adjacent to a vehicle repair shop with mechanics on duty. Not only did they have the tires he needed, but also a new rim. Matthew could not help staring at the young man who, knowing he had a plane to catch, helped him right away, for he had an uncanny resemblance to Russell, both in looks and character. Thanks to him, Matthew made it to the airport just in time to park his truck and board the plane. *I did play a part in helping you out...guiding you, we can appear in many ways. Those in our lifeline, it is easy to know when lifeline partners need an intervention...u know me, I network.* Matthew told Russell how grateful he was for the help.

Do u believe in 2 miracles? Russell, my ring! How did that happen, was that you? *Wasn't me, it was his spirit guides.* You mean Refugio's? *Yes, u know me, I can sell anything.* The analytical part of our brain continually questions and I was anxious to talk with you. Russell was surprised at my "doubting Thomas" attitude. *U know u took it off, left in bin.* Yes, I do, babe. It's just hard to believe, even for me. I have heard before of material objects being transported from one location to another, called apport, is that what happened? *Call it what u wish, just be glad it is yours again, baby. There was 2 much energy connected 2 u and it. It was transported at the molecular level.* A few years later, my son, Christopher, would lend me a book from the library of the school where he taught. He was startled to discover it sitting on the table where, a few minutes earlier, he had seen nothing. Lending it to me he said, "Mom, I think I'm supposed to show you this book." The 2008 published version of *Scientific American on Cutting Edge Science, Extreme Physics* had a blurb about the subject of quantum teleportation: "the science fiction dream of beaming objects from place to place is now a reality—at least for particles of light. From the beginning, theorists realized that quantum physics led to a plethora of new phenomena, some of which defy common sense." Quite possibly in our future, teleportation will become commonplace as we learn more about the nature of light itself and its relation to matter.

Lee Ann was curious as to what Refugio thought happened to the ring. *Hang on...*The oracle circled for a few seconds...*His girlfriend lost it.* Well, thanks, babe, for trying so hard and helping me get it back. *There are good souls among u...*Dad? *Your Dad, yes...he is 2 funny.* The oracle moved quickly in the other direction... *Christmas needs to be special for my girls this year. Make my favorite cake, love my lady.* Hey, Dad! Then Mom said, "I love you, honey." *I got the mike from Rusty.* We laughed and said, "What are you doing over there?" *Teaching how to expand the mind.*

Mom spoke up, "Wick, if you got Kent's ring back, where's the diamond that was taken from my place?" Having been diagnosed with Alzheimer's, Mom sometimes imagined things. *Honey, it was misplaced. Shoebox, it should turn up.* Then Dad was obviously talking to us saying, *she is the only diamond that I care about.* Lee Ann quickly chimed in with yet another question for Dad. "John wonders why you appeared to him several years ago." *2 make a believer out of him, one more question, I have to go. By the way, urs is not the only solar system. If u just knew.* "You have to go so quickly?" *Yes, sorry, but God calls.* Russell then gave me an opportunity to ask one more question too. *Ask...* The grey house in Toronto where we will live, the picture with the orbs. *There were spirits around me all very excited u were home.* Who were they? *Patrick, Thomas, others have been...will be again there. Just got a glimpse of Julian, 11 years; girls 16. He looks a lot like I did as Russell. Tall like his Mom. Wow, if u could see what I can see. It's like being allowed to pull up the blinds a second at will sometimes.* Are our twin girls tall too? *Afraid so...that's ok, beautiful like their mom. Wick said tell my honey I will be in her dreams. He is a busy guy 2. The shuttle is awesome to see in orbit. No damage.* Interestingly enough, Russell must have shown up early and heard us talking about the shuttle mission, STS-116, then going on and how they were using the orbital boom sensor, a robotic arm extension, to look for any damage to the orbiter tiles, the thermal protection shield used when entering the atmosphere. *Wish we had the same view in orbit, thanks, we're glad to hear there was no damage during launch.* A guy I had worked with was on this flight and I wanted him and all the others to return safely. *One day humans will be traveling to other planets.*

This statement sparked a question from Ron, who said, "Russell, was my experience an OBE the other night? It seemed I was being shown some planets, including Mars, and was actually standing on another planet. What was this about, was it just a dream?" *No, spirit guides were showing you that life does exist elsewhere.* What was I standing on, was it a planet? *Light energy like concentrated lightning.* Will it happen again? *Open your mind.* At times, we were in awe and didn't even know enough to ask more questions.

Love Promised: A Future Life Revealed

I will be by your side this week, don't stress, babe, light a candle 4 me. Get a spray of red. With the cologne on your shirt, I can close my eyes and almost feel you there. *There u go... We got 2 go babe...Angels calling, kisses 4 u.* Russell knew this was going to be a tough week, the first anniversary of his accident. Indeed, the memories were still fresh in our minds and the trial had not been scheduled yet for the girl who caused the accident. As with any mourning process, getting through the first year of significant milestones, birthdays, and holidays is always a challenge. At least we were communicating with Russell very often, unlike most get to do…but our hearts missed him all the same.

Russell's daughter, Chelsea, visited during the holidays and even though she was only 14 years old, he told us she had an open mind and would be okay communicating with him. He spoke with her about people and events that her grandfather Ron and I did not even know about, and then told her how much he loved her. He answered some questions she had and passed along information he knew she wondered about. The surprised look on her face confirmed she was talking to her father. In simple terms, he would explain to her…*Heaven is all around u, thin veil separates u and me. The love of God shines everywhere here. We have body but no weight. We do wear clothes. When u cross, u are at your best. There are many levels. As a soul progresses, they move up to higher levels. Be my good girls…I love you much.* Thank you, babe, and good night.

Ode to a Celestial Butterfly

A butterfly am I, or so it appears in the sky
Let me go, Scorpio, so I can spread my wings and fly
Into the subatomic, changing forms as I flow
Then reappear another year as mankind likes to show
Though time, like form, is ever changing
And one day all will know
That the only true bliss comes as a kiss
From this Universal Abyss

Love Promised: A Future Life Revealed

Chapter Five

A New Year, Another Adventure … in Canada

Do not go where the path may lead;
go instead where there is no path and leave a trail.
—Ralph Waldo Emerson

The beginning of 2007 brought over, for a few sessions, friends who were very open to spirit communication. They were fascinated by the ease with which we were able to communicate with Russell and wanted to get a board of their own. Naturally, with them came several on the other side who were hoping to get a message through to their loved ones. As we all squeezed around the table, the oracle began...*Don't worry about me; I will stand...*Russell would say, joking with the crowd. These fun sessions would have turned into more but it was time to focus on our next trip to Toronto.

In future sessions, Hemi-sync music would be turned on to help raise our vibration, with those on the other side trying to lower theirs, to better connect the wavelength of our communication. A short prayer of protection would clear the space as we asked for all those on the other side to respect this sacred space we had created to communicate. Sometimes, if the oracle moved more slowly than usual, Russell would say *Interference* or *having trouble focusing* because so many would crowd around him. And at times, I called on Thomas to assist. *Thanks 4 the clearing, babe, it helped. Can u feel the ease that it is moving?* And we actually could.

On January 28, Russell began our session with *Happy B day to me...* What? Your birthday is not until April. *I'm waiting for next 1...another layer in what u call time. I am excited 4 u to make the trip. Take my shirt, red and white...*Okay, babe, we know it still retains so much of your energy. Over the next several months, Russell started giving us more clues about our next trip to Toronto and this time Oakville too. Since I had a busy work month that included a business trip, we decided to go in March instead of February. *Canada will not be as cold but you all will have a neat experience.*

This trip, I decided to leave something special behind...a gift for Mark and Eva to find in the future. I had their married names inscribed on an acrylic ruler dated long before they will be born because it occurred to me that it may set off a scavenger hunt for them someday. For the reader, unfortunately, this endearing story of leaving the plaque in Canada cannot be revealed since we've been asked to keep its location a secret for obvious reasons.

Mark and Eva Wexford
aka - Russell and Kent 2007

Plaque with names from current and future lives

We naturally became very inquisitive about this next trip. Not only were we interested in finding other locations about which Russell had given us clues, we also truly had a goal to accomplish, which included some responsibility on our part.

Russell had told me in the spring of 2006 that we would grow up together as childhood friends on a street named Little Oak, which was not yet built. When I asked for more information at the time, he said that it was too soon for me to know. Can you give us more clues now, babe, is it indeed Oakville? *Yes, Yarbrough... Watson.* Are these people's names or a street? *Street. There will be a sign for you there.* Exciting, can you tell me where we will go to high school, is it there now? *I can't tell you that... U are gorgeous, hmmm, long blonde hair. Taller, I can smell you.* You have to tell me that again, I just don't understand, how can you actually smell without the physical senses? *I can smell your spirit and now...mind. U just can't imagine. I never would have either.* Any other place we should go while in Oakville? *Regents place to eat, look for Regents Street. U may not have time 2 eat, ha, ha, school.* Oh, is this where the school is that we will attend? *2 cool 4 school...* There you go again, teasing me with no answers! *2 Blondies, later baby, when you walk into that store, listen 2 music, Regent.*

Russell knew to change the topic because if I didn't get an answer I thought I needed, the question would usually be asked in a different way, but no fooling him. And truthfully, it would not be a scavenger hunt if you are given all the information up front. I also remembered the few clues given to us before and just how much we found. That next week, however, I was not able to find on Google Maps a street called Yarbrough, only Pine, so I asked once again…*Just go looking Oakville for Pine and Little Oak streets, Pine and Little Oak intersection.* Okay, babe, I can find a Pine Street and will look at this intersection where you said Little Oak will be built. Are our parents there now as kids? *No.* Did you once say they are living? *Yes.* Russell would then tell Vickey, who will be his sister Yvonne, that their father Andrew would have a twin brother named Adam. Ah, the twin gene, interesting… it makes sense that we could have twin girls. He said the twin boys were 9 years old now and would move to Pennsylvania with their family. We assumed that at least Andrew would eventually end up in Oakville. Should we go to Oakville on our way to Toronto, or wait till on the way back? *Less traffic on Monday…* You're right, thanks, babe.

Go 2 Commonwealth…Church St. Which one? *Go 2 both.* Any more information you can give us about this? *Go walking up Commonwealth, cold, cold; you will see some place special while walking, church.* Is this the church we will be married in? *Good babe, u will think it is not the place but it is… ornate. Yep, it isn't a place u would pick in your present life.* What church or religion? *Different church, just not a traditional…Wrought iron, decoration on building, near downtown.* I immediately became excited by the thought of seeing the actual church. *Blue door restaurant, next morning go out look 4 gov't building.* Of course, that's after we sleep in, right? Being an earlier riser, JR makes a frowning face. *That is a great idea, sleep in…what can I say those late mornings were great.* I smiled at JR and felt this high pitch in my right ear. What's that? *Blew you a kiss, wish u could feel my hugs. I will try to have more about Toronto, try to relax, babe. You are the best.*

Clues and More Data

Russell would again entice us with some clues while planning our trip…*Go to blue restaurant, Toronto, blue, you will know it when you see it. Music 4 u there…I will arrange 4 u to hear at restaurant, baby.* And then another time, *blue bar, eat 2, lights 2 blink…make a toast 4 us.* Russell, can you tell us where it is? *Fun place, searching is half the fun. I'll be right there behind u.*

You mentioned Church Street earlier, anything else about that? *When u realize that u are at right place, u will have rush of peace, crossroad, corner baby. U will say, let's dance on street corner.* Sounds enchanting…*Yes we will be…won't care what others think.* Will Mark and Eva have the same personalities as Russell and Kent? *Some traits same, both of us great fun.* Will you be a practical joker like now? *A little, but only all in a great sense of humor…Take lots of pictures, I will be with you a lot 4 sure. Hat…*Hat? *Take one, could snow.* Should we go into the Flatiron Building? *If u can, go 2 your dad's office, third floor.* Which office will be his? *Whole floor…*Wow, really?

We then called Vickey. One afternoon earlier in the week, she had drifted off to sleep on the couch while thinking about her son-in-law's brain cancer. When she awoke, she was startled to see Russell standing there as if in the physical. He had on his red and white striped shirt and his smile was downturned. *Didn't mean 2 scare her but hair scared me.* We all laughed and I was envious, of course. *A lot of my energy is still in that house. Each attempt to get your attention is hard 2 do for us.* Where are you right now? *Sitting on bar…Have you smelled rain and lemon?* Well, I smelled rain last week when sitting on my back porch reading while it rained. *Baby there is often a smell like lemon when spirits are near, a brief whiff.* I'll try to pay more attention to that. *Patrick says you have made progress…you have both opened a link. U should go to a place known 4 thin veil.* Where? *Sedona.* Ah, Arizona, well, that makes sense, it's the New Age capitol of the world, or at least in the U. S. *Rock formations, castle.* One of these trips we will do that. *Take lots of pics for orbs. There will be a row of flowers.* Where? *Toronto, pick red one 4 me, place in book.*

Russell, we want to go back to Washington Avenue for sure. *They have been doing some work on the house.* By the way, will we have a hot tub in Toronto since it is so cold there? *Tub will be hot all right.* It is still so odd how we got a picture of those orbs on Washington Avenue. *Spirits follow me because of this; they are looking 4 way 2 communicate always. Some are related.* Is there anyone in this lifetime who will be our kids in this next life? *Not finalized. It has to be approved. All will be good, Dad's soul has agreed. I am peeling layers. I can see them, blonde kids, tall 4 age; straight hair, your eyes, playing upstairs.* Oh, tell more! *Smell of lemon, lots of pictures of us on walls. We all learn 2 ski.* How exciting, what about ice-skating? *Yes, and Rachel will have a birthmark on leg, looks like a small star. The smell is strong, clean freak, ha ha.* Who? *Maid, Nanny, more 2 come, there is another pet.* Oh, in addition to our cocker spaniels? *Cat, Cassie.* How cute, I like that name.

When in our next life will we find the book that we write in this one? *After Julian, he will be 1 who brings it to our attention.* Who's Julian? *A coworker of mine…*How old will you be when the book is found? *43 years*

Love Promised: A Future Life Revealed

old. How does he bring it to our attention? *He is an avid reader and finds the book in an off-the-street bookstore. He will wrap it as a gift for me and bring it to my 44th birthday party. I have to close pages, love you.* As always, we were amazed by the information given. Russell said that as Mark and Eva, we will resonate with the information in the book, filled with wonder but skepticism too.

Girl, I will be with you on trip. Dad, this must be you? *Wick...*Great, I want you there too! *Mark invited me, don't know if I can get used to calling you Eva.* Yes, Dad, odd for you. I can't imagine you being called anything other than Wick even though I call you Dad. *Smith lifeline is huge. Watch 4 a sign from me on trip. Tell Momma to get warmer slippers.* How come she and I couldn't get the Ouija board to work last night? *We were in another space, a different level; there was not a way to get thru 2 you. Being in the presence of God, there is no outside connection then.* Not sure we understand, but that's okay. *We cannot talk with u in the presence of God.* Thanks, Dad. Love you. *Love my girl.*

Help Us Understand

Russell, often you mention the grandmother that I never knew coming around for our sessions. She died in her early thirties. Can you confirm for me what Judy once told me, that my son Chris is her reincarnated—my mom's biological mother, Bonnie? *Do u want to know?* Yes. *Yes, part of her spirit still here, long hair.* For the benefit of those here, will you explain how this can be? If Bonnie is reincarnated, how do you see her over there, if she has already come back as my son? *Only last form, she has come back, and I have not. When I come back as Mark, I will leave a part of me here, a shadow of Russ. The learned records remain in heaven, the grand total of your soul's experience. 4 this lifetime, I am Russ. We can assume other shapes if we interacted with them in another lifetime; if a soul needs to be recognized by another lifeline, then we can be seen as that other.* Thanks so much, babe, and another question. In this dimension, sometimes we hear of a soul being seen as an apparition, and then there was Dad, who looked very much in the physical when he appeared to John, and you appearing to Aunt Vickey. Can you explain? *We appear as ether or plasma depending on the density that we wish to be seen or experienced. Ether is more ethereal, plasma is more dense. As the spirit slows, there are photon-like particles that adhere to the slower energy, that's what can be seen with the human eye.* And you appear to other souls there as just an orb or a light body? *Both light body and soul, there are antimatter atoms. Time does not exist. There is matter offset by antimatter.* Yes, you've said before that time does not exist and that is a difficult concept to grasp. *Events and experiences never go away; they are layered on each other. Time is only relative in measuring your soul's experiences. Think of this, the light reaching Earth now is millions of years old, but if you could back up light, u would see that it simply is.* Wow, the concept for most humans is barely conceivable. But I do look forward to talking with both you and Dad about quantum physics to understand that as much as possible. Also, I have recommended to some that movie, the *Celestine Prophecy*, based on the book by James Redfield, as it has a great message. *See it, have an open mind.*

Russell never hesitated to let me know he was around, such as in Washington, DC, on my business trip in February 2007. During one of our sessions, I told Ron that at this space conference there were some beautiful pictures of the aurora borealis and Russell chimed in. *Beautiful moment in space, this second is only like a grain of sand. If u close your eyes, is everything still there? Everything you have ever experienced is still here.* I've always heard and read that all our experiences are recorded…do you look into what's called the Akashic records that we've heard about? *When I get to look in records, I still am astonished.* So there is a Hall of Records, an actual building that we've heard some speak of and write about? *It is immense, all history is kept there, not only 4 Earth but 4 all species in the universe, all levels. No one thing gets the breath of life without it being in book. In fact, babe, you were once the soul in charge of books here. Why do u think u like to read? You were a heavenly librarian assigned to allow access to records over here. One of many duties souls can have in between lives.* That's incredible.

I've always thought it was symbolism in the Bible when it stated that heaven's streets are paved with gold? *From the bright lights; not really a mineral, the spectrum of light is a millionfold from what u now see. I enjoy mountain views KB8414, it is a glorious system, beautiful name of Sun.* Is this what some call the great central Sun? *At the center of everything, light in the center of darkness.* Can you tell me the coordinates? *114 point 999 by 85 point 73. It is outside of your solar system, too far for scientists to record until a more powerful scope is in deep space.*

Do you recall someone that bumped into u…I walked in 4 brief second to touch u. Oh my goodness, I walked through these large doors coming out of the conference room at the hotel and my shoulder hit another person's shoulder as we passed by each other. Neither of us could see the other one coming. Is that what you are talking about? *Yes…How did you do that?*

For me, I batted blue eyes. As always, Russell makes us laugh. *Now u know 4 sure I am always near u…your scent is so calming and full of love. Like I said, the colors n smell are incredible here, if u only knew.* Your feelings are still so real there, as if you hadn't left. *It is strange but the sensations are instant and intense, like electricity.* So you hear us every time we tell you that we love you even if you are not around? *We know when u say it, great sensation 4 us.* So you hear our thoughts all the time? *Like background noise, we have 2 tune in.* One more thing about DC at dinner u looked so great. That's so sweet; you know there was an empty seat next to me. *A sign that I am there sitting… Baby, try to catch the strange scent later, it will be me.* Russell, it means so much having you watch over me. The other day at the office I again had the pressure in my left ear; this time it lasted for 30 minutes. *In office 2 watch u work, I also love 2 watch u sleep and try to make pillow bounce.* Playful you still are…and the pressure in my left ear was immense. *I was very close 2 you.* How many feet? *1 foot away, plus no one else in room…Funny how smell can be so vivid like colors.* Russell, can you tell me how Mom's test will turn out? *Can't, just love her.* I just don't want her to suffer. *She won't, Wick will pick her up n his arms. She will be happy, they will dance again.* Will she cross soon? *Don't ask…her light is beginning to fade; it is as it should be. She has a fan club here, will keep us laughing.*

All of a sudden, Russell's dogs started barking while looking out the back screen door. This seemed odd because my yard is fenced in and there was no one out there…or so we thought. We put our hands back on the oracle…*Kent, I am on your porch…they can c me.* Do you want us to let them out? *No, love you.* Boots's ears were standing straight up as he stood on his hind legs with his front paws on the door. Ron laughed and made a joke about his big ears saying, "Boots needs to stay out of the wind." I couldn't help but laugh out loud and Russell said, *Don't make fun of my boy!*

Off to Canada We Go…Again

How quickly a year had passed. It was already time for our trip back to the Northeast. Before packing the board, we chatted with Russell the night before we were to meet Vickey at the airport. *Baby, be careful in Canada, there are some steps steep that u will climb, wear shoes with traction.* Is this on the steps in the church? *Government building, loose rail. Look high and low…tell Vickey to bring her good-luck piece, gold flower from Grandma. She will know.* Vickey indeed had packed Ann's white gold and mother-of-pearl flower-shaped pin. *Govt bldg; look carefully 4 your likeness.* Is there a name on this print that we can see, this picture with my likeness? *Name, initials, CS...*Date? *Original has date 1948, artist's proof.* *Again, babe, search 4 street corner, will feel very, very familiar.* Is this the street corner you talked about before, where we will dance one day in the snow? *Right, near old town, yep, it will feel as if the wind blew right thru u and the smell will be strangely familiar.* Sounds like another scavenger hunt and you are going over the clues one last time. *More like an adventure, u will be amazed again. Babe, wear my favorite ring.* The one you helped me get back? *Uh-huh...Don't think that miracles can't happen. Canada, get on board when u get to hotel, night.*

On Thursday, March 15, 2007, Ron, JR, Vickey and I took a 7:15 a.m. flight out of Houston's Hobby Airport, bound for Canada. After arriving in Buffalo, New York, at 1:33 p.m., we rented a car and crossed the border, heading to Toronto once again. We checked into the downtown Clarion Hotel that afternoon, then set out to look for the restaurant with the blue door though we didn't find it right away. Surprisingly, we did run across Church Street, where Russell had said we would one day be walking in the snow, holding each other to stay warm. And though we hadn't noticed it before, it was right in front of the Flatiron Building!

The Blue Door

We slowly perused downtown but not finding a restaurant with a blue door, we finally stopped to eat at a place called O'Grady's. Vickey and I sat in a booth across from Ron and JR and very soon, they started snickering. "What's up?" we said, but they just continued to grin. We had been given many clues for this trip but soon realized we goofed on the very first one. Having settled into our rooms for the evening, we decided to have a chat with Russell. *Ask for protection, clear space.* And we did, since the very room we were in was called the Hadley Hemingway suite. Named for his wife and him, it was where Ernest used to stay when visiting Toronto, before this beautiful old home was turned in a hotel. *You guys are 2 funny. I give you clues, and bingo.* Uh oh, we were supposed to get on the board in the hotel after we checked in, right? *Yes.* Sorry, Russell, we couldn't find the restaurant and ended up at a gay bar, ha. *That was 4 Dad.* Where is the blue door restaurant? *Close.* Sorry to keep you and Dad waiting. Should we go Friday night? *2morrow ok...*Any other clues for the day? *Drive down Commonwealth, look 4 unusual building, like church. Does not look like a church.* Can you give us an intersection or where on Commonwealth to find the church? What is the number? *27, I can't see the other numbers, E, that's all I see.* Okay, what about the painting? *Fountain walkway; Government building by University of Toronto; Old Hall; Streetcar next to it.* Vickey then asked about the significance of having their mother's pin with them. *Sign she is with us. She loved her trip to Canada. Rose pin, she bought it.* It then made perfect sense, but surprisingly neither Ron nor Vickey knew that their mom had actually bought the pin, which still carried her energy, in Canada. *Wish we had found the restaurant tonight. God, we hated being stood up.* Did they play the song we were supposed to hear? *Saved it.* Can you tell us more about this government building where we are supposed to find the Eiffel Tower painting? *Trees in front, you will know by the wrought iron.* Thanks, babe, we'll try to do better tomorrow.

Touring Toronto

We started our day early on Friday, March 16, anxious to see the inside of the historic Flatiron Building. The sweet girl who greeted us at the door said she didn't typically give tours on this day but since we had come all the way from Texas, she would be happy to show us around. She began by letting us know the Flatiron was built in 1892, 115 years ago, to house offices for the famous Gooderham Distillery. After showing us the oldest working electric elevator in all of North America, she pointed out the original brass railing leading to a main office on the first floor, and the original chandelier above our heads. We couldn't help but notice a huge white sign against the dark-stained wooden walls over the elevator with the word "Belong" spray painted on it in blue. We were then told that the recent owner of the building had found original graffiti from around the world and displayed it on the walls for all to enjoy. I was anxious to head up to the third floor, where my father would one day have his law office, so I asked, "I heard there is a lawyer's office upstairs, can you tell us exactly where?" The young lady smiled and said, "Yes, there is, the whole third floor." Ron and I just looked at each other in amazement.

We continued to walk up the staircase toward the second floor and found a second piece of graffiti, taken from an old, white frame home. It was spray painted "I love you" and had an acrylic coating. And, on the way to the third floor was the word "Her" written on a section of old, bright red brick. This graffiti was amazing and it was almost as if Russell had guided us to see the message…you belong here, I love you. Our guide then took us for a ride on the elevator to the fifth floor, with its large conference room and huge windows, where we looked out over the downtown park on this cool, sunny day. We thanked her as we left and walked back outside, still mesmerized by the unique shape of this building. On the back, the flat part of the "iron," an artist had attached a painted mural that appeared to be a curtain giving the illusion of many windows where there were actually only three. This trompe l'oeil mural definitely added to the building's unique character. What was even more exciting was that this building was now part of Toronto's historic district, a guarantee that it would be standing during the middle of this twenty-first century. This left us believing even more that my future father, Ben Stone, could be working one day on the third floor as a lawyer.

Kent and Ron on the stairwell inside the Flatiron Building

Since we were so enthralled with the history of this building, for more reasons than our tour guide could possibly imagine, it was recommended we walk over to the St. Lawrence Market close by. Celebrating 200 years of operation, it was one of the oldest in North America. Before the market, however, we would cross Church Street, take a few pictures, and mosey inside the Flatiron gift shop. That street corner brought a sense of wonder and excitement and felt strangely familiar as I gazed at it. Inside the underground market, we window-shopped before trying the famous Peameal Canadian bacon sandwiches. Off to find another part of town, we drove past the downtown open-air ice-skating rink where, as childhood friends, Russell, my brother, and I will one day ice-skate. Next, we went inside the former city hall, now the Criminal Court building, where Vickey will one day work as an attorney. As we made our way through security,

Love Promised: A Future Life Revealed

it was obvious this building demanded respect, with its massive staircase and wooden stair rails in the center of the marble floor. The split staircase led to the open second floor. After traversing the widest formal hallways we had ever seen, we continued looking on all the walls for a watercolor picture of the Eiffel Tower. We then went inside the new Toronto city hall, a multistoried C-shaped building. Again, we had no luck finding a picture of the Eiffel Tower, but how neat it was to walk around inside a new building that I might be working in one day.

We continued on our way to find yet another impressive government building, one that we had driven by on our last trip. Russell had told me I would work there when moving up to "statehouse." This colossal building with high ceilings was in fact Ontario's Provincial Parliament Building, we soon learned. By the time we arrived, tourists were well into the last official guided tour for the day, but as we strolled around inside, we were given directions to the second-floor gallery, where the parliament members' seats were located. We did find some attendants who were able to answer a few questions about the building and the fire that had partially destroyed it. It was quite interesting to see how the half that had survived had walnut-stained square columns and hardwood floors lined with dark emerald-green rugs, while the new half was built of white marble and painted white on the inside. I did not know for sure if this was the statehouse Russell was referring to, but walking through this building left me with a feeling that was almost indescribable. As we were close to Washington Avenue, we drove by it once again to relive the joy of our first trip's findings. As Russell had told us, work had been done on the house—the unpainted wooden steps and porch banister had obviously just been built.

After an afternoon break, we talked with our spirit team, who was with us throughout the day...*Did you feel comfortable?* Yes, and the lure of these buildings was surreal. *Vickey works high office criminal lawyer.* Jokingly, she puffs out her chest, smiling. *How did u like private tour of Flatiron Bldg., I love you graffiti?* It was probably the most special, babe, and what a coincidence to get that tour. *No coincidences. Great, "Her" is u, your energy will remain there. Ann didn't care 4 history lessons. She loved the shop. Hey, baby, Wick said the sandwich was awful.* Love Canadian bacon but we sort of agree, is he here? *Gone now told me to tell u that he will be there tomorrow 2.* Ah, yes, the Hay House conference, Dad would want to attend it. Is the Parliament Building where I will work? *Eventually at Parliament, start at city hall office, move up ladder provincial seat.* Wow! On which side of the building will I work? *Both offices...Go have a nice dinner.*

On to Find the Church

We kept looking for a painting of the Eiffel Tower in just about every government building we could find. But it was now time to shift our focus to the church where Russell and I would one day be married. We decided to search for a street called Commonwealth, which we had found on Google Maps before leaving the hotel that morning. The only Commonwealth Street in Toronto, however, took us to the outskirts of town so we were a little skeptical when we found a fairly modern but run-down-looking church. Perhaps we were too focused, disregarding the other clues given, it now seems, such as *downtown, walking down Commonwealth, different church, not traditional, wrought iron, red door* and *decoration on building.* Other than the fact we were on a street named Commonwealth, none of the other clues fit at all and we were a little disappointed, to say the least. Sensing we were not on the right track yet, we pulled in at a convenience store, only to hear the song "Collide" on the store's sound system. Understanding my frustration, Russell was trying to console me once again. It did make me feel better. We drove back into town, again, looking for the painting, but no such luck. In spite of some pretty good clues we were getting nowhere, it seemed, and the clue *Commonwealth* would continue to confuse us. Also, with Friday coming to an end and offices closing, we might not find this Eiffel Tower watercolor painting after all. There was something we were not getting right, some miscommunication. We headed back to the hotel that afternoon to talk with Russell but just before we did, Ron had the idea to Google just the words *Commonwealth in Toronto.*

Sorry u had to run around but it is part of the intrigue… Gosh, it would be so much easier if you could just give us the address, babe. *I can't tell every detail, not allowed but Commonwealth Church is not the name.* So the church today was not it, just to be sure? *God no, this church is a part of the Commonwealth, St by it… Queens at this church.* What? *Babe, Commonwealth Society runs this church; St. P…* We got off the board for a moment and went on the laptop. Then Ron found a Web site that excited us. We quickly got back on the board. Is this it, Russell, St. Paul's? *Bingo …dark red doors, big, prestigious, next to Queens.* Looking again, we realized this street was next to Queens Street. We are finally getting somewhere, thanks for the extra help. By the way, did you send that song to me in the convenience store today? *Uh huh…Collide, u were feeling down.* I thought so, yes, and the picture? *U will b fortunate 2 locate it but look close, it's there, a government building old and new, look high and low, hmmm.*

That evening this keyword, Commonwealth, finally led us to the Web site of the Toronto branch of the Royal Commonwealth Society, where an international meeting had just been held. The address was St. Paul's, downtown Toronto, 227 Bloor Street East. What we also learned was that this Commonwealth Society represents 53 countries of various faiths, races, languages, and cultures "linked through shared traditions and the belief that their interests are served by partnership." Each year this society meets in a different country. What a relief to find the church! We couldn't wait to see it.

We also found the address of what we thought might be the "blue door" restaurant, and hopped in the SUV, excited to go out for the night. Just a few blocks from the Clarion Hotel was a beautiful church of English grey stone. There were ornate concrete arches over the windows and doors and the solid wooden doorways were painted a dark red, with lanterns above. The surrounding yard was outlined in wrought iron. In front of the church was a large sword mounted on a cross, honoring members of the Queen's Own Rifles of Canada who fell in battles fought between 1866 and 1953. How could we have missed this, focusing on one clue only and making assumptions? Nevertheless, we were elated to find it and knew right away that we wanted to attend their Sunday morning services. It was a very historic church indeed, having been built in the late 1800s, with a beautiful addition that came later. Will this church really host Mark and Eva's wedding on August 22, 2048?

It was now time to celebrate after our long but successful day, even though we had not found the painting. We dined at the *Blue Pelican* restaurant downtown, which had a blue door. This must be it, we thought. Russell let us know, by blinking the bar lights, that we were in the right place but, excited to be there, we didn't listen for a song. When we left the restaurant, we were surprised to find that, this late in March, almost three inches of snow had fallen. Watching the snowflakes drifting among the street lights downtown was an awesome sight, and we understood why Russell had wanted us to get a taste of the Toronto winter. As we walked up the steps at our hotel, a lovely couple leaving offered to take our picture. I couldn't wait to talk with Russell once again around the fireplace, especially when we noticed orbs in the pictures just taken! Worn out from the day, Vickey didn't join us in the session.

Ron, Vickey, JR, and Kent; with Russell, and Ron and Vickey's mother in Spirit

Hello, Dad and Baby... Love you, Russell. *Love you more. I enjoyed today with you. Did u enjoy taste of winter?* How awesome. *That was not easy to arrange, had help of angel.* Whoa! Are you saying that you made it snow? *God did, I'm right over you reading pic.* The orb in the picture we just took, that's you, right? *Right overhead, above baby girl...* that's the largest, whitest one I've ever seen. I just love it. Were you guys with us tonight? *Of course, me and Daddy Wick; two together outside, we followed you all night.* We have pictures with several orbs. *Anna, WJ, Paula, and Shorty went by here.* How can that be? Ron wondered out loud, WJ hasn't crossed over yet? *But a part of him exists over here, part of the light. Just like when u put your energy in the rails at the government building. It's more like in our current world than u can imagine; do you think that what you did an hour ago does not exist now? It still exists, just a few pages back.* Someday, we hope to understand this all. So, it's okay to leave the plaque in Canada? *Angels Michael and Gabriel have already approved and it will be found no matter where u put it. A young girl will find it, that's what I see.* We stopped for a moment, just staring at one another in amazement, and soon decided to call it a night.

Later, Vickey had an emotional healing when Russell told her that the flower girl in our wedding would be the daughter that she had aborted in this life. It also stands to reason that although on a physical level abortion may seem like a fetus or child has been killed, that soul just decided to come back in another lifetime, in another physical body, to have Vickey as her

Love Promised: A Future Life Revealed

mom. A soul is a part of God which, like energy, can never be destroyed and a human body is nothing without the soul that inhabits it. The little girl's name will be Julia. My sister Lee Ann was told that she too would be attending this grand wedding as a 13-year-old with her father, a successful businessman and owner of the Drake building in Montreal. As Cammy Braken, she will wear a blue dress to the wedding and have blue flowers flowing in her golden locks of hair.

Daddy Wick

On Saturday, March 17, we were at the Hay House I Can Do It! Abraham workshop all day, along with approximately 300 people, listening to Jerry and Ester Hicks with Abraham talking about the Law of Attraction. It was an interesting day and a learning experience for all since the information given could be applied to anyone's life experiences. We then went to celebrate

Sign from Kent's father,
Wick Smith

St. Patrick's Day with some green beer at the Firkin pub in the basement of the Flatiron. This small pub seemed to be the happening place so space was limited. While we were waiting at the bar for a table, I was shocked to see this sign from my Dad. The large oval black-and-red beer siphon bore the name *Smith Wicks*. As I grinned from ear to ear, I was certain my father, Wick Smith, was letting me know he was indeed there, as he had promised to be.

Saint P's

The next morning, Sunday, March 18, I was awake, but my eyes were still closed as I listened intently to a song that would not stop playing in my head. "Into the Night" is a passionate love song by Benny Mardones about a 16-year-old girl who was obviously too young for her admirer. The song must have something to do with our next life, as it seemed Russell was sending me a message. Then it occurred to me, if the age difference between Mark and Eva is five years, he would be 21 and she 16, making it illegal for him to be with her. If they grow up together on the same street, this might very well be the case. Having been so much older than Russell in this lifetime, I do know that age is not a factor when it comes to being in love. Russell later verified he sent the song…*Foolish kids, once we realize it, we will be one heart; a love that will be enough 2 take your breath away.* The lyrics, "I can't measure my love, there's nothing to compare it to," practically lifted me out of the bed to stare at the plaque sitting on the table next to me, the acrylic ruler made for Mark and Eva.

Excited, we all prepared to attend worship services at St. Paul's Anglican Church on Bloor Street. I was amazed when we went inside what seemed to be more like an old English cathedral than a church. Greeted with a smile by one of the church attendants, we were taken on a short tour prior to the service, since we were visiting from out of town. Just inside the entrance was a beautiful stone statue of Jesus preaching to men, women, and children on their knees. There were also two striking life-sized statues of the Archangel Michael and St. Paul. The interior was breath-taking. Exquisite stained glass windows depicting biblical scenes adorned the body of the church. The dark walnut pews and ceiling were a striking contrast to the white stone walls, columns, and carved, pointed arches. Lighted sconces hung above the plaques that lined the walls, and simple but elegant lighting hung low from the high ceilings. Leading to the ornate altar were approximately ten very wide white marble steps. On the right was a massive pipe organ and against the back wall were even more majestic pipes that reached the ceiling. Artifacts from all parts of the world had been sent to decorate this beautiful church.

I could hardly focus on the words in the sermon. Sitting through the service in this glorious church put me in awe at the thought of what it might feel like to walk down the aisle in a bridal gown one day. I could feel Russell's energy next to me and the pressure in my ear…It was as if he was saying, "Wow, look, babe." And I now understood why he had told me, months earlier, that I too would have a grand wedding one day. That night on the board he said the church is used a lot, but that my guide, Saint Thomas, has connections to God and to Anglicans, who helped him arrange for the wedding. Hearing this was surreal indeed. Where will we go on our honeymoon? *Bali, r u ready? Dream about me.*

Exploring Mark and Eva's Hometown

After leaving the church and grabbing a quick bite, we couldn't wait to explore our future hometown of Oakville, the birthplace of Russell, Vickey, and myself. On the way there, we went over the clues and the maps I had printed out. Though we never found a Yarbrough Street, we did find Pine and Watson Streets which, as we had been told, intersected. A few streets over, I looked up to see yet another surprise, Kent Avenue. This had to be the other "sign" that Russell told me I would find.

Streets in Oakville, Canada

How ironic, I thought…close to where Mark and Eva will grow up is a street with my name. And where they live as adults is a street with Russell's name.

In comparison to Toronto, driving around the small town of Oakville was quietly exciting. Russell had said we were to look for the intersection of Pine and Little Oak, even though he mentioned Little Oak is not yet built. So we drove down Pine Street looking for an area that might one day become an intersecting street and we did, in fact, find just one. This had to be it, and its current name is Perkins Passage.

Perkins Passage, where a street named Little Oak will someday be built

One day, Russell said, he and my brother Karl would pick me up from a birthday party at another new home and street not yet built, 1890 Beach Walk. Along this street, not far from Little Oak, a new seawall will be built because the water level would be higher than it is now. He said it would be cold and there would be lots of kids on the deck overlooking the water at this party being held in honor of twin brothers Rick and Nick Lowderback.

We decided to try to find the high school Russell, Vickey, and I would attend in Oakville. We could not get very close to Trafalgar High School since a gate blocked its entrance, but we could see a very modern red brick two-story building outlined in royal blue tucked away in an area completely surrounded by woods. Russell would later confirm that this was indeed the school.

At Lake Ontario, we drove past some beautiful homes on the water and stopped for a while to walk around. From here, we could look back and see the city of Toronto. Russell later said that one day we would build a lake house on this very spot of land. I wondered how it would remain empty for so long, as it seemed prime real estate, but he said a shack would be built that we would later tear down. *Our lake house will be 15 feet out over the water on one side, right where you saw little jetty. Lots of open view, glass on water side, rock jetty supports pilings.* Russell went on to confirm this house would actually be more elaborate than our home in Toronto. I'm sensing, Russell, that this house will be built about the same time this book is found, is that true? *Yes, about same time, around 2067.*

On this last night in Toronto, we decided to celebrate the evening at the uniquely decorated Spaghetti Factory and reminisce about our adventure. Later, we talked with Russell. We felt our trip had been successful, except for not finding the painting of the Eiffel Tower. Russell did tell us that the original was now crated and stored away because the art museum was being renovated, but that there was an artist's copy in a store in Toronto. *Guys I wish I could disclose all, some things I can't reveal yet.* Were we close today looking for it? *Close.* Russell, before this, I've had ringing in my ears and felt your vibration while scavenging around but I didn't sense you at all when looking for the picture this morning. *Yes, our presence. Spirit Guides ask me to stand back on this one; they say if you saw yourself, it might change your perspective. The guides will eventually allow it.* I didn't quite understand, but would have to accept and trust what I was being told. *Don't worry, when angels say it's okay, you will eventually see*

it. Sensing my disappointment, he went on to say...*Babe, this life u are experiencing is only brief, we will be back 2gether before you know it and 4 sure no one will be happier than us.*

On Monday, March 19, we left for the airport in Buffalo just before dawn. As we drove south past the town of Oakville, I contemplated in silence what had happened over the last few days. Then it occurred to me just how much more we had learned about this future life on our second trip to Canada, and how much more familiar this place had become.

We stopped by Niagara Falls, and were once more immersed in the beautiful view and sounds of nature. This time we each tossed a red rose in the Falls, saying a prayer for the ones we loved in spirit who accompanied us on the trip, and sending them light, as they asked us to do. *We do hear your prayers,* Russell says. They thanked us by showing up in our pictures. *Orbs are the spiritual energy of the soul, u see the ones that will affect next chapter* (lifetime), *moving ones are going around in circles fast. Bigger ones are closer 2 your lifeline. An orb may appear still, but energy of each soul is moving.*

Niagara Falls, Buffalo, New York—March 19, 2007

While on the plane, we searched our cameras for all the photos we could find with orbs and we had plenty. It was the first time I saw a photo of moving orbs.

Waves of Energy—Strings of Light

It wouldn't be until we got home that I noticed several very unusual photographs taken with my camera while dining at the Blue Pelican. Russell had said we should expect something special from the trip, and when first opening a couple of digital pictures, I deleted one, thinking it was somehow ruined.

Looking closely at the others, I noticed something very unusual. There were waves coming off the overhead TV in the bar, and what seemed to be heat and energy extending from the ceiling lights. (See cropped photograph below.)

Cropped picture showing the ceiling of the Blue Pelican, Toronto, Canada, above Ron's head

Lights like concentrated lightning in Toronto's Blue Pelican sports bar

Another photograph revealed evidence of something I later confirmed with Russell, that Ron's guardian angels were all around him. We were amazed

Love Promised: A Future Life Revealed

to see this photograph and grateful for this special gift he had promised. And indeed, it looked like what Russell had once mentioned, *light energy like concentrated lightning.* It wouldn't be until the following year, when we were getting some similar pictures that we attempted to understand the scientific nature of what we were capturing in these photographs.

There had also been some questions about Toronto I forgot to ask while there. One night, before the question was even posed, Russell said, *Sky Club, u asked.* Yes, I was wondering! Is that where our wedding reception will be held? *Yes, the reception will be held in tower…* The CN Tower, oh my. *Cool, huh, we will have a caravan of limos 2 take everyone to the tower.* That's one place we missed… *Wait till u see 3 carats.* What! You give me a 3-carat-diamond wedding ring? *Yes…* Wow! What shape will it be? *Pear…* Sounds beautiful! How many people will be at our wedding? *Over 100 people.* Vickey asked Russell about their future father's profession. *Surgeon, Pediatric…It is so neat that u got the plaque placed.* Yes, that's a relief!

More Obstacles

After this second trip to Canada, Russell never left my mind and my life revolved around communicating with him each week. Some family members were naturally concerned, not fully understanding the impact of his presence and the purpose to all that was happening. There was more to discover. I wanted to understand these unusual photographs and this world where he and my father now existed. It wasn't a game we were playing, for this board was a tool that truly connected us to this other dimension. And the longer we communicated, the more important our messages became. I wanted to understand, too, why street lights went out right in front of me, and why the repetitive numbers continued on a daily basis. Ron too enjoyed the sessions, still having experiences of his own. As Russell had said would happen, this communication brought us peace. In addition to documenting the sessions and preparing for future ones, work and family filled my waking existence.

It was also during this time that my daughter's drinking problems started up again, when she was laid off from a job that she loved. Both this disease and her depression took their toll not just on her, but on her father, brothers, and me as well. The stress of long work hours, Mom's worsened Alzheimer's, and living with the physical pain of having had two back surgeries, due to an injury, came to a climax. My primordial urge to exist was waning when I picked up my prescription of Darvocet and headed home. Without premeditation, I sat down at my kitchen table and opened the bottle, laying all the pills out at once. I just stared at them. How easy it would be to just go to sleep and not wake up, at least not in the physical body anymore. There was no such thing as death, for slipping out of my body many times had proved this to me. My heart longed to be free of any future pain and suffering and possibly, my time could be better spent helping my loved ones from the other side. And being with Russell again was an alluring thought. I gazed for a minute out my dining room window then looked back at the empty bottle on the table…and quickly put all the pills back. This would be the easy way out. It was not in my nature to give up. If I'm still here, there's a reason…this difficult time would pass.

After some prayer time and relaxing with my favorite Enya music during dinner, I slipped into a much-needed deep sleep. The next morning, while stepping out of the shower, my mind began to focus intently on the radio and the words to a REM song, "Everybody Hurts,"[1] that I knew Thomas had sent. Wrapped in a towel, I leaned against my bed, weeping.

When your day is long
And the night, the night is yours alone
When you're sure you've had enough
Of this life, well hang on

Don't let yourself go
'Cause everybody cries
And everybody hurts sometimes

Sometimes everything is wrong
Now it's time to sing along
When your day is night alone (Hold on, hold on)
If you feel like letting go (Hold on)
If you think you've had too much
Of this life, well hang on

Everybody hurts
Take comfort in your friends
Everybody hurts
Don't throw your hand, oh no

Don't throw your hand
If you feel like you're alone
No, no, no, you are not alone

If you're on your own in this life
The days and nights are long
When you think you've had too much of this life to hang on

Well, everybody hurts sometimes
Everybody cries
Everybody hurts sometimes
And everybody hurts sometimes

So hold on, hold on
Hold on, hold on, hold on, hold on, hold on, hold on
Everybody hurts

My devoted guide was next to me another time when my burden seemed much heavier than I could bear. Driving home from work one evening, my thoughts and emotions overwhelmed me again. The pavement was difficult to see through my tears, along with the falling rain, so I briefly pulled over on the side of the road. At that very moment, I glanced down at my digital screen, surprised to see only the word *Thomas* displayed. Part of Rob Thomas's lyrics to "Ever The Same"[2] filled my soul:

Just let me hold you while you're falling apart
Just let me hold you and we'll both fall down

Fall on me
Tell me everything you want me to be
Forever with you forever in me
Ever the same

Man, this doesn't need to be the end

Just let me hold you while you're falling apart
Just let me hold you and we'll both fall down

Fall on me tell me everything you want me to be

Forever with you
Forever in me
Ever the same
Call on me
I'll be there for you and you'll be there for me
Forever it's you
Forever in me
Ever the same

You may need me there
To carry all your weight
But you're no burden I assure
You tide me over
With a warmth I'll not forget
But I can only give you love

Fall on me tell me everything you want me to be
Forever with you
Forever in me
Ever the same
Call on me

This message comforted me beyond words and, once again, gave me the strength to endure yet another day. As with the ebb and flow of tides, life got easier and I got stronger. And soon, we were given yet another task. One that sounded exciting, but Ron and I also knew it would be a real challenge.

The Time Capsule

Hey babe, I got to look in the book. You mean our future life? *Yes, can't wait for Toronto. Yellow is definitely your color. I've been watching you as a teenager; you are alpha female, a real take-charge girl.* Well, I'm definitely garnering strength in this lifetime to carry forward.

It was now the summer of 2007. *I can see another trip to Canada in 2010. U will have another task.* What's that, babe? *Time capsule.* Are you serious? *U 2 need start work on book and capsule contents.* What do we put into the capsule? *The book, seal it with silicon in bag; thumb drive pictures;*

labeled jar with strands of my hair and yours babe; where my body is buried; addresses of interest; genealogy of both families, more later, babe.

We sat there stunned, thinking only that a book would be written someday and discovered in the future. Now we realize there was more to the story, and a deadline. Russell stated we would bury the capsule on our last trip to Toronto and that it would be found mid-year 2067, two and a half years after Mark and Eva had read the book, the one his best friend Julian would give him for his birthday. *When the contents of the time capsule are revealed, as Mark and Eva, we will not be able to ignore it, the details of our previous life and the one we will be living.* Russell continued... *The subject of reincarnation will present itself to the public which cannot be denied but will cause much scrutiny among the followers of Christianity.* Interviews with the media will include Mark and Eva, he said.

This was another session that left us speechless but the thought of a time capsule intrigued me, as it made even more sense if it proved the theory. Very soon, I remembered the end of a psychic reading with Petrene in 2002, before I met Russell, when she told me there would be something very significant happening in Canada in the year 2010. At that time, I never imagined it involved me personally and it was so far off, the thought never entered my mind again until now. My mind started to whirl and another piece of the puzzle came together.

During our next session, we asked Russell what he had been doing. *Teaching arts; helping new arrivals. It is still strange a little; I feel like I can reach out and touch you. The veil is so thin.* Where are you right now? *Sitting on the kitchen counter...* When can we see you? *When I get approval and you will see me dense as before.* Russell, I'd like to talk a minute about what happened the other night. I was home from work not feeling well and had an OBE while resting in bed. I was a little nervous at first when the vibrations started up but decided to go with it. Soon after floating out, all of a sudden, I was looking around in what seemed to be someone else's place, an awkward feeling because they were not home. It was like looking through a light fog, though I definitely could see furniture, items on a coffee table and an end table, a kitchen and counter. Nothing looked familiar to me. *Hazy experience...* Yes, very much so. *Did u recognize the picture on the wall?* No, I didn't see a picture. *You were at our house.* You mean I have a house with you over there? *Kind of, you were in this space. Your face... It was the one I drew of you.* But I have the picture here? *I have one here too. First time u crossed 2 here. Fuzzy...* Yes... Hours here but seconds to you. Were you around? *I was not allowed there. Later, I will be able to be there when you visit.*

But…why? I asked, tears starting to form in my eyes. *It would have been too emotional for you. See what I mean. Don't do that, baby, I am with you.* Okay, is this place connected to another room, because it seemed more like apartment-style living and not on the first floor either? Also, when I went out the front door, it was very bright and there were many people passing back and forth all around me. *Like 4-story condo. Bright pastel doorway. I painted door blue.* Yes, I saw that! *Feels high 2 you, high up, 3rd level. Smells citrus, many are busy here.* Was I alone? Because it seemed someone was with me but I don't remember seeing anyone, I could just sense someone. *Thomas was there.* Oh, wow, why was I there, why did it happen? *Portal opened. Thomas took you by the hand and asked you where you wanted to go. U asked 2 to come here. U left energy here. We loved it.* Who is "we"? *Me and your dad, we watched you travel all over here in awe. You felt we were watching but did not see. You sat on high rock to watch oceans. Do you remember holding a wild animal?* No…*Ok, I will tell you. Do you recall holding the bird?* No, I don't. *It was a spirit guide.* You're kidding! This reminds me of a classmate at the Monroe Institute who coddled a little wild sparrow that flew down on the deck railing. Several of us stood around in amazement as this little bird perched there being stroked for literally fifteen minutes. *The same one…*You are saying that was the same bird? *One and the same.* Oh, my. When I left the body, did I stay on Earth or go elsewhere? *Another place, when portal opens, go with it.* What is a portal? *At some places events allow the electromagnetic field to weaken and the soul energy can escape. Remember, most OBEs are not remembered. Often it is to remind your body and brain what is right and wrong to refocus u.* Sometime you will have to tell me more about the spirit guide posing as a bird, and portals. *There will be another one in November for you.*

Bathed in Light

Almost exactly two years after Russell's death, the girl responsible for his accident would finally go to court. It was an emotional time for his family and for me, as we relived the experience. Russell reminded us often that it was time for him to leave and prepare for Canada. On weekends, we found time to talk primarily with Russell but also with Dad, though starting the book seemed an impossible task. Sitting up in bed each night, if for only a few minutes, my body and mind could relax while reading one of my metaphysical books that were stacked on the nightstand. But late one evening it was enough to just crawl into bed. I even forgot to turn on my

Love Promised: A Future Life Revealed

Hemi-sync music that usually put me to sleep. Lights out, my body sank down between the sheets, and then all of a sudden it was slowly lifted up by the waist while the rest of me folded over lifeless.

Gently I was laid back down on what seemed to be my bed, but my senses let me know something was very different. I heard someone to the right side of my head walking around the bed toward my feet. How could that be, I was clearly hearing the sound of footsteps like shoes on a hardwood floor—but on my carpet? This person continued walking close around me, as if on a massage table instead of my queen-size bed. Even more bizarre, I lived alone but was completely unafraid. I could hear the breathing as they slowly walked behind me, placing their large hands over the top of my head. The warmth and relaxation throughout my body was indescribable and I could smell, feel, and hear the warmth of their breath as they leaned over and kissed me on the forehead. It was then that I knew it must be Russell, though my imagination was blown away trying to figure out how this was happening. Then very suddenly, there was complete silence in my bedroom; no one there. Enchanted, I wondered what had just happened and, opening my eyes saw the night-light on in my bathroom.

Whatever it was, I was sad that it was over and lay still to see if it would happen again. That weekend we got on the board. *You are curious about the other night.* Unbelievable, please tell. *Well, we knew your energy was real low. Michael allowed me to borrow you.* Archangel Michael? *Yes, I have been a good boy.* Babe, you were at my house, stone floor, sandals made a flopping sound. Exactly! How did this happen? *Instantly, he helped me bring your thought waves under control to get you up to my vibration.* I could feel the warmth and slight pressure of your hands on my head and when you kissed me, it was as if you were here in body. *You could smell me, citrus smell.* Yes, I'm totally in awe. Was that Reiki? *No, I bathed you in light and it allowed me to know your touch again. I tried to get your Earth brain to relax but you woke up.* How long was I there? *Your brain only perceived 10 minutes, but really 3 hrs.* This experience bewildered me, but I woke up the next morning feeling very energized. If I had opened my eyes, would I have seen you? *Yes… Kent, have I whispered how much I love you…I do.* I miss you, Russell, so very much. With new lighting in my bathroom, I can hear the popping noise that you make only somewhat faintly now each night. *Harder to make…I am the sound you hear; shadow by your side.*

It wouldn't be long before the popping noise was loud again as he told me goodnight whenever I crawled into bed. Once he popped the lights so loudly, it startled me and woke me up. I frantically looked up at my altar, the little sacred corner in my bedroom. *Babe, don't fall asleep with candles lit next time,* he told me. And later, he would have to mention the same to his Aunt Vickey.

Planning Our Next Scavenger Hunt

With the Christmas holidays came time for family and a relaxing break from work. Ron had time off too so we talked about our overseas trip since Russell had mentioned the year before that we should go to Ireland. *Go in springtime,* he said, so we planned to spend St. Patrick's Day in Dublin.

While at Barnes and Noble shopping for presents, books about Ireland had practically jumped out in front of me. How uncanny that this country was showcased that week. Beautiful pictures of the landscape made me drool, especially since we were actually going there. I couldn't leave without buying *Ireland for Dummies*…and for that matter, the ones for London and Paris too. We had decided that if we went overseas, we would visit some other places we had never seen. This time my daughter would go with me, along with Ron and Vickey.

We also received a special gift in the mail this season. During most of the seven years that Russell had been in prison, he developed a brotherly relationship with Chris, better known as Toucan. More than friends, they actually guarded each other's life in a place where survival of the fittest was the norm. Toucan had been deeply affected by the news of Russell's death and wrote a beautiful poem about him for Ron. Using a favorite photograph, he also had an inmate draw a beautiful pencil portrait of the two of us and asked Ron to make me a copy. He told us Russell hadn't belonged in prison but had made living there more tolerable for him. He called once while we spoke to Russell, and was not surprised to hear him say, *U take care; I miss u bud. You know I have the best game and am most handsome.* We laughed and to our surprise, Toucan said they used to tease each other about which one was better-looking and, as a favorite pastime, competitively played basketball.

Many times I thought how difficult it must have been for Russell's family, especially his parents and daughter, to have missed seven years of his life and then have the joy of his freedom for only three more. Russell told us that he chose the prison experience not just for himself, but for his parents as well. I guess we can never judge the roles that one may choose to experience on Earth. In the larger scheme of things, every experience and every relationship is to embrace, challenge, and then benefit all those involved...*to help us all spiritually evolve*, he says. Thanks to Ron and his American Express points for some hotels, we planned for a less costly trip. And planning our trip on a day-by-day basis was a must.

My dad came through at one session and said, *Once upon a time there will be a princess named Eva and her prince named Mark.* I couldn't help but grin and I loved watching movies about royal history. *We've had many past lives 2,* Russell then said. Yes, and how odd, when you confirmed our future last name would be Wexford, then we find there is a town in Ireland named Wexford. Is that a coincidence? *Again, there are no coincidences.* And amazingly, he went on to tell us there is a definite connection between Toronto and Ireland.

We can't believe that day is almost here, have you been watching us plan the trip? *I got an agreement with a soul 4 walk-in. Ireland, it is on, babe.* What? You will briefly enter another's body? *With their permission...* and we might somehow be able to see you in them? *Yes...If all goes as planned, I can't wait.* We can't, either!

By the way, you told me just the other day to listen for a song from you. Driving home the other night, while switching radio stations, I looked up to see the street light ahead of me go out. Then Shania Twain starts singing this really upbeat song with the lyrics, "We will be together and for always." I was overwhelmed with emotion. *Didn't mean to upset you.* Your spirit definitely lifted mine and I love it when you let me know you are still around. *I am sometimes so very close to you at night. I want 2 kiss u, we had passion; I still do for you.*

Chapter Six

Past Lives—Our Irish History Comes Alive

Plato affirmed that the soul was immortal and
clothed in many bodies successively.
—Diogenes Laertius, from Plato 40

O ur scavenger hunts would continue and this time our journeys
would uncover the past. Before we had made our second trip to
Toronto, Russell had told us we would also be making a trip to
Ireland. Just the thought of it excited me as my love of Celtic music, Celtic
jewelry, emerald green, and longtime attraction to this beautiful land now
made perfect sense—I had lived a lifetime in these lush, rolling green hills.
Now, my favorite musical artist, Enya, lived there, in addition to an Irish
author, Patrick Francis, who wrote, under the name of Paddy McMahon, a
notable two-volume metaphysical work entitled *The Grand Design.*

The beginning of 2008 would bring several sessions to gather clues
for yet another scavenger hunt, this one expected to be just as adventurous
as the earlier ones. *Babe, pack new sweater, green.* I did just buy a new green
sweater. *Green for Irish… Look for red canopy, have a Gulliver for me. Like
Toronto, I will make lights blink.* We grinned.

As we had three countries to visit, our minds raced to plan the perfect
trip. Sensing our confusion, Russell stepped in to help us out one session.
*Babe, go to Ireland first. Go to Wexford, then Dublin, and then fly to London,
train to Paris, back 2 Dublin via train 2 London and plane to Dublin.* The
big picture helped immensely. Another session, he helped us pick a hotel
online in Paris. *Good job. U will love Paris. Call my name while walking along
river.* "The River Seine?" asked Beth. *Yes, Paris, plan to stroll along river, very
unusual food. Don't eat the fish, nasty water. Throw a penny in river.* What else?

Try to find downstairs pub in London. Drink a Bass for me. Okay, a Gulliver in Ireland and a Bass in London, got it! Can you describe the person who has agreed on a soul level to let you walk in briefly while in Dublin? *36, blond and good-looking...* Oh, wow, so similar to you, I could get arrested! My witty daughter sarcastically laughs, then quickly chimes in, "Wow, Mom, 36, you are moving up. Sure that is not too old for you?" *Give your momma a break... but luv u 2 Beth—BTW, go to old theater north of town, dirt floor, wood seats, guys dressed as women.* Beth exclaimed, "Yes, Russell, that's the main reason I was so excited when Mom asked me to go, the replica of Shakespeare's Globe Theatre is in London! You are right, back then women were not allowed to be actors; so at that time, men dressed up as women." *And when you are at the theater, you should take it all in.* "Does she have a past life there?" I asked. *Front right bench, she will walk where she once did. Her brother was an actor, her name, Katherine Welsh.* Smiling at Beth, I asked Russell if she was from an affluent family during that time, since she was sitting in the front row. *Yes, that big headpiece blocked the view.* We laughed. *Funny, looked like a dunce hat. Grandpa says he is excited 4 u on trip. Buy green socks. Sunny days will be hard to come by.* So it will rain a lot? *Some... cool and wet. Black coat, take it, Dad... still has my energy.*

More Clues for Our Biggest Scavenger Hunt Yet

Hey, babe, we found two neat places to stay in Wexford, one called McMenamin's. *Cool place to stay, u will be led; one of them will be booked.* Okay. *Honey, there is a moment on trip that will take your breath away. U will really sense it in Wexford, both of us had past lives there, one significant 4 u.* Oh, a past life in the town of Wexford? *Once upon a time a princess went back to her roots.* Me? *U, babe. We all have roots there. Yours and mine are on the Nordic side.* This concept of past lives has always made so much sense to me. *All to get where u are now—Oops, 2 fast, all to get your soul 2 where u are now.* Russell, you told us we would go walking up "Kilkeny." On Google Maps, I found a town and street close to Wexford named, Kilkenny, is that it? *Yes, you know my spelling.* And, you've used that word "princess" twice now...you have my curiosity. Are you meaning that specifically, by any chance? *The lady of the castle...*Wow, I saw a neat castle in the same area that I would love to go see, they give tours, and in fact it's called Kilkenny Castle. Is this the one you are talking about? *No.* Were you with me then, during this lifetime? *Was born as Arthur William Morse... There is a cemetery* *named Kings Cross in Dublin.* Is your body known as him buried there, and what was our relationship? *Yes, and we knew each other as land owners.* What was my name? *Constance McFarland.*

The following week we were anxious to get more information but shocked we were. Russell told us that his father in our next life was in body now as a 10-year-old boy living in Ireland. Moreover, this trip was to become quite intriguing. You did say one time that our future parents were living now as kids. *Yes...* Where are they? *Mine are Ireland, yours from Vancouver.* Wow, where in Ireland? *Belfast.* What does Andrew's father do for a living? *Engineer for BP...* This may be a stretch, but are they going to the Mardi Gras festivities in Dublin, where we will be this year? *Yes.* We immediately looked at one another, astounded. You mean there is a remote chance Vickey and I could see our future father and father-in-law as a 10-year-old boy? *Possibly.* Russell went on to tell us that his future father would be transferred to Pennsylvania in the United States when he turned 17, and from there would one day move to Oakville, Canada. Once again, our session ended sooner than we had hoped. We were told they were being called by angels, as newcomers were getting ready to cross.

Just before the trip, we visited with Russell and Dad once more even though we planned to take Russell's "cell phone" with us. *Well if it ain't the Griswolds, ha...* Hey Babe, yes indeed! Any messages before we leave? *Relax and let it come to you on trip. Little things add up. Don't look too hard. Watch 4 coins. Be sure to watch out for pickpockets. I will be enjoying flight with u. Dad, bring Chelsea something special 4 me from each country and buy tapestry on trip, it will remind you of something. For Vickey, Grandma will have birds in London. I am excited about trip. Take an open mind. Walking is on the horizon, wear comfortable shoes. I love you, baby girl... I just had to say it.*

Ireland...Like Going Home

On March 12th, 2008, Beth and I met Ron and Vickey at the airport and Ron adorned us girls with silver plastic crowns encrusted with fake emeralds and diamonds. He bought himself a white, orange, and green cowboy hat. Indeed, we were ready for the parade. Whether or not I had once been a princess in Ireland, I would for sure be one in Dublin for Mardi Gras this year.

We had a layover in New Jersey and when getting off the plane there, a penny on the floor caught my eye. Getting off the plane in Dublin, Ron spotted a penny on the floor. We then gathered our luggage and as we headed for the vehicle Ron had just rented, I found a five-cent euro on the concrete walkway. Russell had said watch for coins, and so far we were finding them everywhere!

Driving around the quaint little coastal town of Wexford, we found McMenamin's House bed and breakfast but no rooms were available, and we chose not to stay at the place where we had reservations. By this time, we were getting really tired and sleepy, having been up now for over 24 hours, so it wasn't by chance that a jolly, white-haired gentleman carrying boxes into a pub walked over to our van. He responded very kindly to our questions and, surprisingly, happened to own a B&B with his wife, Angela. At first, he gave us directions but quickly noticed we were weary American travelers new to town and decided to lead us there instead.

John and Angela Doocey's B&B

If ever there was a bright-eyed, friendly, outgoing Irishman, it was John. And though it was not the Victorian-style B&B we had had in mind, what we did find was a lovely, modern two-story brick home with beautiful landscaping. John and Angela's children were grown, so what better use of their upstairs bedrooms than turning them into guest rooms. After settling in, we went into town for a bite to eat at O'Brien's. We then crashed for an afternoon nap and got up to talk with Russell for a while before going back to bed.

Russell, were you with me watching *Celtic Women* on PBS when packing for the trip? *Yep, lights blinked.* Then they switched back and forth from dim to bright and dim again. *You are connected to the Celtic lifeline.* My, have I ever felt that, and I can hardly believe we are really here…Any messages? *Go to museum and then the Abbey, see castle, look 4 messages. Get an Irish flag for my headstone and a flower from beach.* What's the purpose? *Carries energy…* And our past lives? *Yes, having your energy here in Ireland makes past lives come in…your individual energy will always remain here. The lady is a direct link 2 u.* Lady? *Barren land, ask about the Lady of the Castle…* In Wexford, babe? *Near…* Which castle? *By water…sign.* That's all? *Fox Hunter…* What does that mean? *Just another sign…* Can't give me the castle's name? *Won't allow…* These sure seemed like too few messages to find a castle, but we would have to go with it.

We enjoyed the rest of our conversation as Russell continued with candor about lifetimes lived here by several members of our families. He told Vickey that she had once lived in Rosslare, which we remembered was a town between Dublin and Wexford. *You owned a bread bakery, eat all u can and sell the rest, ha.* "Thanks, Russell!" Vickey said. *Sorry, but you were a big girl.* What about your dad? *1340, a printer of books, named Master Palmer, u did this again in 1790.* "Both times in Ireland?" I asked. *Yes...Did I know Ron then? U asked him to write history of family. Remember read. Dad u are 2 find the book, grey binder, old.* You mean a book that Ron wrote about Constance McFarland's family? *A book that quotes him...*Can you tell us any more about the walk-in? *He will be tall, have a vest on. Big hug 4 u all, we have to go.* Can you give me just one more lifetime, this one about Beth, since she is still snoozing, so I can tell her tomorrow? *She was later than Constantine, 1611, lived in Wicklow, ran an inn for sailors. Named Beatrice Genovese, called BG. She fixed a mean Irish stew.* Wow, thanks, babe, this is all amazing. *More than u know, let's talk later, love you.*

Abbey Ruins and the World's Oldest Working Lighthouse

On March 14th, after a good night's sleep and the delightful Irish breakfast that Angela cooked for us, we were well on our way to exploring this little town of Wexford and the surrounding area. We started by visiting the thirteenth-century Selskar Abbey ruins in downtown Wexford, which had been destroyed during the Norman invasion of Ireland. We then traveled south to see the oldest working lighthouse in all of Europe. Hook Head lighthouse, on the southernmost tip of Ireland, was built in 1201 by the Normans to prevent ships from crashing into the narrow, unseen Hook Peninsula at night. We took a tour that led us to the top, where we walked on the balcony to see the magnificent view of the ocean waves crashing upon the black rocks below. Amazingly, before electricity, there was a group of monks who lived in the lighthouse and kept coal burning constantly to provide the light that shone out over the ocean. After leaving the lighthouse, we stopped along the road to take a closer look at the ruins of a church and cemetery from the 1300s. Touching something so ancient left us in wonderment.

A Ship and a Crystal Factory

The next morning, we enjoyed Angela's homemade Irish bread and jam, then set out on another adventure to see a replica of the ship *Dunbrody* in New Ross. For 30 years in the mid-1800s, the original cargo ship took over 3000 Irish men, women, and children to America to escape the potato famine in Europe. As a donation for the upkeep of the ship, for 15 euro I purchased in the gift shop a tree to be planted to help replenish a forest used to build the ship. With this donation came a certificate with a place to honor anyone you chose. The saleslady was quite intrigued with my request to have "Mark and Eva Wexford 2048" written on the certificate. It occurred to me that this would be an excellent item for the time capsule, possibly enticing Mark and Eva on a scavenger hunt someday. On the back of the certificate is a handwritten number corresponding to a purchase receipt in New Ross that has my current name and address on it.

We soon arrived in Waterford, home of the famous Waterford Crystal Factory. An extraordinary tour showed us how the world-famous crystal is made by technicians who spend five years learning the trade to become master certified in working with glass. If these skilled craftsmen were to make a mistake, the piece has to be broken since flawed pieces are not allowed to be kept or sold. Afterward, we browsed their store to see the beautiful artwork on display and took the opportunity to purchase pieces unique to Ireland.

Finding My Castle

We left the crystal factory hungry, hoping to find, off the tourist path, a special place where we could eat. Angela had given us directions for the more scenic back roads and, though picturesque, there were more roundabouts and crossroads than we could have imagined. As we quickly rounded one corner, Ron noticed a restaurant called Fox and Hound. Remembering what Russell had told us about "fox and hunter," we decided to turn around, excited that this was it. This Irish pub-restaurant combination was classic, with many Irishmen stopping by for a beer after work. As we were finishing our meal, I felt inclined to "ask about the castle" and the thought wouldn't go away. Believing it was Russell doing the nudging, I bravely asked a gentleman sitting at the table next to us if he knew of an old castle on a hill close to Wexford, and near water. Perplexed, he didn't offer any information but another at the table behind me overheard our American accents and Ron asked him the same question. This Irishman said, "Yes, there is a very, very old castle called Ferry Carrig nearby and it is near water and on a hill." We thanked him and followed his directions to get there; fortunately, it was not far away. There indeed stood a large castle tower upon a hill, overlooking a huge river. After we parked, Beth was so excited for me that she took off running up the hill to get a closer look at this abandoned structure.

It was now dusk and as night would soon be upon us, we all started taking pictures at every angle. Holding the camera out in front, I snapped my first shot and could see two large orbs in the LED screen immediately. It was then that Russell let me know we had found my castle. "A moment that will take my breath away," he once said, and I thought he had meant the beauty of Ireland's landscape. But nothing can compare to being in the same spot where you feel yourself having lived almost 1000 years ago. Call it vandalism, but Ron and I jarred loose a very small piece of stone from the castle as a keepsake. Being there was almost like collecting a part of me, the energy of the "Lady of the Castle." Unfortunately, the only wooden door on this abandoned stone castle tower was locked. At one point I held on to its walls, trying to see if any visions or memories would come to me but no such luck, possibly my emotions were too high. Vickey kept hearing birds singing in a bush nearby, but neither she nor Ron actually saw them. Taking one last picture, for it was now dark, I was aghast at the number of orbs that showed up on this cool, clear night. We left and drove past the Ferry Carrig hotel, which was further confirmation we had found the right place as there was no sign at the castle itself. Considering how close we came to missing it, I felt extremely grateful. Still in awe, we drove back to John and Angela's Townparks B&B, anxious to talk with Russell before going to bed.

You did good! Did I find my castle, babe? *Ferry Carrig, yes.* For some reason I always wanted to know where Russell was in the room, so again I asked him...*Beside u on right.* Hey babe...*Hey 2 u, didn't you love the view?* Yes, it was beautiful! *U r not afraid of heights.* I guess not. Beth then exclaimed, "I literally ran up there faster than I thought I could." *Energy pulled u up. There used to be a boat dock.* Did the castle extend to the other place that we saw across the river? *Rope and wood bridge, there was a stone tower at each side.* Was it the castle, then, that we saw? *Was more to it than that, wall around and stone fences for animals.* I'm so glad you gave us the clue, "fox and hunter," we would have missed it! *Thank goodness, my guidance was good. Street by water.* We missed the Wexford Museum, was that it? *U all walked right by and missed it.* Oh no, tomorrow we leave for Kilkenny, then on to Dublin. *It's okay, baby, don't sweat it. Did u get flashback at tower with smell of oxen?*

Love Promised: A Future Life Revealed

No, didn't, babe, guess I was so overcome with emotion. *Wait...when u stood on flat rock u were in exactly same space that u once occupied...*Flat rock? At door, u did. *You sat on shore crying over lost son.* Okay, yes, there was a flat rock just in front of the door....amazing. What happened to my son? *He drowned...*I then wondered if my soul remembered this experience, since I shed a few tears there. *You and Will had good relationship.* Are you talking about yourself, you said your name was William Morse, who owned land nearby? *Yes, lived close.* Did we have a romantic connection in that lifetime? *We had those lingering looks at each other but u were married, u were a real lady.* Did you have kids then? *No...your husband bought u, u actually descended from a family up North.* What was my husband, if I was a princess? *Son of a king, his dad died young and you were only 14.* How long did I live? *51...I am excited.* We are too, babe. *Mamaw sang for Vickey, sang like a bird.* Oh my goodness, she heard it, how funny. *Dad Wick was there.* Great, thought he might be...oh, and the orbs! I took several pictures and the more I took, the more there were, I'm amazed. *Hundreds came to welcome u back.* People I knew then? *Your workers loved u.* Well, that's good to hear. Was Dad one orb in the picture with Beth? *Yes big one was Wick.* Can I research more about the castle? Is there any information about it online? *Look deep.*

Russell, can you give us any information about tomorrow? *Find that place on way, look south and see my land, look on way there 4 sharp curve next to hill and stone fence.* Okay...How old were you as William in this past life, when I was 14? *21 years, a babe then 2...Watch 4 signs at castle, red room, tapestry. Dad, to remind you of me, see me in it.* With Russell, we started talking about the next day. *Just enjoy castle...leave 2 pennies there, put 1 on top of tall chest and 1 under the red rug.* Is there a reason? *Red has a connection 2 it, was in that lifeline, I will come get them later.* Why? *Put in silver box...box will be sold at an antique store in Toronto.* Wow, I have a surprise for you too. Did you see what I did today at the Dunbrody gift shop? *Guess not, tell me, babe.* I purchased a certificate and put Mark's and Eva's names on it with the year they'll be married. *Cool, babe, put in capsule.* That's what I thought too!

Beth, make them stop in store with red awning in Dublin, wellow letters, crap, yellow letters. "Maybe they will listen to me next time," Beth said jokingly. *I yelled shit on your shoulder.* What, who is this? *Wick.* OMG, Grandpa, was that when I was sitting up front and we were going the wrong way down a one-way street, about to collide with an oncoming car? *Yep...* Because that's what I yelled! Ron and the other car both had to swerve to keep from hitting each other. Grandpa, will there be any signs from you in Dublin? *Okay, u will see a man in a wheelchair. Ignore him, it's not me. How's that.* Grandpa! Dad! Ron bends over laughing and can hardly contain himself. And that was my Dad, the big jokester. *Seriously, nothing would keep me from trying to show myself. We are trying to get more information. Berry Store, Dublin, I will be there reading books. Step it up, girls.* And we knew what that meant. Ron and Vickey had had to wait on us a couple times while getting ready. *Russ back on...he's yelling later, gator, accident in China, being summoned by angels.* Bye, Dad! *So much learning; there are so many spirits coming.* At times like this we just looked at one another, dumbstruck. *Castle surprise tomorrow, sleep good.* Okay, babe, thanks, we will look for your castle tomorrow.

On Our Way to Dublin

Bags packed, we visited with this sweet couple, John and Angela, the next morning over breakfast and said our goodbyes to them and Wexford. With more instructions in hand, we were headed now for Kilkenny Castle. On the way, we looked for all the signs that Russell had given us about where we would stop by the side of the road and look back and see our ancestors' land. Other clues included a sharp turn and a stone fence. We stopped once, thinking we had found the place, as there were a lot of stone fences and sharp turns. However, we did get excited at one point because he had said *there will be a place to stop on the side of the road* and, a little further down, we saw it...a picnic area by the side of the road, with the most beautiful scenery in Ireland yet. Trees, green hills, with sheep and cows surrounded by stone fences that partitioned the property; a beautiful river that ran slowly but aggressively under a stone bridge still used today; and finally, in the valley was the bottom half of a castle overgrown with ivy. We pulled over to photograph the land and what we suspected were the ruins of the twelfth-century castle where Russell had once lived as William Morse. Hopping back into the vehicle, we continued driving toward Kilkenny, still staring out the window at the beauty of this land.

Arriving in Kilkenny, we quickly spotted the castle. This very large medieval castle had belonged to the Butler family, who lived in it for almost 600 years. It was originally built by the Normans—our ancestors, Russell says—after they landed there in 1069 and took over much of the land. The interior had been restored to its original look but had only a few pieces of the original furniture, since most had been auctioned off when the Butlers became bankrupt and left. The last living Butler practically donated the castle to the city and county to restore it for historical purposes. We decided

Love Promised: A Future Life Revealed

to have lunch while we waited for our tour. Soon, it occurred to us that we were walking up Kilkenny Street as Russell had told us we would, one year before we ever knew there was a Kilkenny Street, castle, or town.

After a delicious lunch, we returned to catch the tour, where we watched a 10-minute video of medieval times and the passage of almost 1000 years in this historic castle. Armed with two pennies and looking for a red rug and a tall chest to hide them in, we began the sightseeing tour. Only pictures can truly describe the lavishly decorated 25-foot ceilings of this fortified castle where royalty once lived. Besides buying a memento of the castle, I bought another book that included all the ancient castles in Ireland and enjoyed reading about Ferry Carrig. Ron lagged behind the group to place the pennies and Russell confirmed he got them. I could only imagine that it might be the Wexfords being drawn to purchase this silver box in a Toronto antique store someday, continuing the journey to collect a piece of who they are—us in this lifetime.

Arriving in Dublin, we soon found the Kilronin House, the very first B&B where we had made reservations. Greeted with a friendly welcome, we were offered a cup of strong Irish coffee, which I had come to enjoy with some tasty sweet biscuits. Our rooms were newly decorated, but in keeping with the Victorian style. It was dark by the time we settled in and we were anxious to know if that was indeed Russell's castle we had found that day.

Hey you all, I was impressed with you and Vickey driving. Funny he mentioned that, as we had bravely tried our hand behind the steering wheel. *Way to go, Dad, got pennies done. Did u like the view?* Was that your castle, babe; were we at the right place? *Bridge, yes, in valley by itself, it went from town back to castle.* And what's its name? *Was called Celig...* How far was it from your place to mine? *By horse it was 3 days, 41 miles, one and one-half days downriver. I would often take river down and buy horses 2 take back.* What did you look like in that lifetime? *Hold on...Long reddish-blond hair, beard. U were darker skinned, light brown hair. We were both short.* We all laughed! *But go ahead.* Beth then asked, "And the tapestry, we did not find it?" *I can't tell u now. It hasn't been seen by u yet.* Did we know the people at Kilkenny Castle, since it was built when we lived in our castles not far away? *We were both there for a coronation party. How u could breathe with that corset on I will never know. But it was hot.* Too funny! Russell, did you ever marry when you lived in that castle? *No.* When did you die? *45, I died in winter, infection in leg, got cut bad during battle.* Jokingly I said, so you never got married because you couldn't have me, right? *Pretty much...why buy the cow when u can have the milk for free, ha. There was a son by another woman. I thought you mentioned not having any children? When he was* *10, she told me...he was raised as an O'Conner and killed in battle.* Did I have any other children that lived in the castle after I was gone? *Yes, two more sons, one lived in the castle, one went to England.* Who was your dad that I asked to write the history of my family, and where did he live? *Town of Cork, name Mister Morrisey, Edward. You gave specific instructions.* Can you tell us the year of death or when he lived? *1364 died, he was 51.* After Vickey asked a few personal questions, she told Russell to tell her mom that she loved her. Russell then said, *U tell her, she is sitting next 2 u. Tomorrow go have fun and look 4 guy.* You mean your future dad, Andrew Wexford, or you through the eyes of another? *Me, smile at me, while I work.* Can you tell us where that will be? *Not far from a Guinness.* So, it's in a bar? *Pub, fun behind bar, u huh.* Red awning? *Red and yellow letters.* Is this guy going to feel any different? *If all goes as agreed, he won't realize.* Okay, you said he will have a vest on and a scar on his nose, right? Can you give us the guy's name? *His guides say no. Go to bed, baby, rest, luv u more, Kent.* Love you too, oh and my right eye hurts, but your dad gave me some medication. *Babe, you have an infection, keep up meds 3 days, got it on plane.* Vickey then asked if Russell had a message for his dad. *Thanks 4 sticking with this, luv u. Now go and enjoy tomorrow but remember I am watching, ha.*

St. Patty's Day 2008

Waking up early the next morning on St. Patrick's Day in Dublin was surreal. Each of us dressed in some variation of the color green and we all met in the small dining room for an early breakfast. Every room in the hotel was booked and we knew it would be crowded. The food was delicious and between the four of us, we tried just about everything on the menu. Before leaving for the parade a few blocks away, we pulled out the board to talk with Russell one last time. *Kids with fun hats...* You mean Andrew and Adam? *Yes, walk right by them.* Are they blond-headed? *Blond* Will there be a way to talk to them and take pictures? *Stand in front of them to picture, don't freak them out.* Can we ask their names? *Their parents are very protective. Be cool.* Don't worry, we will. *There are a lot of people in this scene. Pay attention, many chances for this to not work out...A lot of freedom of choice.* So it may not work out? *True...easy to miss, so many people; they are on holiday.* Where do they live, here in Dublin? *No, Belfast.* Oh, I think we've asked you that once. We've asked a few people, but no one is familiar with the last name Wexford, only the town. That surprises us, is this not a common name? *No, not a common name; there is a part to the story that I don't have permission to see.* Is it still agreed that this will be your dad? *Agreed.* What about permission for us to get a picture and put in the book? *Again, part of the story, I do not have permission to see...to tell you.* Okay, babe, we won't push it, understand if you can't answer. Can you tell us during the parade, on this main street, where might we see them? *Mid route.* Looking more at the map, we tried to strategize. *Good choice, they are staying in hotel near river.* Any more information you can give us? *Near Castle Street, near where you will be walking.* Can you tell us which side? *No, both, parents will have them up high...now go.* We knew it would be difficult to spot them in the crowd—like looking for a needle in a haystack—but the anticipation of the possibility still excited us.

The weather was beautiful, 65 degrees and sunny. We ladies joined the festivities by putting on our Irish tiaras and Ron, his colorful cowboy hat, bringing a little bit of Texas to Dublin. We happily watched the Irish take in all the fun and excitement of this event that celebrated their heritage. But as the afternoon progressed and we hadn't yet found the twins, our excitement started to wane. Beth, understandably, was not fanatical about looking for the boys and wished we would have stopped to enjoy the parade more. If I had been more relaxed and in the moment, I would have taken my camera up the steps to the porch of a bank building where I was inclined to go, thinking this would be a good place to video the parade. I hesitated, though, not wanting to get too far from the group because the steps were very crowded. As we found out later, that's indeed where the boys were standing. When the parade was over, we decided to give up looking. Russell was right, there were many chances for it not to happen due to free will.

Royal Dublin Society...Then Off on Another Mission

To my surprise, Patrick Francis, the metaphysical author, planned to be in Dublin at the Mind Body Spirit Festival hosted by the Royal Dublin Society that afternoon. It was probably the only thing that would have pulled me off the streets of Dublin in the search for Andrew Wexford right after the parade. After the presentation, we browsed the many exhibit tables, which gave me the opportunity to meet Patrick and thank him for his work.

Back at our hotel room, we rested and caught up with Beth's afternoon before heading out on another pathfinder mission. Our disappointment in not locating the twins quickly faded in the excitement of hoping to find Russell. Possibly there would be a moment of with recognition. We moseyed downtown again, enjoying the nightlife this time, with bandstands, a one-man band, or jugglers tucked into a small crowd on the sidewalk. The streets were filled with couples holding hands and it reminded me of moments Russell and I had shared, that were still sorely missed. It was fun, though, to be with his dad and aunt, who were also enjoying this adventure, and with my daughter, who wanted so badly for me to find what I was looking for. The first pub we came to was downstairs and while it had a red awning with yellow letters, we didn't see a bartender with a vest on. I quickly discarded any other clues like blond, tall, good-looking. There were many more pubs to explore and the night was young. Much to Beth's dismay and despite her encouragement to stay at that pub, we continued to go from one pub to the next. None had all the clues we were given. Again, except for Beth, we let our heads lead us, instead of our hearts.

The walk back to our hotel was rather somber, especially now that the city was settling down. I knew Russell was with us, sensing our disappointment, and the serenity prayer popped into my head. Truly, we needed strength to accept the things we could not change, courage to change the things we could, and wisdom to know the difference. With all that we had endured over the last several years, we would be patient for that wisdom. We talked with Russell once again before bedtime. *Even agreed-upon situations are subject to free will. The guy took off his jacket.* What? Where? *The one downstairs.* Beth immediately asked, "The first one?" *Yes...* I quickly chimed in, "What did you do?" *I left when you did.* Russell, I'm so sorry, babe...and my frustration escalated. My "whatever will be" attitude quickly left and my ego's guilt stepped back in. Why, I thought, is it so hard at times to live in the moment and not regret the past or worry about the future? Listening to my daughter and staying for a while to see what might happen would have been so simple. I was too determined and she was just going with the flow. No wonder she was more open to hearing Russell at that moment. It takes a real balancing of the heart and mind to be human, for sure. *Babe, don't sweat it. Let me try again in London. I will try to give more info.* Vickey said, "Thanks." *Don't give up yet. Hold on, if u cry u hurt me 2. London area by Trafalgar Square, I am working on it now.* Okay, thanks, babe... What about kids? *They were up high on steps of building.* You mean the bank building in front, the one where I started up the stairs, then hesitated? *U did, close 2 them. Their Dad made them stay up there…Shiny cowboy hats, blue aura.* Did we get a picture? *U have to look close, but yes.* Blue aura, you said? Whose camera? *I think u…Light blue light or aura around Andrew, one was looking away. Dad had light brown coat on.* And the dad works for BP? *Consults 4 Royal Dutch Petroleum 2. The kids looked at Dad's hat…*We did walk by, down in front of the bank! Beth switched the conversation again and asked, "What color of jacket did the guy have on in the bar and did he see us?" *He did see u…black.* "Did you enter his body and did he feel it?" I asked. *Yes, only a moment, like a hot flash…*It later occurred to me that this could have been why he took his jacket off. *Please don't be too upset, freedom of choice can screw up plans. U all should trust spirit guides, I did ask Beth to stop u all there. Hey, I love you, let's try again; look in his eyes. You are the one living this life, live, learn, make good decisions, sometimes make bad decisions; learn to not repeat the bad ones. I had 2 learn this 2. I'm going to work on this while u all get to London.* This message from Russell helped us all to calm down again, and I would later ask if there is any way to verify Andrew Wexford's existence. He had told us that he's 10 years old and his middle name is Clark. *Andrew was born September 19, 1998, in Belfast, Ireland. Look on the Web for birth records.*

"Was Dad with us today?" I asked. *Watched when u nearly tripped, he softened the fall.* Immediately, Beth and I stared at each other, remembering what had happened earlier that day. While walking down the steps at the Kilronan House, I tripped on the sixth step up from the bottom, losing my balance and falling gracefully down the carpeted stairs. The reason for saying "graceful" is that it seemed I was floating on air as I bounced off each step. "You should have seen her going down the steps from our room, she kept falling and falling then hopped up and smiled," Beth said. And there wasn't a sore bone in my body the next day. *Go to London have good time. Let it happen if you can make it work. Try.* Vickey had a question. When you cross over, do you know it right away? *No, but u sense things are different, that your vibration has increased.* Can u still see a body? *Yes, each time ur soul crosses it is a different experience. Let me know the plan, let's talk after ur dinner 2morrow.* We plan to tour three areas. *You 4 sure need 2 be conservative when u can.* Russell, was that our first lifetime we had together here in Ireland, the one with the castles? *Yes, because it was not a lifeline link, but not the last, baby girl.* What do you mean by "lifeline link"? *Like a walk-in. Not really a part of that lifeline. With an agreement it is possible to link to another lifeline in order to have a special experience, one that has not been experienced before or that has not been planned.* Thanks, babe...*Nighty night.*

It was only when I arrived home that I found the picture Russell was talking about. Beth had photographed the crowd in front of the bank, and when zooming in there stood a man in a beige jacket, who appeared to be a father with two boys who looked around 10 years old. And now I knew why the twins must have looked down and noticed Ron's hat when we walked by. They too had cowboy hats, only theirs had sparklers. Russell had told us that Andrew would be the one with the blue aura looking down. In the picture, the light blue aura above the green cowboy hat is not as obvious, due to the daylight and light background of the bank building.

St. Patrick's Day in Dublin, Ireland, 2008—Andrew and Adam Wexford

Traveling to Europe and being that close to someone who will be significant in Vickey's and my future lives seemed incredible. How often do we cross paths with someone we may never know who might have been in our past life or, for that matter, will someday be in a future one? Without a doubt, we must weave a tangled web.

A Glitch at the Airport

The next morning we packed our bags and left to catch our flight out of Dublin to London via Ryan Air. It was another pretty day, yet getting north to the airport was a struggle. Streets were crowded as many people had come into town for the festivities and, like us, were headed out. I wondered

Love Promised: A Future Life Revealed

if the Wexfords were also in their vehicle, headed back to Belfast. A week in Ireland was not long enough and we still wanted to find the Berry Bookstore, supposedly in Dublin, and the King's Cross cemetery where Russell had once been buried. These plans, however, would not materialize on our trip back.

At the airport we found out that our baggage was over the limit and we would have to pay a large fee. We were told by airport officials and Ryan Air that our tickets could be canceled prior to flight and the majority of the fare would be refunded. We decided to do just that. Ron then found us seats on a British Airways flight allowing more weight per bag and a flat minimal rate for additional bags. We were tremendously relieved to have the issue resolved, even if it meant waiting six more hours and leaving at 9 p.m. It seemed our best deal at the time, though, after many attempts, we would never receive our refund.

We proceeded to the restaurant area upstairs and after eating, used our tall luggage and a brick wall to seclude ourselves and talk with Russell. *Pretty creative; sleep good tonight.* Since the board was not stable on the jacket that propped it up, it moved slightly up and down. *You are making me seasick.* I think he knew we needed a laugh. "We love you, Russell," Vickey said. *Love you...u will need to be wary of how much u spend in London.* Have Adam and Andrew gone back to Belfast? *Yes...Be ready for bumps, breathe y'all, it will be okay.* It had been a stressful afternoon, to say the least. *Relax, this is only a test.* Test for what? *Just when you can't find the way, God opens a door and we help it work out. Try 2 book a bus trip.* "You mean a day excursion in London?" I asked. *Yes, 777.* Hmmm, okay, besides the excursion and Globe Theatre that Beth wants to tour, what else do you recommend? *Abbey and go see Buckingham Palace...in this life, none of u will be back together here. Go, go dance r.* The board was starting to sway again. Jokingly, I said, "We should see a go-go dancer in London?" Russell tried again on this wobbly board, as Ron and I too were getting uncomfortable bending over. *Oh God, own no, go down st air...*Go down St. Air while there? *My God, one more time, go downstairs, hello...Hurry.* We quickly looked at our watches and realized it was time for our flight! The line downstairs was definitely boarding and we had just enough time to get through security and get on the plane.

Off to London...Finally!

As we settled into our comfortable leather seats, British Airways announced free wine was being served, so Ron and I indulged ourselves.

With the lights down low, it was time for relaxation and possibly a nap. Though tired and exasperated, we were slowly getting our second wind and the excitement of getting to London started to build. Gatwick Airport offers a train into the city, so we gathered our luggage and took off. Soon we were on the streets of London at close to midnight, along with several others waiting for a taxi. But not just any taxi would do, we needed a huge one to accommodate all our luggage.

A large taxi finally did stop. Driving it was an older English gentleman who maintained a very pleasant manner in spite of our tired attitude. After we had packed ourselves in like sardines, he welcomed us to London with his calming British accent and light-hearted conversation. The London Hilton South Kensington was a welcome sight. It was all we could do to unpack, clean our faces, brush our teeth, and crawl into bed. The next day we realized that perpendicular to the hotel was a street called Russell Road. We grinned broadly—we knew why Russell had picked this hotel for us online.

One of the Oldest Rock Formations on Earth

Relaxed and back at the hotel after a good first day of sight-seeing in London, we decided to get out the board but Beth would call it a night. *That was a really long day.* Yes, getting here was not easy. Did you tell me, Russell, tonight while walking out of Harrods, that someday as Mark and Eva we would be shopping there? *Our daughter will buy wedding clothes there.* Exciting! *Glad u caught it, babe.* Russell then quickly jumped into the next day's clues.

There is the shape of a cross waiting 4 u at Stonehenge. What do you mean? *For u, four feet and below, look for a cross.* What for? *4 me 2 know and u 2 find out.* Ah, the hunt is on! *Kiss pence, a coin, and leave at rock number 3.* OK…druids at Stonehenge. Oh, the druids? *Race and aliens originated on a different plane.* Vickey's eyebrows rose. *There was a whole civilization b 4 u, u don't really think you are the only ones?* To say the least, we all were very curious for the rest of this session.

Indeed there had been a sect called druids that lived in Ireland, supposedly in the final centuries BCE. They were considered Celtic, and were also thought to be a learned, priestly class of seers who believed in reincarnation. We know of them today only because of what the Romans had written about them, as the druids' knowledge was passed down solely

Love Promised: A Future Life Revealed

by word of mouth, as is the case with the Mayans, who lived in Central America centuries ago. It is believed, however, that the druids were suppressed by the Roman government who feared them and disappeared from written record. Is this what happened, Russell? *Run out country for survival and some remained underground. Druids lived in Ireland, but that place was visited by space people.* How was Stonehenge built? *Faraway stones brought by levitation. Space visitors helped druids set up stones.* Why there? *Just like astronauts who want a place to mark their visit.*

Wow, tell us more! *Druids made Stonehenge an altar; they considered it a holy place to call the visitors back. Druids did tell the story of space people but it died with last druid.* Was this stone configuration supposed to be the actual landing site? *No...* So they landed on the ground? *Hovered...* How did they get out of the spaceship? *Star Trek...* Are you serious? *Yes, teleported.* And the story was just that they visited? *They came on a chariot of fire.* Based on limited knowledge at the time, I guess, this was the only way they could describe a spaceship? *Right... That is how and what they saw, described.* What did it actually look like, alien spaceships that have been described today? *Oval with pencil-shaped engines on all 4 sides...* What was their method of propulsion, not liquid-fueled rocket motors? *No, silly.* But, what was it? *Antimatter; made sky look like sparklers.* This is fascinating! Do you have any more to the story? *Druids built walkway, road to river, altar, other huts around it.* It sounds like they built a whole city around where the visitors had come. *It was much bigger then.* When exactly? *4812 B.C.* But it was druids that carved the cross. Though a holy place, the cross couldn't have been to signify Jesus on the cross, since it was before his time? *The fire looked like a cross ship. The craft the visitors came on left trails of gases in shape of cross, it was marked on stone as a symbol and as the mark left for us to see.* Vickey went on to ask, "What did the aliens look like, were they human-looking?" *Do u? Russell! I am saying, who defines human? They have 2 legs, 2 arms, 1 nostril, no hair.* Did the druids leave with the space visitors? *Most...* You once told us the Mayans left by "flaming chariots" in the sky because they thought the world would come to an end. I thought you were crazy when you first mentioned that, Russell, but now I see books have been written about chariots in the sky. To survive, where was it the Mayans went? *Dropped off at 479...* Is that a constellation number? *Point 33 star system, 311 light years away.* Were the druids and Mayans the only races to be visited by space visitors? *Heck no, one other, the early Chinese. They referred to visitors as animals; they asked to be taken quickly, like a tiger, to preserve their race of people.* "This is incredible," we said.

Remote Viewing and Our Government

Though hard to believe from the outset, it wasn't the first time I'd heard aliens described this way, and not by the tabloids either. I went on to tell Ron and Vickey about the talk given by Joseph McMoneagle while I was at the Monroe Institute, and how the government had used his and other psychics' remote-viewing skills to see things at a distance with their mind's eye and spy on foreign countries for 18 years. McMoneagle writes about this topic in his book, *Mind Trek*, first published in 1993. He also mentioned remote-viewing on the planet Mars and saw what some aliens looked like, describing them in the very same way.

Our discussion with Russell continued…"So does our U. S. government know of aliens visiting here?" asked Vickey. *Of course.* Very much intrigued at this point, I too brought up having recently seen a TV documentary where a former secretary, now much older, at Wright-Patterson Air Force Base in Ohio, decided to reveal all that she had once kept quiet. She said they actually had an alien in a freezer underground, and that not many there even knew about it. *Too much publicity, Reagan had it moved 2 Barksdale Air Force Base, that's why Bush went there on 9/11 in case we had 2 use the IR technology.* Is this infrared technology and is it fairly new? *Oh yes.* Is it supposed to save, protect, or defend us somehow? *Yes.* You mean other defense technologies that we could possibly learn from aliens? *Shield, an area of a craft we haven't perfected.* Is this to protect a person like Bush or a country like ours? *It's enough to protect USA.* It made us wonder if new technologies are being transferred by thought to the mind of man from another source, this other side, or possibly from others in the universe. *And God has allowed Earth to advance; they have almost figured out how to suspend a body 4 hundreds of years. Three awaken.* Wow! Who is doing this? *Air Force and CIA.* Vickey, being a nurse, spoke up and said, "Well, surely we could learn how to cure disease if we can do this?" *If people had worked together, those questions would be answered.* How are they doing this suspension? *It revolves around use of magnet energy to slow movement at subatomic level, stops cellular death.* Oh my, this is amazing! Speaking of subatomic particles, I wanted to know about the super-collider that was canceled in Texas but started later at the CERN institute in Geneva, Switzerland. This is more about accelerating particles, not slowing them down. *Same group scientists working cellular regeneration.* At CERN? *Partly.* How long were the bodies suspended? *One was for 2 weeks, another for 46 days. All had some tissue death.* Are they okay? *Yes.* Is the US working with other countries on that, Russell? *Yes, UK.*

Okay, back to Stonehenge, you are going to pick up the penny I will leave? *I will and it will be a kiss from u. Babe, Wick said to look at orbs, 2 big ones.* These are two of the largest I've ever seen that showed up on a picture of me sitting at Ferry Carrig castle. Who are they? *Wick and Pearl...u can barely see the smiles in orbs.* Vickey asked, "Why do some people have so many orbs, like Kent?" *U have many also...Call on them more often.* How come Mom doesn't speak to Ron through the board? *She must evolve to higher plane. Her conception of God was closed-minded. For now, she is content.* Are you and Mom together? *Near but different, lots of lifelines. Babe, get rest.* Okay, Russell, love you...*Love you more.* After our session was complete and we had bombarded him with questions, we forgot to ask how we would know rock number 3 at Stonehenge.

An Old Cathedral, Roman Ruins, and Ancient Stone Artifacts

On March 20, we met downstairs in the Hilton Hotel for our Evan Evans bus driver to pick us up for the tour. Ron had had an early breakfast and couldn't wait to tell us that there was a Russell Boardroom in the hotel. Also, he had discovered a room called Chelsea Borough...synchronicities abound once again!

After our visit to 1000-year-old Winchester Cathedral, we stopped at a nice place to purchase sandwiches for lunch and were asked to meet back on the bus in 30 minutes. After getting my sandwich, I decided to quickly browse one of the shops and was surprised to see a slot machine. Hurriedly, I tossed in a coin. The next thing I knew, my daughter came to get me as everyone on the bus was waiting. Now I knew what Russell meant when he had said 777 in the Dublin airport...this very slot machine! Well, he didn't tell me *not* to play it. Another 30-minute trek and our next stop was Bath to see the ancient Roman ruins that had been unearthed in 1986. It was absolutely fascinating to walk around these stone structures, Roman busts, and natural spring baths that had been in use during the time of the Roman Empire. And like our natural spring water today, the baths were used not to cleanse the body but for relaxation, purification, and meditation.

Our last stop was Stonehenge, which left us speechless. These large stones are thought to have been arranged some 5000 years ago, or as Russell said, in 4812 B. C. To our surprise, the pre-recorded, handheld tour guide told us when giving the history of the stones, which numbered stone to stand by. Hoping no one would see me, I did kiss pence at stone three and quickly threw it into the circle of stones. Ron did the same, and pointed out to me what seemed to be a cross carved into the stone. We were told by the automatic tour guide that these stones were thought to be a landing site for vehicles long before man knew how to fly machines. None of the audio information, however, came close to the depth of information we had been mesmerized with the night before.

After what seemed to be a long trip back on the bus, we were dropped off three blocks from our hotel. Having an uncomfortable feeling, I looked back twice at the bus as we walked away; something wasn't right, something seemed missing. Later that evening while eating pizza in our hotel room, Beth discovered she had left her money pouch on the bus… with her passport that she would need the next day for our plane trip to Paris! Now, on the eve of leaving for yet another country, we were greatly challenged once more.

Leaving London for Paris

Fortunately, we were able to speak with someone from the Evans bus tour that night, but it was not until the next morning that we knew the pouch was in their possession. We left at 9 o'clock knowing we had to be back at the hotel by noon in order to grab our luggage from the concierge and leave for the airport. The theme song to *Mission Impossible* must have been playing in our heads. After a long hike by foot, railcar and underground metro, we finally made it to the tour company's central office and were relieved to find the pouch, with everything still in it. Nervously, we waited for the C-1 bus, which was the fastest way to return to our hotel. We made it back at 11:59 a.m., just in time to grab our bags and a couple of taxis for our trip to the airport. As we headed off again, this time for Heathrow Airport, we had fun snapping pictures of one another in these solid black, 1940s-style vehicles.

It was a beautiful sunny day on March 21st, as we flew out of London. When we landed in Paris at Charles de Gaulle Airport and retrieved our luggage, a kind man asked if we needed a lift. He went on to convince us that the metro would cost as much per person as his van would for all of us, so we took him up on the offer. We enjoyed the 30-minute ride into Paris as our driver told us about his city, of which he was obviously very proud. As we came closer to our next place of comfort, Hotel Splendid at 1 Avenue Carnot, it was exciting to see one of the most famous of monuments there, the Arc de Triomphe built in 1806 to commemorate Napoleon's greatest victory, the Battle of Austerlitz. Amazing it was to watch the traffic maneuver around this pentagon-shaped avenue, with many lanes of cars weaving in and out so quickly. Vickey was feeling under the weather that evening so she decided to stay in the room while Ron, Beth, and I found a quaint little pub and restaurant two blocks from our hotel to have dinner. Oddly enough, takeout was not available so Ron stopped to grab Vickey some fast food nearby and told us not to wait, knowing we were tired. Though I wish we had…Ron told us that while he stood in line, a guy showed up looking so much like Russell that he could not take his eyes off him. And the guy, about the same height as Russell, with an uncannily similar physique, was staring back at him. We settled in the hotel to get some rest but had to talk with Russell before going to bed.

*Another day, another thousand dollars gone, ha…*Practically! Ron reiterated the story of how amazed he was to see this guy, who looked so much like Russell, staring back at him. He'd stood there astonished. Wanting badly to have been there, I asked, "Russell, was that you?" *Just for a second. Love you; I will try to walk in again.* Vickey asked, "What was the purpose for you to walk into his body, did you plan this?" *Just to be there, no, just a quick opportunity.* I went on to ask Russell if he had been with us at the restaurant…*Just watching u eat, could have had a vino for what the water cost.* Yes, we could hardly believe our bottle of water cost a half euro more than the wine did. *Hey, Dad, how did you like the practical joke?* We were surprised to hear Ron say, "You mean the streetwalker woman that hit on me?" *Set up…*Thanks, Russ! *Babe, don't give up, I just had to be there after that joke; it was a spontaneous opportunity.* Russell could sense my disappointment at having left but I was very happy that Ron, obviously still mesmerized, had had the experience. Vickey went on to ask about their future mother, Olivia. *Travels for work; as a child, her parents move often.* What do Olivia's parents do, and where? *Military, UK.*

Russell, are you always with us or do we have to call on you? *I am with you now whole or part at all times. Again, it is like background noise, I have to tune in.* You mean your energy is attached to our energy, you can sense our emotions right away? *And I can ask your angels to help, you don't think that the bus came in time by itself do u?* Are you talking about the C-1 bus? *Yes…* Oh my, in London we were getting so anxious! Hey, I have a question. *Ask.*

At Stonehenge, did we toss the pennies at the right place and was that the cross we saw on the stone next to it? *Yes and I got 2 pennies beside rock, the 1 that Dad threw also. They will go in silver box.* Do you mean the one with the red lining? *And has red ribbon. I am kissing your ear…* Now? *Yes.* Right one? *Both, feel it?* Not sure, babe, can't tell and my energy did feel low. *I love to watch u get ready.*

[At a future session Russell told me … *Your great-great-aunt Dolly will sell a box of books to a bookstore and in it, for you, will be the silver box with the coins. The silver box will be at the antique shop near the office in Flatiron and Church Street. One is stuck in the side, u find it.* What is the significance of this happening? *Transfer of energy; the angels have met at Stonehenge, where the penny landed.* Phenomenal how material objects can be apported, but it occurred to me that as Eva, I will end up in the future with the very coin tossed by Kent. Will it help Eva to remember who she was in a previous life? I wondered why.]

Have any of us had lifetimes during the Roman Empire? The ruins at Bath were fascinating, it was just absolutely amazing, standing there thinking this was where Romans actually stood so long ago. *Caligula, Rome.* Are you saying that was someone's name? *No, lived when he was Emperor.* Which of us? *You and Beth, Roman soldiers.* We both were men? *Yes.* And, we took baths there? *You washed your feet in the dugout stone beside pool. You lived in town.* Bath? *Yes, outdoors, one of your favorite rings is still at bottom of the pool. It had emeralds, like colors of your ring now.* Amazing! Were you there in this lifetime? *As an old man in Senate, you came 2 hear me speak.* What were our names? *You were called Flavia, Beth was Brontus.* What was your name? *A local politician, Horace of Callus.*

Before ending the night, Russell told us to enjoy the Louvre museum the next day. Knowing art was his passion, we weren't surprised when he said… *I get to draw and paint too. I have done a few murals here, angels; one of them is a copy of a Michelangelo. It's funny but he still has works not discovered.* Whoa! As Russell said goodnight, he mentioned that for safety reasons, we should not sleep with the tall windows open in our room on the second floor, even though it was nice having a cool breeze in our sufficiently heated rooms.

Two Churches, a Museum, a former Brothel, and a Tower

Though the weather had been cold and drizzly the day before, the next morning was sunny and cool as a van picked us up for an exciting tour of the city with stops at three special places. The beautifully designed Roman Catholic Basilica of the Sacred Heart of Jesus, better known as the Sacré-Cœur Basilica, sits on the summit of the highest peak overlooking the city of Paris. This church, built of limestone, took 54 years to construct and was finished in 1919, after World War I. Walking into this majestic building, I stood there speechless, admiring the breathtaking apse, or semi-circular dome, of the Christ Jesus, which is among the largest in the world.

Next we were dropped off at Notre Dame (Our Lady) Cathedral, which has the most stunning French gothic architecture in all Europe. When inside this 1000-year-old church, one can't help but stand in reverence. What was even more special about this day of viewing the churches was that it was Easter, the day of celebrating Christ's resurrection. The pews in Notre Dame were roped off—one side was for those attending, who were listening to the sermon in classic Latin, while the other side was for tourists like us, who came in adoration. As we neared a lovely statue of Mother Teresa, a special moment occurred. I asked Ron to help me look for a picture of St. Thomas of Aquinas, my dear guide in spirit, sensing one there. He turned around to look at me and, when he did, his eyes glanced up and over my shoulder right away. As it turned out, I happened to be standing right in front of a beautiful large painting depicting St. Thomas preaching to a crowd, with angels on either side of him. I looked up in awe and later Russell told me that Thomas had been tapping me on the shoulder. We meandered through the large crowd, mesmerized by the chapels of numerous kings and queens of France, we also marveled at Saint Germain.

As our tour continued, we stopped to look at and take pictures of the famous Moulin Rouge, built in the late 1890s. It was first known as a high-class brothel but evolved to become a fashionable place for French society to visit and see the spectacular cabarets. Beth particularly enjoyed this stop, since in her theater days; she had landed the role of the lead actress, Sally Bowles, in the musical *Cabaret* at a local community college. The last place we enjoyed was the Eiffel Tower, known throughout the world as an entrance arch to the 1889 World's Fair. In the evening when it gets dark, the tower automatically lights up with fast-blinking lights every twenty minutes. Later that evening, I would accidently see the tower up close while it lit up, something I had wanted to do, just not in the way it happened.

That afternoon, we took a taxi to the 200-year-old Louvre, knowing that it takes two full weeks to tour the entire museum, the largest in the world. I couldn't imagine all the artwork and riches that lay in this half-mile- or kilometer-wide stretch of palace that had started as a fortress in the twelfth century. Entering from the glass pyramids, now most famous for the novel and movie *The DaVinci Code,* we traversed the halls to ensure we saw Leonardo's famous *Mona Lisa,* as well as the armless Venus de Milo. Among the other famous historical paintings and artifacts we admired was the Winged Victory. We gazed intently at the statue, trying to imagine it being sculpted on a remote Greek isle in 200 B.C.

We left the Louvre to warm up a bit and have coffee and biscotti before taking a taxi back to our hotel. On the way back, I pulled my small camera bag out of my backpack, prepared to take any last-minute photos since this was our last night in Paris. It was always a challenge to be on the go and keep up with one's coat, scarf, hat, gloves, umbrella, camera, and video camera, and I had done so well…up till now. At the hotel, I climbed out of the taxi, forgetting that my camera in its case had been sitting in my lap. In the room, I soon realized that it was gone. My heart sank as there were over 500 digital pictures from this trip on that one-year-old Sony digital camera. I asked Ron if we could quickly get on the board. Russell, indeed, told me my camera fell onto the floorboard of the taxi when I was getting out of the car. He told me this taxi driver was stationed at the Eiffel Tower area and gave me the first two letters of his license plate number. He also described the vehicle, make, and color, which was vaguely remembered by me, so I took another taxi to that area and hoped to find the one with my camera.

Acrim to My Rescue

As darkness fell, it became cold and wet and was now starting to snow more heavily. Throngs of people were everywhere and many were starting to line up for a taxi, due to the weather. I let others go in my place while standing alone on the curb, away from the covered area, umbrella in hand and watching feverishly. Surely, the four-door silver Peugeot with the letters ET in the license plate would soon pull up again. Most of the crowd spoke French, with only a few having British accents. Many did not understand why I was just standing there. Waiting and watching, for hours it seemed, I waved others to go ahead of me. Then over my head, as grand as seeing it from a distance, the twinkling of lights above me on the Eiffel Tower lit

Love Promised: A Future Life Revealed

up like a Fourth of July sparkler. It was stunning, though when turning sideways to look up, I lost my balance on the curb. All of a sudden, I could feel myself start to fall into the street almost in slow motion, it seemed. As I was unable to brace myself, my head bounced lightly off the concrete, hitting the pavement once. I could feel the whole right side of my body now cold and wet. Gazing ahead, all I could see were headlights coming my way as I lay in the street. Then all of a sudden, I looked up to see a handsome, dark-headed, well-groomed gentleman in dress slacks, shirt, and a brown overcoat between the cars and me. Surprisingly, while bending over he spoke to me in an American accent saying, "Ma'am, are you okay?" "Yes, thank you," I said, as I looked down quickly and got back up and on the curb. Strangely enough, no one was standing there beside me. I looked all around for this gentleman but could not see him anywhere. How could he have disappeared so quickly? Feeling how cold and wet I was, and now noticing how dirty my pants were, I decided to take a taxi back to the hotel.

It would be after arriving home that Russell told me how he tried to stop me from falling but could not. He said…*it was so cool to watch, babe, as Archangel Gabriel quickly summoned an angel named Acrim, as soon as you lost your balance. It seemed to you time stopped for a second and he was there to keep you safe. He extended a hand to you…*"Wow, I never saw that he did," I said quietly, still in awe. In thinking back how it all happened, I was not surprised to hear what Russell told me and wondered how often this must happen to so many on Earth who are not even aware of it, like me at the time. What about the taxi driver, the one with my camera? *He left before you got there.*

Earlier that day, while eating in a restaurant off the Champs-Elysées, we started thinking about how little time we had left on our two-week trip. Since we had spent a week in Ireland, we decided to stay over in London another night after leaving Paris, before heading back to Dublin to catch our flight home. There was still much left to see, but our time was limited. I alerted the front desk about my lost camera, while Ron spent time on the hotel's computer booking us rooms in London.

Europe's Speedway

Our first experience of riding the Chunnel, the sleek Euro rail, the next morning was like gliding almost at the speed of light back to London. I tried very hard to put the depressing thought of my lost camera behind me. Fortunately, Beth had her Sony camera and had taken some of the same pictures as I had. Arriving back in London, we settled into our hotel around 2 p.m. and decided to split up to see some of the things we had missed. Ron and Vickey would make their way to tour Westminster Abbey and Buckingham Palace while Beth and I left to find the Globe Theatre, a real treat for any theater major whose idol is Shakespeare. After being engrossed in the origins of drama and acting, we decided to see Madame Tussaud's wax museum. Afterward, we hopped into the front seat above the driver in a red double-decker bus and gazed out the window. Mesmerized, we watched the falling snow, which made the antiquity of London's streetlights under the night sky look even lovelier. Unfortunately, when we arrived at the famous London Eye Ferris wheel, overlooking the River Thames, it had just been shut down due to technical difficulties. Disappointed, we decided to take some pictures of the area before heading back to our hotel.

The next morning, March 25th, the skies were clear and sunny as we dropped our bags off in the hotel lobby. The four of us headed off on foot to tour the Tower of London. We explored this castle fortress that began with William the Conqueror in 1087. Since then, it's expanded over the centuries and has served as a royal residence, a prison, a refuge, an armory, and even a treasury, and still today houses the Crown jewels. Famous kings have claimed their glory there, while some queens, such as Anne Boleyn for instance, definitely met their fate there. The history within these walls was indescribable. In the gift shop, we each bought a souvenir, and Beth's and mine being a spiral writing tablet with an unusual metal cover design of a Knight Templar holding his princess. Ron finally found his tapestry, which had a similar design since, as Russell had told us, he used to be an early Knight Templar. Later, Russell would tell Beth and me...*yes, write how you felt on trip... C'est la vie, love you and yes, in French it means "that's life."*

We met back at the hotel around noon, just in time to retrieve our luggage and take a taxi to Heathrow Airport. Stuffing two carry-ons into one, we made our way through security and onto the plane. Arriving back in Dublin, we were able to book an earlier flight back to the States. Again, at the Dublin airport, we called Russell on his cellphone... *Weary travelers.* Babe, some clues you gave us just didn't seem to work out in the latter part of our trip...*kind of funny how we got off sync after Ireland.* Yes, you mentioned that Beth would run into someone that she had spent a previous life with at the Globe Theatre and strike up a conversation. What happened there? *He left before you got there; he was in the previous tour.* What about the picture of Andrew Wexford, now that my camera is gone? *Look on Beth's camera when u get home.*

Back Home Again — Looking Back at the Real Aoife

The long flight home made me think about all the hits on this trip, but also the misses. And one thing was for certain, I still missed Russell. The next time we talked, he started out by saying...*I wish I could be there to pick u up, u know I love u; you have my heart. We are like a rock split in two.* If there is anything that continues beyond the veil once we experience this so-called death, I'm convinced it's our feelings of love and how to express them. Ron and I both commented that we each had a high-pitched sound in our ears, only it was his right ear and my left. *I have my hands on both your ears.*

This time, I was anxious to talk about my previous life as a princess in Ireland. Researching the name he had given me, *Aoife*, I learned it was the name given to a maiden in Ireland. But there was one particular maiden who had a significant lifetime there, or so the research showed. Russell had told me that during my lifetime in the twelfth century, I came from the northern part of Ireland and my father, who was a king, had promised my hand in marriage, and also land, to one who would fight and help him reclaim his territory. Indeed, research showed there had been a princess named Eva McMurrough, or Mac Murchada, whose father, the King of Leinster, had promised land and castles plus his daughter's hand in marriage to someone who would re-conquer his territory. The Ferry Carrig castle outside Wexford was one that he was given. Interestingly, there was a striking resemblance to her story with regard to what Russell had told me about my life as Constance McFarland. What I also found online was a picture painted in the 1800s, portraying Eva's marriage to a well-known early Norman knight-soldier named Richard de Clare, better known as Strongbow, who led the Norman invasion of Ireland back in 1170 A.D. So what was the relationship, I thought, between Eva and Constance? Could they in fact be the same person? I was anxious to find out.

Over the course of several sessions, Russell did reveal to me that as Constance, I had been born into a poor family. My father had died and my mother could no longer take care of me in the fields of Dublin. Since I had such a strong physical resemblance to the king's family—same hair and complexion—my mother dropped me off at the castle, hoping they would take me in, and they did. I was adopted at the age of seven, Russell said, and given the name of Eva Mac Murchada. Del Roach was also a family name. Overnight, I went from pauper to royalty, which is also why the date of my birth is still in question. As Arthur William Morse in that lifetime, Russell said he was one of three other knights who led the invasion alongside Strongbow. He said that in the wedding picture online he was the short one with pulled-back hair. As Will Morse, he was wealthy and owned two other castles besides Celig—Castle Kildare and Castle Duns. After Strongbow died he and I, as Eva and Will, met at Ferry Carrig. I asked if we became lovers then and he said that we didn't, it was not safe for me to stay in Ireland. He went on to tell me that King Henry II brought Eva and her daughter Isabel to England, and that we stayed with him in the Tower of London for a few weeks before I settled in Northern England. According to history, King Henry eventually gave my daughter's hand in marriage to William Marshall, who later became known as the last heroic knight in all of Europe. Russell would go on to give me more information about Eva. Due to her wishes to lie in Ireland, her daughter Isabel took her back when she died at the age of 51 and buried her at an undisclosed location, on account of the family's enemies. Her body, Russell said, is buried underneath a large tombstone bearing the letters AOE, which stands for Ancestor of Endicott and is near Endicott castle. The burial site can be found near a Y-shaped tree, 22 feet NNW, and 4 feet underground. Russell said I was buried with four gold rings and a gold necklace.

Ron and I both stated how we someday would enjoy going back to see the King's Cross Cemetery in Dublin, where Russell told us he was buried. Also, he would later tell us, when we visited the old church remains not far from the Hook lighthouse at the southernmost tip of Ireland, that we stood 15 feet from where we were once buried as children in a subsequent lifetime after Eva and William. I thought how odd it was that we were inclined to pull over by the side of the road at that church when there were several other stops we could have made. When I asked what our relationship was at the time and how we died, Russell told me we were brother and sister and that our lives were not as colorful as before. He went on to say that he was my older brother and we died very young, one year apart, from cold weather.

Another clarification was needed about information regarding a previous life Ron had in Ireland around 1340 as Mister Edward Morrisey. I wondered how it was that I had asked him to write about my family's history when I lived in the 1200s. Also, Ron was supposedly a printer of books, and named Master Palmer in 1340, so I was a bit confused. Russell clarified by saying...*Pseudo name.* Okay, so they are the same person. *Mr. Morrisey was called Master Palmer.* Good, that explains it, but what about the hundred-plus-year time difference? Was it another reincarnation? *Mrs. Morrisey had a past life as you.* Ron and I looked up at each other with peculiar looks on our faces. Oh wow, you mean I was married to your dad then? *Yes, and had dreams about past life.* So when I was his wife in the 1300s, he wrote about the dreams I used to have of my previous life? *Like Casey, you would go into a trance and tell details of your previous life as Eva.* Oh my! You mean like Edgar Cayce, the man whom they called the Sleeping Prophet? *Yes.*

Russell went on to tell us that the little grey book was first published by Mr. Morrisey in the 1300s but reprinted in 1897. He said it has PLR in the title and now, more than ever, Ron and I wanted to find this little book written so long ago. How many copies are left, Russell? *6.* Where are they? *One in Dublin family bookstore boxed in back of store, one in Wales.* Do you mean the Berry Bookstore in Dublin, where Dad said he would be waiting for us but we never went there? *Yes.* Groaning, I said, "I don't imagine there are any in the U.S.?" *No.* Also, by any chance, does this little grey book with PLR in the title stand for Past Life Revealed? *Yes.* And we are now collaborating on revealing a future life in a book that I'm writing? *Bingo.* The moment of this revelation was just too surreal. History, without a doubt, does repeat itself.

Before we ended this session, Ron said, "Russell, I want to ask you about my vivid dream. When waking the other morning and looking up and to the right, I could see this big, beautiful tunnel with different colors of blue. This whole experience seemed so real, can you explain that?" *You were on your way back looking up at heaven, the blue represented peace; you had gone out for a while and walked with me.*

It had now been over two years and our sessions were becoming light-hearted, with some on the other side showing up when necessary. *This is Thomas; the boys will be here soon.* Or another saint or angel would show up and identify themselves. It was as if they were keeping the connection open till Russell and Dad arrived...*Sorry, can't be in 1000 places at the same time, ha.* This session, I wanted to ask about the board in general, one question that a healthy skeptic had posed to me. "If it was not Ron and me moving the oracle, then why couldn't we blindfold ourselves and have it still work?" To this question, they answered…*Energy thru u, u have to be able to spell what your mind receives.* Well, that makes sense. This person then said, "It must be like mental telepathy, your mind receives the message, which then tells the brain what to spell out and moves the muscles in the arms and hands." We didn't exactly know how it worked; we just knew that it did. Russell went on to ask, *Babe, do u remember seeing a red bird in your back yard?* Yes, as a matter of fact, I saw two red birds together, I was so intrigued by them and once there was a blue bird. *Red was your Dad and me.* You can transform into a bird? *Take over it for a minute…just so we could see you through the eyes of a bird.* Wow! *Pour a Bud in the bowl, and if it drinks, it is me.* The small group broke into a roaring laugh, but it did make me wonder if his comment had anything to do with a carry-over of his addiction in this life. He stated it didn't, though, that he just enjoyed making us laugh. With each session, we awaited more information and guidance from the other side, but we also looked forward to the clever wit that came through from Russell and Dad, and how they even seemed to enjoy teasing each other.

The Words Begin To Flow

In the fall of 2008, I finally sat down at the computer to begin writing the book. I had barely laid my hands on the keyboard when, all of a sudden, application after application started opening and closing right before my eyes. Staring in astonishment, I finally realized what was going on. It all stopped when I said out loud to Russell, "Glad I'm finally getting started, eh?" He later confirmed his excitement and when I asked for some direction, he told me…*Thomas will give it to you.*

Many years before, in prayer, I had surrendered my will to God's will: whatever my mission in this lifetime, please allow me to know and, even more so, give me the strength to follow that guidance always. I realized now that everything experienced, both the good and bad, put me on the journey of my highest good even if it meant dealing with pain along the way. In December 2005, I sat up in my bed sobbing…and sincerely prayed to be able to help those who had been in my shoes, dealing with the loss of a loved one.

Now, almost three years into our communication, the subject came up once again from an outside source as to whether it was safe to communicate through this game board, and the possibility that we were opening ourselves up to negative energy from the other side. On January 1, 2009, Dad and

Russell started the conversation by telling me I had a special visitor. The oracle paused, and then started up once again with what would become a beautiful message. *This is Thomas. I am your guide. This is a holy moment. I have Russell and Wick, one under each arm. We are here together to give you all serenity and the everlasting knowledge that all is as it should be…Go do this with love.* Ron, Lee Ann, and I sat there in awe. No more would we question, based upon others' feelings or our own, what was right or wrong about how we were getting the information…the board was simply a tool with which to communicate and we felt it was in our highest good to do so. Russell went on to say more than once…*Baby, this is a unique link, this communication is rare.* And we knew it was, since we never quite had the same results with any other combination of people playing "the game."

Cruising with the Writer's Workshop

The year 2009 turned out to be a busy one both personally and professionally. Trying to work on the book in my spare time, in addition to keeping up with sessions and notes, was a challenge while staying busy on my job, which included some travel. And family always comes first. In the spring, Lee Ann made me aware of a Writer's Workshop sponsored by Hay House that would be held on an Alaskan cruise in July. Though money was tight, this experience would offer an opportunity to progress with my writing adventure, for I was a novice. Lee Ann was hesitant to go with me, as she needed new carpet for her house, which would soon be on the market. But one afternoon in a session, when she posed the question about going, Dad offered his advice… *When you are on your deathbed, will you say to yourself, "Damn, I sure am glad I bought that carpet."* It seemed as if the house shook with laughter.

As fate would have it, in midsummer, the two of us were sailing away from the harbor in Seattle and I was off on yet another scavenger hunt. Russell offered more clues since he said, in my future life as Eva, her family, the Stones, would come from Vancouver. As usual, the trip was not without some synchronicities. On my list of places to see during our brief stopover in Sitka was the small but charming St. Michael's Church, with beautiful artifacts and paintings. And it wouldn't be until I returned home and looked at my pictures that I discovered two beautiful white circles of light in the photographs of these life-sized portraits of the Archangels Michael and Gabriel. I would later ask Russell if these were indeed orbs. *Hang on…they were exposing their hearts to you.* And hearing these words melted *my* heart.

What's the glow across Michael's picture, which extends to the other pictures next to them? I don't see this glow on the same picture that I took from a different angle. *Secondary angels, not identified, accompany them. You see the energy as a blur; it's the other angels who travel with them.* Do they show their hearts to everyone who takes photographs there? *Only to those who believe.*

Our stopover in Ketchikan the next day gave us a rare opportunity to take a small boat out on the waters for whale, eagle, and otter watching. As we climbed aboard, the local teacher introduced us to his beautiful, sweet, blonde labrador called Eva, oddly enough, who accompanies him while he takes tourists out on guided summer tours. Undoubtedly, we enjoyed the magnificent creatures we saw. Once the tour was over, we hurried back to catch the *Amsterdam*. Entering our cabin, we noticed the name "Russell's" in big green letters on Lee Ann's white plastic shopping bag of souvenirs. The synchronicities continued during our last port of call while in Victoria, Canada. Off on another side excursion, we took a bus down a busy main street and looked over to see a store called Artwick, then another called Thomas Sounds and Music, and across the street was a gift stand with books and snacks called Russell's. It was exciting to see that our dad, my spirit guide Thomas, and Russell directed our eyes to these signs, letting us know they were there with us.

The tour of the Craigdarroch Victorian mansion built in the late 1890s by a wealthy coal baron was enchanting. After the tour, Lee Ann and I quickly left the gift shop to make it back to the bus on time. We took off running down a steep hill and, in slow motion it seemed, my prescription glasses, which were hanging on the front of my sweater, went flying into the air. If I had lunged for them, my face would have hit the sidewalk. I watched as they slid downhill along the concrete walkway, glass-side down. By the time they stopped, so did I in order to scoop them up, but I hated to even look at them. A few minutes later, when we were seated on the bus, I sighed when opening up my hand to evaluate the damage. After a minute, I turned to my sister in amazement and said, "You're not going to believe this. I just watched the lens of my glasses slide across concrete and there is not one scratch on them, nor are my wire rims bent from the fall!" Naturally, she stared not knowing what to say. It was one of those little miracles Russell later told me… *Your glasses were moving one-tenth of a centimeter off the ground.*

And you can thank your guides for that. Practically unbelievable, it seemed, but I was truly grateful.

Later that evening a friend of ours from the ship met us for dinner in downtown Victoria. We took a glance inside an exquisite Irish pub before walking across the street to dine. Before our meal was served, however, I was inclined to walk back across the narrow cobblestone street to where a large building stood across from the pub. I stood there in silence, feeling the energy while staring at the building. If not limited by time, I would have loved exploring it. It was the last leg of our journey home now, and it had been a while since I had thought about the clues given, which were...*old stone building, narrow street, cobblestone, across from pub.* Later, when looking over my notes, I realized this must have been the old Stone house from my Stone lifeline. Russell later indicated this was the place. "Was it Stone because of my future family's name or stone because it was built in stone?" I asked. *Both...It once belonged to Douglas Stone, two generations back. The Stone name came from old French and your future parents, Ben and Heather, will eventually migrate to Ontario from here.*

Seeing Victoria lit up at night was stunning and surreal though sad in a way, for the next day we would be arriving back in Seattle and our cruise would be over. We also had met some dear friends on this trip, especially a couple from Australia, and the Writer's Workshop had been very informative. During the plane ride home, I thought about all the trips taken over the last few years. Everywhere linked me to a past life, or I had left energy in a place where my future life or family would be located. There had to be a point to it all...and people must be doing this all the time without being aware of it. Are we drawn to certain places, collecting pieces of our soul to become whole again? *We are a product of each bit of energy left behind each life experience.*

Dogs Play in Heaven Too

In the fall of 2009, the health of our family's 14-year-old English sheep dog was starting to decline rapidly. She could no longer walk, and it was time to put her to sleep. *BTW, Bailey has a place here, sweet dog. She and others will run and play, no worries.* Russell told us once...*Look into eyes of an animal, there is much you don't know.* Knowing how emotional I'd become while holding on to her as she went to sleep, the next day on the board my father would speak first...*My dear daughter, God has his hand on you. Honey, it's Daddy.* Solemnly, and with a tear in my eye, I said, "Hey, Dad." *The dogs are having fun. She can run and is even chasing rabbits, no pain now. Bailey wants you 2 know that she is thankful 4 great life.* Though I knew she was okay, hearing this from my father made me feel much better. Russell then made us laugh...*Your Dad almost said a cuss word when Bailey crossed the veil and about knocked him over.* It seemed they always knew the right words to lighten our burden or make us chuckle, in addition to giving advice. Just to be sure, pets don't reincarnate, do they? *Man alone has a conscience. If u give love 2 one of God's lesser animals, then u are blessed.* Also, I knew Russell wanted to cheer me up when he said, "*Hey baby got another glimpse of Toronto.*" Now smiling, I said, "You did? Please tell." *U standing in front of the house wearing running clothes...*You mean on Washington Avenue? *Yes, what a hottie, so cool...*And make me laugh, he did.

That day Dad talked about Mom, stating that they visit often. They were married for 47 years and adored each other. I asked him, though, how he could be around her so much in spirit but he still missed her too, he would tell us. *It's like smelling an orange but you can't taste it. There is an essence of each life lived here. But when in body, she, the soul, is in body.* Though a wonderful analogy, he could still see our puzzled faces. *There is still a veil of sorts that separates us as long as the cord is attached. It is being there but still having a cord attached...u can only get so far while still physically in body. Not distance, levels.*

Reflection

That evening once again, I reflected on my trips to Canada, Europe, and Alaska. How exciting it had been to be on these extraordinary scavenger hunts, with clues close at hand and a fun way to get more. Learning such specific details of my future life in addition to a significant past life was a truly mystical experience. My mind was now long past proving to itself that our communication was real, though how all this could be happening was something my left brain desperately wanted to try to figure out.

Looking at photographs and reminiscing about our experiences while continuing to work on the book, I was somehow drawn again and again to those bizarre, colorful ones taken at the London Eye on the Thames River.

Love Promised: A Future Life Revealed

The snapshots somehow seemed related to the one we took in Toronto, only these were more distinctive and colorful. I was intrigued beyond words and over and over, we were told…*the answers are in the light, dig deep.* This time much more research would be needed and afterward, the questions really began to flow. I intended to learn as much as possible about the subject of quantum physics.

Chapter Seven

Cords!
Our Link to Each Other and to Our Universe

*The process of scientific discovery is, in effect,
a continual flight from wonder.*
—Albert Einstein

O ver time, I would come to believe through personal experiences,
philosophy, metaphysics, and quantum physics, that not only are
we attached ethereally (i.e., via a silver cord), without material
substance, to the unobstructed universe, but we are also attached to all forms
of life, including those in spirit, via etheric cords.

This more recent understanding came very slowly to me and only
over the last several years, as my analytical mind had a hard time wrapping
itself fully around this thought. I certainly believed, and knew, from having
OBEs, that another dimension existed, the one we inhabit before and
after we shed this physical body. And I had grown to embrace authentic
psychic communication, things told to me that no one could have known;
a link of some kind. Emotionally, I know we are affected by others, sensing
positive or negative energy…Or our intuition kicks in by thinking of
someone five seconds before they phoned you or walked through the
door. However, my left brain still had a hard time understanding *how* we
are attached to other forms of life via cords of ether, in spite of the fact
that I felt it to be true.

Ether is described in Webster's in different ways, i.e., "1a) the rarefied
element formerly believed to fill the upper regions of space b) the upper
regions of space: Heavens 2a) also aether: a medium that in the wave theory
of light permeates all space and transmits transverse waves b) such as airwaves

Love Promised: A Future Life Revealed

3a) a light volatile flammable liquid $C_4H_{10}O$ used chiefly as a solvent and especially formerly as an anesthetic." The type of ether referenced here falls into the descriptions of both 1 and 2 above. The famous philosopher Aristotle, in approximately 350 B.C., introduced ether as a fifth element along with fire, earth, air, and water as a divine substance that makes up the heavenly bodies. He was also known for stating that this heavenly element has perpetual circular motion.

So, how is it we may be attached to everything and others ethereally? This is where the theory of quantum physics may play a crucial role in helping us understand the seemingly paranormal. Dr. Michael Persinger at Laurentian University in Sudbury, Canada, who is doing research on OBEs in the scientific community, has stated, "For the last 400 years, the paranormal included what in large part is science today, so that's the fate of the paranormal, it becomes science and it becomes normal." And Einstein himself speculated, "We still do not know one-thousandth of one percent of what nature has revealed to us."

Not being a physicist, scientist, mathematician, or even philosopher, I appreciate wholeheartedly that there are some today who are trying to help the layman such as myself understand the very difficult concepts of the quantum theory. This subject has fascinated me for several years, so I've tried to learn more, especially after discovering these unique digital photographs encompassing the quantum field, I'm told. It seems hard to believe, even for me, that a digital camera could capture this…which is why I've tried to understand the concept of quantum mechanics, or how things work in the quantum field, to better understand what's being conveyed from the other side.

The Quantum Theory

The quantum theory, I found, is based on some factual and theoretical science, which is an attempt to explain natural phenomena that scientists are still trying to understand. I might also note that we still don't fully understand electricity although its energy is harnessed every day for the good and sometimes for the not-so-good. So my discussion with regard to quantum physics will move toward a very basic metaphysical model on a microscale as I try to connect the dots, so to speak, with some ongoing scientific research and my own personal experiences and beliefs. A metaphysical model is one that seeks to explain or "represent reality in the broadest possible way with *meta* in this sense meaning "to go beyond physics or the physical." For a hard-core scientist, this link may be quite a stretch; however, what follows is my simple explanation of the connectedness of all things in nature, starting with a little history.

Quantum comes from the Latin word *quanta* (plural) first coined in 1567 to describe "how much." Quantum means "any of the very small but measurable increments into which many forms of energy are quantized *or subdivided*." The word "physics" comes from the Latin word *physica* which was first used in 1715 to describe the science of nature. For centuries, astronomers, alchemists, mathematicians, physicists, and scientists have philosophized, researched, and studied both light and matter; thus many theories have been written. As mentioned, Aristotle was one of the first to philosophize on the nature of our universe, along with Plato and Socrates. And today, we are still searching for answers.

Isaac, Albert, and Max — A Little History

Isaac Newton, during the 1600s, gave us the laws of motion and gravity. His third law of motion states that for every action there is an equal and opposite reaction. In other words, with regard to two objects, any force exerted upon one of them has an equal force exerted back onto the other. A classic example given is how the force used to propel a bullet from a gun is also exerted back upon the shooter. The extent of that force is determined by the mass or weight of either object. Newton, after studying the early astronomers Copernicus, Kepler, and Galileo, went on to establish the law of gravity, which simply states that any two objects with mass are attracted to each other by some force. Although Newton's work was immense, he never offered an explanation for the force that caused the gravity, even though it is thought his equations implied one. He stated this "action at a distance" was contrary to sound science. Later, when he referred to this force as "invisible," he was criticized for attempting to introduce the occult into science. Newton also studied the refraction or bending of light and determined that a prism could decompose white light into a spectrum of colors. He was also the first to determine that light is made up of particles, which were named photons in 1925, and to this day are considered the smallest particles in the electromagnetic field.

With regard to matter, it was once thought that the atom was the smallest of particles, but we amazingly learned in the early 1900s that it

Love Promised: A Future Life Revealed

could be broken down into subatomic particles such as electrons, protons, and neutrons. Still, at the time, some physicists didn't believe this to be true. Much more research followed over the years, with Einstein's work in the early part of the twentieth century being the most notable. He is probably best known for his special theory of relativity, adding time as a fourth dimension by which all things can be measured spatially, i.e., length, width, and depth. He also showed how time is relative to the observer, furthering the concept of spacetime, whereas time was once thought to be absolute. Einstein went on to postulate the formula $E=mc^2$ to demonstrate the equivalency of energy to mass, relative to the constant speed of light, 186,000 miles per second. Later came his general theory of relativity regarding gravitation and its distortion of spacetime (gravitational lensing) regarding the basic structure of the universe. But it was his research and discovery of the Law of Photoelectric Effect that earned him a Nobel Peace Prize in 1921. His work in this field led to the discovery that electrons are emitted from matter when its energy is absorbed with light. I think it is interesting to note that Einstein, one of our most famous scientists, also wrote papers on the arguments for the existence of God.

Max Planck, a German physicist who received the Nobel Peace Prize in 1918 for his work in physics, is known as the founder of the quantum theory. However, Einstein had laid the groundwork for more research in this field as well. As a result of the photoelectric effect, the wave-particle duality theory came about, stating that photons can act as a particle or a wave. Not long after, in 1927, physicists were astonished when they verified that electrons can also act as a particle or a wave. Research has continued to baffle physicists for almost 75 years with what is called the double-slit experiment—shooting electrons or photons at two small holes or slits. They wondered which hole the electron or photon would go through and expected many to denote or create a single pattern on a back screen beyond the slit. But to their amazement, what they found was that the electron particles became waves and went through both slits simultaneously, creating an interference pattern on the back wall. The observation of photon particles in the same type of experiment created the same results. As mentioned, these experimental results continued to shock physicists, who observed that subatomic particles do not adhere to the same laws of physics as those of atoms and molecules in the atomic world. The most mysterious was the uncertainty principle devised by Werner Heisenberg, who stated it was impossible to measure the speed of the electrons or where they would end up. At best, only probabilities could be calculated. This became known as superposition, which indicated that all possibilities in regard to where the electron could end up did, in fact, exist. The subsequent theory of the wave collapse function put an observer in the equation, and showed that when the electron wave pattern was viewed through the eyes of a person, all probabilities collapsed into one.

Since then, both objective and subjective experiments, observations, and theories have continued, with one particular experiment being called the Einstein, Podolsky, and Rosen (EPR) Paradox. A paradox is something that is considered to be true but contradicts logic or intuition. This experiment showed that two particles can become entangled and that it was possible to predict the measurement of one according to its spin, if the other had already been quantified. This indicated that what affected one particle instantaneously affected the other regardless of the distance between them. This interaction of particle exchange is called "entanglement." Einstein was perplexed, however, and called this exchange "spooky action at a distance." Also at that time, it seemed to imply that light may travel faster than the (constant) speed of light, which violated his special theory of relativity. Max Planck passed away in 1947 and Einstein in 1955, but their basic research on these scientific theories was monumental and is still being expanded upon today.

Scientific Research Continues

In the 1950s, using high-energy particle accelerators and atom smashers, scientists were able to observe atoms moving at high speeds, and discovered even more composite and elementary particles such as hadrons, bosons (thought to transmit particles), and fermions. With improved particle accelerators, the 1970s brought about the discovery of even more elementary particles such as quarks and leptons. Numerous other particles have been theorized but haven't yet passed the Standard Model of Physics. Thus far, quarks are found to be the only elementary particles that, according to today's science, engage all of the four known universal forces, i.e., electromagnetism, gravity, and strong and weak (nuclear) forces. Quarks are still being studied with regard to their mass, spin, electrical charge, symmetry, and color charge (though it has nothing to do with color). The interaction of these particles is held together by what are called gluons, which came from the English word "glue."

Additionally, since 1973, the string theory in physics has been established. It states, according to Webster's, that "all elementary particles are manifestations of the vibrations of one-dimensional strings." This thought has now been *super*seded with the same concept, only made multidimensional. The superstring theory is "an attempt to explain all of the particles and fundamental forces of nature in one theory by modeling them as vibrations of tiny supersymmetric strings." Ed Witten, a theoretical physicist who some speculate could be the Einstein of our time, postulated in 1995 the concept of 11 dimensions, "using the M-theory to explain a number of previously observed dualities." He is currently a professor of mathematical physics at the Institute for Advanced Study in Princeton, New Jersey. Witten has written over 350 publications regarding the quantum field theory and the string theory. Numerous awards have been bestowed on him, two of which are the Einstein Award in 1985 and the Isaac Newton medal in 2010, for his contributions to the particle theory, quantum field theory, and general relativity.

CERN, the 18-mile underground supercollider in Geneva, Switzerland, has ongoing research with several experiments in particle physics. The goal is to study the world of antimatter, the opposite of matter and all of its antiparticles. Why? Quite possibly, like electricity, understanding this energy and how it could be harnessed might someday advance and better mankind. It could also help us understand the cosmos, from which we are not separate, as metaphysics postulates. And, if you can believe what I've been told, antimatter was once used as an energy source to propel space vehicles during another evolution of mankind on Earth. It has been thought for some time that there may have been advanced civilizations on Earth prior to the one in which we are now living.

So, quantum physics has to do with the attempt to find the smallest particle known to man and understand its behavior and relation to everything else. Brilliant physicists continue to work toward this goal and scientists are definitely on the verge of making some new discoveries, my father and Russell told me in 2008. According to the *Los Angeles Times*,[1] in November 2010, the CERN Institute delighted in trapping one type of antimatter, "the elusive anti-hydrogen." And on March 7, 2012, it was reported that an antimatter atom had been measured for the first time.[2] Will they continue to search and find what has been coined the God particle? Will the AMS onboard ISS shed even more light on antiparticles than we know today? Inventor Nikola Tesla speculated, "The day science begins to study non-physical phenomena, it will make more progress in one decade than in all previous centuries of its existence."

Maybe on Some Level We Are All Tiny Quanta...
Just Blinking!

Coming from only an undergraduate social sciences background, my brain begins to melt down trying to comprehend even a fraction of quantum physics on a scientific level. Is science trying to discover God? Are scientists trying to get a leg up on religion? Not at all...in my humble opinion. Einstein said, and I do believe, "Science without religion is lame and religion without science is blind." Possibly, scientists just want to prove what religion has told us all along...that we are truly all one. They also know if we are careful and work together, new technology can advance mankind's existence on Earth and move on to other planets as well. New technology has the potential for either great good or great harm, and with it comes the responsibility to use it properly. For instance, the scientists who discovered the process of nuclear fusion that led to the manufacture of the hydrogen bomb never envisioned that it would be used to kill other human beings.

So, what is this energy of which we and our universe are composed? Energy, I might add, is also described in Webster's as "a usually positive spiritual force, (the *energy* flowing through all people)." Examining the human body on the atomic level, we know that it is primarily made up of oxygen, and then carbon, hydrogen, and nitrogen. Then we have smaller amounts of calcium, phosphorous, potassium, sulfur, chlorine, sodium, magnesium, iron, and manganese, along with tiny traces of zinc, copper, fluorine, silicon, and iodine. These are the very same chemical components as all other living and breathing creatures, including the Earth itself.

Russell and my father tell me that there is *"one universal language and one universal set of elements."* So it does seem we, as humans, are very much a part of this ecosystem, not separate from it. An ecosystem is described in Webster's as "the complex of a community of organisms and its environment functioning as an ecological unit." And in order to "function" together, it would seem that everything in nature would have to communicate with one another in some way.

Also on an atomic level, ecologically we know that plants give off oxygen, which humans need to survive, and our human bodies give off carbon dioxide, which plants need to survive. The human body even functions as an ecological unit itself. In our brain, neurons transfer information via brainwaves, synapses, or electrochemical impulses to other parts of the body without our conscious awareness, and our organs work together uniformly. Both are very simple but beautiful designs of how the exchange takes place on an atomic physical level, the one we've known most about for many years.

Will physicists someday soon prove that on a subatomic level there are paths of communication, also simple in design, which allow for exchanges as well? And quite possibly would this be the quantum wave "function"? It does seem that there is a connectedness to all of nature, whether or not we completely understand it yet. And, quantum physics seems to have an explanation, including how we, as the observer, may play an extremely important role in the potential of "what will be" in this quantum field of infinite possibilities.

Russell and Dad say, *"If you remove one piece of the puzzle, it is incomplete. Same with your side, every form of life depends on another."*

Intelligence behind the Blinking

The more I've attempted to understand the theory of quantum physics and the subatomic world we all live in, the more the "idea" of how everything in nature coexists and functions together now makes sense, whether or not it has actually been scientifically proven. If we truly are connected in some way via strings or cords and subatomic waves, then it seems there would have to be an exchange of intelligent information taking place in order to "function" together ecologically.

Interesting to note, a "function" in mathematics, thus quantum mechanics, is called an argument and its description even refers to the metaphor "machine (box) that takes an input and converts it to an output." The vocabulary of the word itself is also referred to as a map or mapping, and even an *image*. Now *imagine* that, no pun intended!

Loosely speaking, isn't this communication about how thoughts turn into things taking place on a subatomic level? Furthermore, isn't it *intelligence* behind the argument (or input), that you and I are co-creators with this omnipotent power we call God? A much-respected doctor of endocrinology in alternative medicine and the well-known author of 57 books, Deepak Chopra, states, "There is a difference between information and intelligence. Information is just data. Intelligence is not only data, it has the capability to feed back information on itself and create and grow. Intelligence is God consciousness. It is the expression of the mind of God. There is intent in the light or conscious energy field. Intent is a force in nature." Interestingly, giving a lecture at the Unity Church in Houston, Dr. Chopra stated that we are all pulses of light blinking on and off. Science knows what the light is, he said, but is still trying to figure out what encompasses the space between the light.

Is this intelligence, of which we are a part, not also our free will, and our gift from God to experience whatever it is we wish to experience with unlimited opportunities? Would this "box" be where we place the *image* of ourselves or how we want things to be? Would this not be how the metaphysical law of attraction works scientifically? There are multiple paths or "superpositions" out there. But whatever we focus our attention on as the observer, our input or "image" is what will be the output *or*, the image is the map to our manifestation! In other words, all potentials hence collapse into the one, the one to which we give our attention. Wow! I was taught 40 years ago in CT to create an image of what it is that I wanted, literally, and to write it down and be specific. If necessary, make it logical so your mind will believe it, otherwise your thoughts of fear that it can't be, may cancel the image altogether. Einstein himself said, "Imagination is everything. It is the preview of life's coming attractions." And, as the Bible teaches us, "Ask and ye shall receive." So if there is something we've asked for, we have surely focused our attention on it. Belief is the key. And so it truly is. Chopra goes on to say, "But there is a trick; it (this intelligence) cannot come from the ego. You know you have gone beyond the need for ego when you can relinquish the need to be right."

Remember Newton's third law of motion, "For every action there is an equal and opposite reaction." If we ourselves are energy in motion, just vibrating at such a low frequency it is not even apparent to us; it makes sense that whatever energy we send out to the universe will come back to us like a boomerang. In other words, this law of cause and effect applies to us as individuals made up of both antiparticles and particles, I believe. That's why Jesus told us, "Do unto others as you would have them do unto you." Literally, we were being told this for our own good.

If energy is always in motion, and we are made up of energy, then we must always be in a constant state of creation. Secondly, using deductive reasoning, if there is a level of being unseen to the human eye, where there is a constant wave or flow of energy exchanging intelligent information, this too helps to explain the connectedness of all things in nature, including the ability to communicate with those not in the physical form. It is certainly no secret today with science or theology that a human is more than his or her physical body. And I do love the quote that is widely used today, "We are not human beings having a spiritual experience, yet we are spiritual beings having a human experience." Once the human experience is over, our true essence is that of a spiritual being, more aware than ever.

Cords of Light

It wouldn't be until arriving home from our overseas trip in 2008 that I discovered not just orbs, but some really odd photographs that had been taken by my daughter and me using only a Sony 8.1 megapixel camera at night. (See endnotes for technical details of camera[3]) It was at the London Eye, a huge Ferris wheel ride for which we had tickets. But it had technical difficulties as soon as we arrived and we decided to snap a few pictures before taking a taxi back to the hotel. At first, I was disappointed that these pictures did not turn out, though I could not stop staring at them or the unique colors and patterns that were displayed. How could these lines be so clear and precise even when zooming in on the fragmentation? What *is it* with these pictures? I thought to myself. My left brain was frantically trying to figure out a logical explanation, so our next session with Russell and Dad would involve many questions. What we were told was that the camera snapped photographs of the other side, or beyond the veil, of this physical dimension. They also stated the camera was not capable of taking a picture of both dimensions at the same time, which explained the physical dimension being not quite focused, although the other side was most definitely crystal clear.

In this first picture, the focal point is my daughter, Beth, who seems to fade into the background. True, there were tiny blue bulbs in the trees at this park, but they were not strands of light. Is this somehow related to the picture we took in Toronto of the lines or cords around Ron? Is this what I think it *may* be?

It was explained in our sessions that the picture below shows etheric cords in different colors, representing souls who are connected to Beth in her current life. *Each cord is a member of your lifeline; the tip is where they cross the veil. The cords are all around you.* Sonia Choquette did tell me in her 2004 Psychic Pathway class that we were attached to others via cords—incredible!

An evening photograph of my daughter, Beth, in the park at the London Eye

In this picture, above my daughter's head, where the yellowish orange seems to form a line, is what Russell says is the *horizon* or what is known as the veil. The *"light yellow orange color,"* he says, *"is from here on this other side. Red, blue, and green are the other brightest colors in heaven. Look at the bottom where the cords curve and where it is the brightest; it takes a lot of energy to re-enter the veil; brighter where most energy is spent."* We were also told that there are four angels to right of Beth. *Can you see how they are the same color as the other side? Many others in her lifeline are there to assist her. She is in a better place today and if photographed again you would see yellow in her aura.* I do remember being told that the light body remains once the physical body is shed, and is similar in appearance to how one once looked in the physical. On the other side, however, Russell says they view each other as unique patterns of energy, much the same as each snowflake is individual and unique.

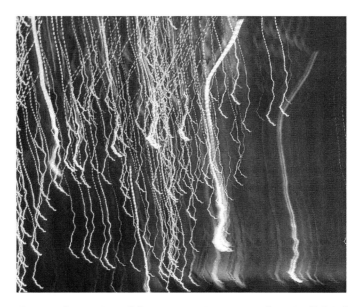

A zoomed-in section of the previous picture, just above Beth's head

A Unique View of the London Eye Park

The previous photograph depicts my daughter at a closer range while the one of me below only shows my aura. My physical body is unseen due to the picture being taken at a distance, I'm told. With regard to the colors, the blue cord represents souls who have already crossed over. Souls who have never incarnated in this physical dimension are denoted in *short green cords. Silver are in body.* The one red-colored cord, close to the neck area, connects us to our source. *Red is the tiny bit remaining when soul re-enters source for good.* Finally, the whitish-silver cord directly overhead connects us, the incarnated soul, with our higher self or oversoul and the universe.

In the picture below, to my right is the shadowy figure of my spirit guide, St. Thomas, with my father standing to his right. Both appear as vertically stretched orbs. I was even told to look for some facial features. Where the snow had melted on the concrete walkway is a reflection, they say, of my silver cord. It was approximately 9 p.m. and, by then, the light snow had subsided.

Photograph taken at a distance of Kent at the London Eye in London, England

Cropped photograph of picture above

Love Promised: A Future Life Revealed

Entanglement and Lifelines

The following pictures were taken of the area, though what was in the photographs was unrecognizable. Russell and my father stated the first photograph below depicts my lifeline, and the second photograph, my daughter Beth's and my lifelines combined. A life*line* might be comparable to each soul's total experience and a life*time* is one chapter in a book of life. *See the turquoise on the left; that is the significant life you had as queen of the castle,* Russell said, speaking of my lifetime in twelfth-century Ireland.

They went on to say that my current life stops where there is an apparent wall or division on the right side of the photograph. To the right of this "wall" is depicted another dimension, showing significant persons attached to me. The fading lines or cords are those individual souls who will soon exit my lifeline or the physical dimension. The thicker, brighter ones are souls with strong connections, those that will soon be entering my life, whether they currently already exist in a physical body or are soon to be born or manifested in physical form. The two bright, thick white cords in the upper right-hand corner of the seventh level of heaven are two angels who always travel in pairs. These angels, Constantine and Enoch, often accompany travelers, we are told.

Still attempting to make sense of this somewhat scientifically, I wondered if by chance these cords or strings that are obviously intrinsically interwoven might depict what physicists have called entanglement. *Yes.* Many books have been written on this topic just in the last decade, and scientists and theoretical physicists today still study and question what exactly is taking place.

My questions continued, as I was anxious to know more about this subatomic level that supposedly had been photographed. *Look at cords, antimatter is in the space where the strands separate, causing light to move faster.* We were enthralled as we were told, *it's what's in between and speeds up the image, every other one due to speed; without it light would not go fast. Antimatter travels three times faster than what you call the speed of light. This spectrum cannot be seen by humans.*

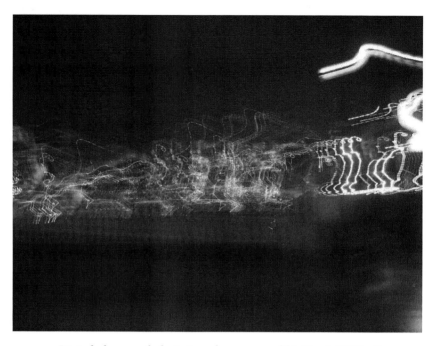

Digital photograph depicting what we are told is Kent's "lifeline"

In the metaphysical world of thought, again, as I'm told, a lifeline consists of many lifetimes that we have had interacting with souls we continue to reincarnate with, as necessary. Regarding the picture above, I'm told... *The current lifeline stops where the vibration increases, the birth line, and you can see how one life flows to next one. You are not alone. See the cords in this line. Relatives are the blue and red cords. The pics are snapshots of rotation, the center of all that there is.* Amazing, can you say more? *Lines spin in and out. Horizontal lines, gravity on your side pulls the lines back straight, gets denser with atomic particles. The light bends too. Quarks are particles of light.* "Lines," you say? *Very thin lines are strings...* We wondered if this might have anything to do with the string theory with which we were vaguely familiar, so we asked, "What are strings?" *Photons that are invisible to humans... Holds all universes together. Strings are layers upon layers of time and space, just a way for you to comprehend. They bend and distort when the veil is opened. Think of it this way, to u a shirt is just a shirt but it is comprised of many strings.* Wow! So, with the string theory of physics in mind, you are essentially saying that we are made of tiny strings of light? *Yes.* Ron and I looked at each other in amazement. This one small analogy seemed to put the larger picture into perspective, even

Love Promised: A Future Life Revealed

if it was still difficult to imagine. And that's the veil between our world and yours. *Yes, there was an abrupt change of temperature at the line... Colder on your side.* Would that be the left side of this picture? *Yes, these are levels 3 and 7 of heaven.* Only 3 and 7, you say? *A snapshot, it is all rotating. Think about an elliptical orbit, there are times when each level is close to the center. These were the two levels that had activity at the moment the picture was snapped. The two mesh, light and matter...if strings didn't encounter mass, entanglement would not occur. Lots of things occur at the place where entanglement is at its max so as each parallel universe gets close to heaven, there are changes and entanglement increases. As level 3 got closer it increased. The experience on Earth is only one plane of existence.* Yes, I would really like to talk more about parallel universes. *Sure...and no one has resolved the gravity issue. Look at the big picture; think about how much the life experience parallels a computer game. There is a God who wrote the program, you are the donkey pong.* And we have to work our way through the levels? *And if you don't reach the goal, you go back and start over. Like a game, many choices of paths. Every experience is really just an illusion. When a soul comes home it is very, very different. All of the senses are enhanced. Light, smell, and touch are a million times better.* And time? *Time is not really measured here. A wink...*

Our Physics Class

Russell and my father are always telling us, *the answers are in the light.* Someone asked, "What answers?" *The proverbial meaning of life,* they said. They went on to say, *Light waves can act as a carrier of other energy. A photon is so much more powerful than scientists know.* I had a diagram of the electromagnetic wave spectrum in front of us on the table for this discussion. *Take a look at the page, imagine a wave compacted so that it is the size of a human hair and that one hair contains a million waves.* It was stressed again that *photons will be proven to be much more important as carriers of information and when they are acting as waves, they attract energy of other forms. Photons attract and yet repel.* Will scientists discover particles smaller than a photon? *Absolutely, they are working on it.* Incredible! What will they be called? *Not named.* Can you tell us more, this is so interesting? *How about a little physics class next time; we have to go now, many crossing over, ding.* Ding? *This class is over...Rusty wants on. Love you.* Lee Ann spoke up, "Love you too, Dad, can't wait, we love talking to dead spirits!"

Honey, sorry to say but you are more dead than me. "Well, that certainly puts a new twist on things!" she said.

Over the next few sessions, Dad delighted us with our physics classes as we wanted to make sense of the data with both our right and left brains. *There are more colors in the spectrum and it is possible to go faster than light. Light can be accelerated, it will be proven... Can create artificial pull of gravity. Matter and antimatter, how can I say this... sucks the light waves faster? Gravity can push as well as pull. The key is gravity's effect on light and temperature.* How does gravity attract light when it has no mass? *Gravity can sling-shot light around. Light is searching for the path of least resistance and it is like its own vacuum searching for mass, it pulls itself. Humans have found a way to slow it down in the very cold. What repels light slows it. Gravity, as you know it, does alter matter, but gravity has its own force and exists even where no matter exists. If light can travel and burn at constant speed at absolute zero, it can be made to act different. Higher temperature speeds... at very coldest, it is slower. It was generated hot and slows in cold... that is what you see, slowed light waves. If it were to speed up, you could see time. Light acts differently. The light you see in sky has traveled in very cold. The level of vibration is so much higher here; if slowed, we would be on same plane. There are planes of light levels. The colors in the spectrum are traveling at different speeds. As a soul experiences and learns, it moves up. Colors are magnified. Think about a prism experiment splitting light. You cannot really see light, but here you can see everything... all pieces of light waves. That is why it is difficult for you to see me. There are many unknown spectrums in light that remain undiscovered. Your reality is what you see, but don't be fooled; there is another reality right next to you.* Where you exist? *Yes. Human energy converts to a form of light at passing. Souls exist with God. Some souls change and are born on Earth, they choose to come and learn, but Earth is not the only place. You have always existed. Like ice changes to water and then vapor. You just change form.* Not the Earth itself, Dad, but is our human experience an illusion, as some say and as you mentioned before? *Honey, of sorts, to the soul it is.* Dad, what do you consider to be the main forces in the universe? *There are 3.*

1. *Gravity and its opposite, antigravity*
2. *Matter and its opposite, antimatter*
3. *Light*

All three fit together equal, but not quite. Einstein was partly right, matter has an opposite unseen density, and so does gravity. The third focus is

Love Promised: A Future Life Revealed

on light. Antimatter equals mc squared over the speed of light. Antimatter is n times mc squared. It is the opposite of matter pushing the universe apart…A very, very simplified statement. Like Russ said, the answers are in the light. N is a factor. What about electromagnetism as one of the forces in nature or of the universe, Dad? *It exists only on planets with hot cores. It is not a universal force. Without light, magnetism would not matter. Light is the ultimate source of heat.* In our universe, what is the percentage of matter as opposed to dark matter or antimatter? *Not equal…15 percent matter; 85 percent antimatter.* How do you compare antimatter and dark matter? *They are similar, yes, dark matter is positive; antimatter is negative…antimatter acts as expanding glue. Antimatter is not magnetic.* And dark energy is by-product, you said once? *Yes.*

Dad, as mentioned, the CERN institute released a statement in November 2010 saying they had captured the "elusive anti-hydrogen," which was exciting news for them. However, it also stated, "The Standard Model of particle physics predicts that hydrogen and anti-hydrogen atoms should be identical…if they're not, everything needs to be reexamined, and textbooks need to be rewritten." My question to you is, are they identical? *No…Look at a picture of yourself, the two sides appear same but if you look at two of the same sides, you look different. Not identical.*

Parallel Universes

With regard to parallel universes, in an effort to make sense of the information provided, I found it helpful to put the data into the diagram below. As we were told over several sessions…*Currently 11 dimensions or parallel universes make up our universe as a whole. A smaller, very unstable 12th parallel universe existed and, like a big wave, undulating vibration, universe one reached out and touched eleven, causing an event which humans call the Big Bang. Parallel universe 12 was absorbed by 1 and 11 and provided more heavy mass to make yours reality. They are dense, not yet stable so there is a veil of separation. At a point, they will become stable and the veil will disappear. Universe 11 is almost a mirror image of 1. Earth is in 11 and 12 is gradually reorganizing. God's favorites are 11 and 1…1 started it all and split into two. They are like twins. Each universe is like a slice of pie pushing outward, expanding universe. The Earth's Sun is just one of many and is a spin-off from the brush of universes. There is a great Central Sun, KB8414, located outside of Earth's solar system. Each parallel universe includes numerous galaxies and there are black holes and then wormholes. Worm holes are smaller by far and are able to bend with dimensions to connect universes. Black holes are much bigger and convert energy from one type to another and generate antimatter, the glue that holds it all together. The universe grows on itself, self-propagating and expanding. All is made up of energy; therefore, all is in motion. But essentially they are in this order with heaven in the center of all, having its own levels or planes of existence. Each parallel is full of tiny strings; the vibrations are different due to mass. Entanglement occurs as you get closer to the center. The gravity on each is different; therefore, each universe has its own mass, thus vibration, which makes time relative on each, except for 11 and 1, which have the same gravity, thus same time. As a soul, we have always existed and are truly a spark of the Divine Creator. We exist on all universes, not necessarily in what we think of as human form. The universes are known only by number. The odd-numbered universes are our past and the even-numbered universes are our future. Each one is a different level of growth. Lifelines are experienced in timelines on each parallel universe. However, time does not matter in heaven, it is of no effect. The present is heaven and the only part that is real. All universes point to heaven. Between parallel universes 3 and 4, there is a planet very similar to Earth except it is much less dense…Same souls; different life outcomes. If you hear of one speaking about their life passing before them when having what's called a near-death experience, this is because as a soul, one has passed temporarily through a tunnel between universes. Life experiences are analogous to a computer game. As a soul, we are the "Mario." When we have mastered one level, we move up to experience a more challenging one but we must experience them all. Eventually, the parallel universes will merge into one, at a time not yet spoken.*

Russell would later say…*Have you ever heard of 711?* Are you being funny? *No, it makes the math work.* Hmmm, okay. Then does the math work with 712 when there is a twelfth universe? *Yes.*

Dad and Russell stepped aside when my guide, St. Thomas, arrived to explain a little more, knowing my confusion. *"My dear, blessed are u. The many universes are parallel, same but different. A universe is only a finite plane with light; 11 and 1 are both dense and reflective of past experiences. They are identical; have the same time; and are reflective of each other. A soul can travel to others and back to heaven without the death experience. Remember, the answer is in the light and the soul has many facets. Ponder, goodbye."* Okay, I thought, that's a lot to ponder!

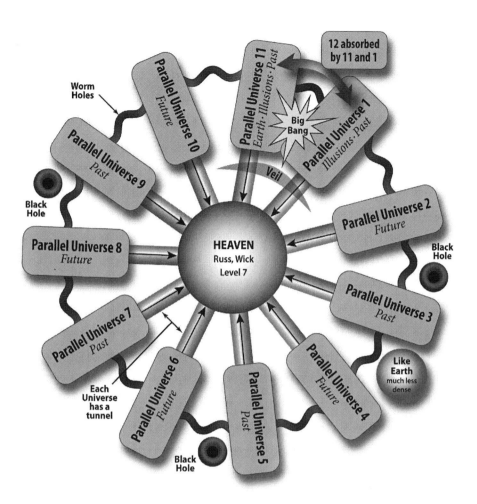

So, to be sure, the human body cannot travel to other parallel universes? *It would break apart. Someday it will be possible for humans to travel to distant galaxies and planets, however.* How's that? *Toyon particles exist in the very cold of deep space and will eventually be discovered to have an application to longtime space travel by suspended animation.* Mind-blowing, can you explain just a little more? *By manipulating the cells at the subatomic level, a body can be resurrected after being frozen. This is being tested today but they are missing this step. It allows for removing ice from the equation. Taking water out of the equation but leaving life and replacing it with something that would not crystalize. Flash freeze for long trips, space travel.* Whoa, Star Wars! Do I put this in the book? *Just that it remains unsolved now but an answer is coming that has to do with toyon particles.*

Lifelines and Timelines

The photograph below is a combination of my daughter's and my lifelines. Russell was eventually given permission to reveal that in the right top corner of the picture, the camera captured five Archangels energetically.

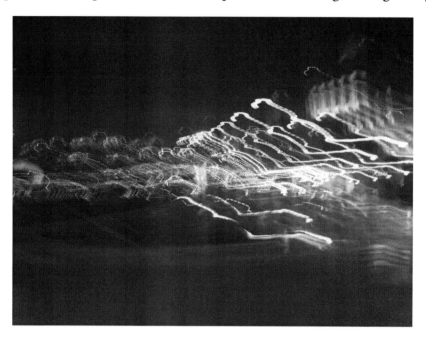

Digital photograph depicting what we are told is Kent and Beth's combined lifeline

Dad and Russell, can you explain more about lifelines and timelines? *A soul experiences a life on a lifeline. And each lifeline exists on a timeline. There can be multiple of each in more than one parallel universe. Picture this—a child goes into a house with mirrors, the sister is with him. Each child lives their own experience as a lifeline but the singular experience of going into the house of mirrors exists in and on multiple mirrors which represents multiple universes. The reflection in each mirror may be different but the image is still the same soul existing on each parallel universe. In universes 2 through 10, souls are aware of each other.*

Past, present, and future are on the timeline. All of the different lives experienced by the lifeline of the human can be contained on one of many timelines, sometimes simultaneously and sometimes back to back—the greater the human understanding, the greater their experiences. A lifeline is the combined

Love Promised: A Future Life Revealed

energy of all souls or facets that made that life possible. A lifeline is not a singular experience. Within a universe, there is a timeline for each soul. It takes many experiences to complete the timeline—Difficult for the human brain to process. Yes, indeed. I could see this concept remaining a fantasy for many until crossing over. But, as you say, shedding this physical body and crossing over does not mean we know everything either.

Mesmerized, Ron and I talked about how fascinating God's world truly is and how interwoven our souls apparently are on this subatomic level. Furthermore, we as human beings are much more incredible than we can realize when viewing life through one facet only. Theoretical science is speculating that we might possibly exist in more than one parallel universe so it makes perfect sense that Thomas would tell me, we are multifaceted beings. Can you tell us more how it works within these human bodies we inhabit? *Plans are agreed upon to accomplish certain things as goals of the life still allow 4 changes. As mentioned, souls exist on all parallel dimensions. Eleven is a significant number. There are four meridians and seven chakras. The eye of the spirit is the first chakra. There are many meridians in the body technically, but four in which 2 negative and 2 positive manage the direction of the soul. However, basically there are four major ones—the brain, heart, lungs, and kidneys that keep the body functioning properly. They all intersect and connect to the seven chakras and the nervous system. The meridians are the electromagnetic lines in the body that move the energy through to the organs. Organs are connected to the chakras. Each chakra is in charge of dispersing energy to those specific organs. That's why acupuncture works so well, it keeps the energy moving through the body and in the proper channels. The meridians are secondary to chakras but they are important to life and life force in the body.*

Oh, by the way, how did I manage to get these pictures, anyway? *The time and place were right, arranged for you.* Hmmm…Just out of curiosity, did this possibly have anything to do with the fact that the London Eye was shut down due to technical difficulties just as we got there? Beth and I saw on one of London's television news stations, when we got back to the hotel, that they did not know what caused the huge Ferris wheel to malfunction earlier that night. *Electricity interruption, same as blowing a light bulb…It could not handle the energy of Thomas, Archangel Michael and many angels in one place.*

Life Plans, Life Links and Walk-Ins

One other session, we were anxious to talk more about lifelines philosophically and, still trying to understand, we didn't mind some repetition. *Lifelines are a spark of creation with intent and purpose. A lifeline is inclusive of many timelines and lifetimes. A soul may plan one or more lives with other souls prior to incarnating. Usually lifetimes are consecutive in order to record the experiences and balance any unbalances for the next experience or enhance their purpose or intent. More evolved lifelines of creation are able to have experiences simultaneously without being in consecutive order, or link to another soul's lifeline for a special experience. An example would be a physicist in one dimension and a poor, starving child in another, one is experiencing how life works and one is experiencing how life doesn't work. Humans may have up to six lives parallel, unrelated to each other but recorded in the book of records. As mentioned, nothing gets the breath of life without it being recorded. Lifelines are the continuity in human experience. Lifelines of different souls can interconnect with each other. Souls come together for specific reasons. We each* (Russell says) *knew many other humans and lifetimes and could get back together with any of them if we wanted. When you and I met in this life, you could have turned around and walked away or I could have only said hi to you and walked away... Or not spoken to you at all. Those things happen every day, but we felt strongly about being with each other, even when it was difficult at times, we wanted a life together. And now we know why but didn't at the time.*

Once crossing back over to this side, a soul returns to its true essence, bringing back all the knowledge and experience gathered in that one lifetime, and becomes a much larger soul. A human mind follows you from lifetime to lifetime. In other words, the memories that you experience go with you subconsciously into your next life. Humans experience their highest level of understanding when they leave the physical dimension and gravitate to the level on the other side with other souls having same awareness. If you have experiences that leave you frightened or afraid, it lowers your consciousness to a different level of heaven where there are not Archangels & where others are frightened and afraid also. Hmmm…birds of a feather really do flock together.

Can we talk about what a life link is? *Just that with another soul's agreement, it is possible to link to another lifeline in order to have a brief, special, singular experience.* Define "special"? *One that has not been experienced before or that has not been planned.* Yes, I think you've mentioned this before. As I hesitated with my next question, Dad went on to give an example…*In a nutshell, Ron wanted to experience being in the military, WWII. He had no plans for it. So he was able to link up with another lifeline.* So essentially Ron's experience of being in the military without being born and raised, was to walk into another soul's body whose soul was ready to leave? *Well stated—a plan is just a plan. Souls plan out their lives with other souls before entering body, what they need to experience. However, if you reach an agreement to have an experience that was not in your plan, it can be a walk-in experience and it cannot change the plan. It is a singular experience agreed upon by two souls.*

So, just to be sure, a walk-in experience is one that is not planned out beforehand? *Right, for example, if u wished to be a movie star, I cannot see that because it's not in your lifeline.* What about walking in to have that experience? *Agreed upon at spirit level, if you want to be a star and the star soul agrees, then you may walk in for that brief singular experience but since being a star was not in your plan, you cannot live that experience, you would only be able to look back on that experience once the soul has crossed.* So, it's not an experience you would be consciously aware of it? *Right.* How much time in human terms are we talking about in order to walk in? *Only long enough to have the experience.* Have I ever been a walk-in before? *7 times… Once you were a run-in.* Seriously, what's that? *Hey, I am making a joke.* And, I should have known!

Russell then joined us in conversation about the different paths a soul can choose to take and what they can see happening. *Can't see things that won't occur…*By that again, you mean something that is not in the soul's plan? *Right, we can see the possible courses that lead 2 another outcome. Paths that are agreed on will play out in some dimension, maybe not Earth. But things that won't occur are not on any path. The paths are like the brain, in a sense, you may choose up to 6 and each path has many neurons.*

So, Dad, regarding our life paths, I guess that's why some predictions you have given others in the family have apparently not come true? *Forgive me, there are so many free wills, we can see all paths because for each path there is another plane where u exist in a parallel universe.* How many? *Honey, there are 12.* Oh, that's right, you mean the parallel universes that we've already discussed; we exist on all 12 at the same time? *Yes, you bounce between universes and one never knows.* And we choose 6 because the other 6 are our past or what has already been chosen, the trail we leave behind? *Right, but not every soul is living 6 at once.*

I did hear Gordon Smith describe a lifeline as a string of pearls. He says there are certain milestones or agreements made and these are the pearls, but there are many different paths on the string in between the pearls. Due to free will, he says, it is easier for a psychic to predict one's future once they have crossed that milestone. *Yes.* But can free will put you on a course where you will not meet that agreed-upon milestone? *Free will is almost as powerful as destiny. It's possible, but only if agreements are changed. But that soul must do that task again.* You mean possibly in another life? *Yes, God gave the gift of free will, but there are expectations that the soul must perform to reach fulfillment. Every soul who has not reached God is moving forward on their path.* So that picture of my lifeline, where you mentioned significant souls entering and exiting my lifeline? *Each is different version of you, same soul at different stages of lifeline.* Well, this is all just simply mind-blowing. Truly, truly what an "entangled" web we do weave!

Time

The talk of timelines made me think about the subject of time once again. This has come up in our discussions often since Russell and Dad state there is really no such thing. Especially with the subject of reincarnation and the supposed coming and going of different lifetimes, one might find the concept of no time very hard to grasp because we think in terms of time when measuring movement and distance on Earth and in space. Also, in this dimension, we are told that *the light you see as humans is actually the past; by the time the brain has processed it, it is the past you are seeing or what has already happened.* This thought may not be scientifically new but certainly coincides with what we are learning about "the observer" referenced in quantum physics and how, through the law of attraction, many believe we are creating our own reality.

With respect to "time," we were also told:

1. *All elements of time are only applied to human awareness.*
2. *There is an event horizon where time disappears.*
3. *Here all events are measured by energy.*
4. *Energy never goes away, only changes form.*
5. *Think how fast quarks move; we are faster.*
6. *Time does not fit unless you are in body at a very low vibration.*

Love Promised: A Future Life Revealed

7. *Time only exists when there is an observer.*
8. *One must remember that the brain is limited by input.*
9. *Time is like flipping pages of a book—when you flip to another page, the previous pages still exist.*
10. *Time does not exist; there is matter offset by antimatter.*

Professor Dr. Wubbo J. Ockels, a Dutch physicist, is also a former astronaut with the European Space Agency (ESA), having flown with NASA on the space shuttle STS-61A in 1985. Currently, he serves as professor of aerospace sustainable engineering and technology at the Delft University of Technology. Dr. Ockels gave what was called a mind-bending talk in 2009 at the Technology Entertainment and Design Conference, better known as TEDxAmsterdam, held in the Netherlands. Sponsored by a private, non-profit American foundation, TEDx conferences are held globally "to share ideas worth spreading."

As a result of his experience flying in space, Dr. Ockels postulates that time is the creation of humans as a way for our brains to make sense of gravity; thus we are what he calls chronocentric beings. He goes on to explain simply how our central nervous system has to generate time as a function of gravity. He further states that "the speed of light is constant because it is made by us; it's the clock by which we have calibrated our existence." People in the Middle Ages escaped geocentricism (thinking the Earth was the center of everything) and we too might someday escape the idea of chronocentricism. Dr. Ockels speculates that "a different gravity, a different life, can generate a different time." Looking at the universe in our time, he says, we may only see a fraction of it. He further postulates that possibly, the Big Bang is just an illusion. Humans go so far as to say everything was created 13.6 billion years ago. "And with respect to what?" he questions.

I'm certainly not alone in my thinking that we are in the midst of a paradigm shift or what's called revolutionary science, which is considered a new outlook on the rules governing science and nature. The research on quantum physics has been ongoing for approximately 100 years but with new technology, more and more research is being done and there could be new encounters that will create a radical shift in our thinking about the cosmos. My guide, St. Thomas, has pointed out to me... *The physical properties of life on planet Earth are in constant flux and that fact makes it difficult to pinpoint with complete understanding which laws of physics are stationary and which are malleable.*

Reflective Propulsion?

Dad, can we have one more physics class? You once gave us a formula that you said had to do with reflective propulsion. *Here is my statement: Light reflected back moves photons faster than speed of light. S equals P squared over N times plus T equals S squared divided by P times N—photons move faster when passing through others. S does not stand for velocity. It stands for state of solid at rest, wavelength, meters per second. It is an aspect of speed not yet considered possible, strange as it sounds, faster than light. It has to do with reflective propulsion, the boost by eliminating gravity.* Someone questioned this equation, Dad? *It is an embedded one. If energy can be at two places at once, then combined energy is greater than a single. The future of travel to go to distant planets will require the use of antimatter. Antimatter is the opposite of most waves but not all. It has a twin; the form existing today is with the influence of gravity. Take gravity out of the equation, and it is moving fast, very fast. Edgar Cayce spoke about it in his case reading 126, in 1927. The formula was once proven by visitors to Hybrasil.* What is that last word again? *Hybrasil—Google it.* I guess Dad could see the looks on Ron's and my faces as neither of us had ever heard of this word and had no idea what it meant. Later, I did in fact research the word "Hybrasil" only to discover it is a mythical island off the coast of Ireland, similar to the mythical land of Atlantis. However, unlike Atlantis, it is thought this island has been visited several times over these last millennia. And by "visitors," again, Dad, you mean space visitors? *Yes.*

Regarding reflective propulsion, we are looking for 2 velocities to create bubble to bend space without changing time. It can be done. The answer is in the light. There is a study of antimatter propulsion given the string theory. It can be done if time is controlled. Light travel is needed to exceed the SOL (speed of light) *with a string bubble in front so time would not change for the traveler. And, someday, undiscovered properties of light will allow for intergalactic communication. Light nanotechnology is the way to travel to the stars. Again, the answers are in the light.*

Interesting Thoughts from a Futurist

Worth noting are statements made by a futurist during the 2009 National Space Symposium or NSS, (the largest annual space symposium held in the United States) in Colorado Springs, Colorado. Approximately

Love Promised: A Future Life Revealed

8,000 attended, comprising mostly the United States military, NASA, and industry contractors. Someone with whom I worked attended that year and said, "Kent, you are going to love this…" One panel during the conference that year was entitled *The Next Space Age* and panelist Alvin Toffler, PhD, a Futurist, made the following predictions with regard to profound changes that are coming around the middle of this century. The following are my thoughts on these predictions:

1. *"Profound medical advances, particularly with the brain."* We do know scientists are now stating that the brain has plasticity. We also know that anything with plasticity means it can be molded or changed. I do imagine there would be profound new findings in this regard.
2. *"Around the middle of this century there will be a worldwide religious war against science."* Dad states: *A theoretical war, yes. Catholics eagerly fight science, struggle to keep it together. Don't want to lose control.*
3. *Knowledge about the cosmos. As an example, the idea that we live in a parallel universe is now receiving serious consideration."* Several respected theoretical physicists today, such as Michio Kaku and Fred Alan Wolf, have been proposing for some time the concept of how parallel universes may very well exist.
4. *"Dark energy is speeding up the expansion of the universe."* This concept already is becoming a more common thought among physicists.

(NOTE: While this book was being finalized, several articles were published in early October, 2011, announcing that three physicists won a Noble Peace Prize in Physics for their observations of "distant exploding stars" which began the discovery that the "expansion of the universe is accelerating." The articles state that this discovery laid the groundwork for the idea that "a mysterious force called dark energy" that has never been detected is "fueling the acceleration." Could this be the byproduct of antimatter, according to Dad and Russell, which acts as an expanding glue?)

Chapter Eight

Do You Have Horizon Wireless on Your Side?

There comes a time when the mind takes
a higher plane of knowledge
but can never prove how it got there.
—Albert Einstein

In 2009, Bernard d'Espagnat, an 87-year-old French physicist and philosopher of science in Paris, won a $1.4 million prize from the John Templeton Foundation for his work on the philosophical implications of quantum mechanics. Under the World Science section in the *New York Times* online article, published on March 16, 2009, Dennis Overbye wrote:

> Noting that the rules governing the behavior of subatomic particles
> contravene common-sense notions of reality, Dr. d'Espagnat, a
> professor emeritus at the University of Paris-Sud, coined the term
> 'veiled reality' to describe a world beyond appearances, which science
> can only glimpse and which could be compatible with higher forms
> of spirituality.

Understanding the larger-than-life picture of our universe and how everything, including ourselves, fits together may be a human feat that some think is unattainable. Looking back, however, knowledge of ourselves and our universe (thus consciousness) has been evolving over the centuries, so who's to say it will come to a halt or that we now understand everything that is possible to know. As Dr. d'Espagnat has noted, science may only be glimpsing what we know of as a higher form of spirituality.

Love Promised: A Future Life Revealed

In this chapter, I offer all that I have learned up to and including my communication with the other side, and how this has impacted my thinking. If through scientific evidence it can be proven someday that we are all connected on a subatomic level and if we believe that we don't die... wouldn't it help to explain things that some of us have already experienced and know in our hearts to be true? Communication has evolved over the centuries from sending messages via doves, smoke signals, pony express, aircraft, telegraph, radio, telephone, and video, to more-advanced fiber optic wires and then wireless connections via satellite signals from space. Today, for the physically handicapped, we have even found ways to turn thoughts into typed words on a computer connected with electrodes hooked up to the brain or head of an individual. And, few, if any, would have imagined 30 years ago that we could write a letter electronically to someone on the other side of the globe and they would receive it within seconds.

Future Communication

There is another information highway just waiting for more people to come on board. If we, ourselves, are energy vibrating at some frequency, then it would make perfect sense how we too could be a medium; both a sender and a receiver. But it will take more than buying a piece of equipment or signing a yearly contract. The service by thought transference will be yours and it will have to be earned or developed. And, I believe the spiritual rewards for having done so will be more than we could possibly imagine, both individually and collectively. Some are afraid of the word "psychic" because of spooky connotations. Now, remember the invisible force of *gravity* was considered spooky by Isaac Newton himself almost 400 years ago, and even others put it into the occult category because it was not considered sound science. Doesn't it make sense, then, that the connotations and skepticism surrounding the idea of psychic energy are due to the fact we don't quite understand it yet? Webster's defines psychic as "lying outside the sphere of physical science or knowledge: immaterial, moral, or spiritual in origin or force." This science of the mind, I believe, will be accepted by modern science in man's future as a verifiable truth due to empirical evidence. But the profession, I might add, is alive and well today. And just as when seeking out services for any profession, choose wisely.

Someday, I believe communication will evolve to include mental telepathy as a more accepted form of communication. And if we don't die, who is to say this mental telepathy cannot reach across to the other side, vibrating at a frequency yet undefined. This communication, like others, may not be bound by material objects, signals from a spacecraft or satellite, time, or space. Also, I believe we will begin to understand that through this communication, our thoughts can affect one another regardless of which side (this or "the other side") you are on *because* we are connected. Lastly, this type of communication doesn't have to be a purchasable one, if we can develop this latent talent with which we are all born. No communication is 100% correct, I'm told, due to human interpretation. And, it's just difficult to stay on the same wavelength. Some may become proficient at it where others may only use it to find their car keys in the morning.

Diversity

Possibly through understanding how everything works, we can better appreciate different beliefs and even puzzling occurrences that happen around the world. The primary goal in some Eastern religions is to meditate and develop their third eye. All over the world, people have claimed to hear a voice when no one is there. And almost everyone who is not too engrossed in what they are doing can sense when someone has walked into the room, even without seeing or hearing them. Studies have shown that the power of prayer by a group focused on a city has actually reduced the crime rate or helped to heal someone. There are numerous stories where people have healed themselves "miraculously" of a disease or injury when our modern science of medicine has given up hope. Some stories include visions of angels who saved people from harm or kept them alive till the paramedics arrived. Other stories describe tragedies where people have died in freak minor accidents while others survived the seemingly impossible. People having near-death experiences (NDEs) in different countries report the same experiences. The International Association of Near-Death Studies or IANDS is an organization that was established in 1978 to provide more research and support for people who have these experiences and who can't turn to anyone else. And, as previously mentioned, the Monroe Institute, based in Virginia, was established to help those who have experienced traveling out of their body while in a very relaxed state of mind. Having stumbled upon the benefits of these experiences through scientific research, they facilitate classes for others who want to expand their conscious awareness. Many over the years have provided testimonials about their lives being changed for the

Love Promised: A Future Life Revealed

better. Paul Elder, whom I mentioned as being a class facilitator, has written his life story in the amazing book *Eyes of an Angel*. He tells about beautiful OBE experiences that eventually led him to rescuing lost souls who didn't even realize they were physically dead, helping them to move out of their stagnant dimension. And it's Bob Monroe's institute and his earlier findings with subject Rosalind McKnight that inspired the class called *Lifeline* to help souls in this predicament. Both Bob and Rosalind wrote about their own experiences in *Journeys Out of Body* and *Cosmic Journeys*, respectively.

Another less scientific group, but nonetheless research-oriented, is an organization in Australia called the Circle of the Silver Cord. They claim certain entities use the ectoplasm emitted from the pancreas of psychic trance medium David Thompson to communicate with a small group on this side. This is done in darkness; if visual evidence is required, and for the protection of the medium himself, infrared video and still photography are used. For this reason and others, participants are carefully selected based on sincerity and the group's desire to help them communicate with their physically deceased loved ones. Many provisions are made to show the participants that there is no trickery involved and numerous testimonials have been given to authenticate the reality of what's taking place. I once asked Russell's opinion about this group and he stated that indeed this is what they are doing. My friend from Australia who participated in the group told me he was amazed. Communicating from the other side to this one, without using the vocal cords of one who channels, Russell said, is as difficult as a human being trying to speak while underwater. Surprisingly, when browsing the group's Web site, I found the communication difficulty described using the very same analogy. Russell also stated that everyone has ectoplasm in their pancreas, with some having much more than others.

Today, there is great diversity on our planet, and how individuals deal with this nonphysical world and many personal experiences are left unexplained. The answers are out there and they are also within, as stated in *The Lion King*—if we can remember who we are. In the past, people's sanity was questioned even if they barely delved into these interests. However, an unexplained personal experience can certainly put a different perspective on one's view about life. And it does perpetuate the need to search for answers outside the norm, since our two main authorities, science and orthodox religion, don't offer explanations. So, interestingly, over the last 50 years or more, people have been propelled to search for truths and to question our limited beliefs, all the while trying to understand these higher forms of spirituality.

Paying Attention

Many believe that an understanding of quantum mechanics explains how our eyes are truly the projector to our world while our thoughts create our reality. The philosophical implications of our behavior alone, I believe, can change our world when this concept is better understood and practiced. For as someone once said, watch your thoughts, for they become your words; choose your words, for they become actions; understand your actions, for they become habits; study your habits, for they become your character, develop your character, for *it* becomes your destiny.

I think it's not only time for us to watch our thoughts but also to pay more attention to what we are thinking, and why. With regard to listening to our higher self, spirit guides, or angels over the horizon, Russell says, *those who have the ability are 90%; out of that 90%, 60% don't hear the message or, if they do, they don't follow their guidance. Only 10% of that 90% try to open their awareness to really listen, following their guidance. The rest, or 20%, blows off the message or experience, entirely as a coincidence. Sometimes u all take it wrong…human interpretation, so hard to keep on same wavelength. Also, there are more interferences than u think, it's hard 4 u to not add your own thought.*

It's through my personal belief and my own experiences that I have real empirical knowledge about those who guide us, called by us "spirit guides" and even "angels," not just on this side of the veil, but on the other side as well. The picture we have of ourselves should be like one of the Verizon Wireless commercials, with everyone in the background just waiting to be of assistance; many times the help is there before you ask. This tremendous help is instantaneous and comes from beyond our own horizon, or the veil. Available anywhere, it would make that 4G LTE network of Verizon's seem like it's moving at a turtle's pace. Plus, the only blackout periods are self-imposed. This horizon wireless network that is accessible to all comes with no fee and you get as many rollover minutes *or lifetimes* as you need. It's like going to school; you can't possibly learn or experience everything you need in one class, in one year in school, or even in one lifetime, *or timeline*.

Unlike the human ego, our horizon wireless group doesn't care to take credit for any beneficial choices we may make. The point is: the message got across. And they will always be there to help but never interfere, due to free will. And regardless of how many mistakes you may make, they will stay with you. This is a part of the game of life that we all agreed to play. Not

Love Promised: A Future Life Revealed

to say that in some cases divine intervention can't happen, because most believe it does. But like the Verizon Wireless group, as the commercials so explicitly show, our support group is there waiting to serve from the other side. Your spirit guides contracted to be with you during this lifetime and will stay with you until the cord is severed and you are home again. Many other guides may come and go as you need them, depending on certain situations and their needed expertise. Nevertheless, you always have a primary and a secondary guide who are with you at any time to help govern your life and assist in making decisions based on your highest good. Also, it would behoove us to listen and watch for signs. Many years ago, I used to think being psychic was a gift that only a few people had. Now I understand it is an untapped area that takes spiritual development and a sincere desire to acknowledge, embrace, and practice working *with energy*. As many say about riding a bicycle or strengthening a muscle, you just don't do it the first time you try. And just like some who are born with natural talents for music, art, or science, there are definitely some who are gifted with this natural psychic ability. Some have developed it to a greater degree and others to a lesser degree, but are still developing. Meditating is the key to getting past the thinking mind and going within. *Be still and know that I am God* (Psalms 46:10). It takes practice to calm the ego mind, the constant chitter-chatter that seems never-ending.

Through impingement on our thoughts without interference, our guides, angels, and many who crossed before us are always ready, willing, and able to help us whether it is a minuscule task or a very complicated one. Furthermore, they can see all the potential opportunities and the agreements with other souls that you made before manifesting in physical form and why, whereas we are limited in that respect. We agreed to the game, we bravely decided to cross the veil into the unknown for experiences we may not be consciously aware of. We are told to ask or pray but we are also told to have faith since we can't see everything from their perspective. Sometimes our egos know what it is we want, but in all cases God knows what we need. Gaining what we think we want at the moment may prevent us from having something much greater downstream. When it comes to relationships, this may be the hardest test of all in this game of life. Or we may feel someone else should change drastically because it's not what we would be doing, or what society thinks someone should do. Yet we don't always consciously know on a human level what another soul has chosen to experience. Where necessary, we can always try to help another to follow their own guidance, but because of free will we must allow another to also experience, learn, and grow. And as a parent, sibling, or even a child or a lover, this can be very difficult...the art of allowing and detaching from the outcome of another's choice. Russell tells me...*What I learned from this side is have all the experiences you can without damaging yourself or someone else. Being physical offers many opportunities for that.*

Our Other Three Senses

Thoughts truly are things. As humans, we have been walking around handicapped for the most part because we've limited ourselves to only the five physical senses, though we have other faculties that can help us in our day-to-day living. Three other senses more commonly associated with this other body, which extends just a few feet from the physical body, are called the three *clairs*, a name used by Doreen Virtue, who speaks with angels. There is clairvoyance or clear seeing; clairaudience or clear hearing; and clairsentience or clear sensing. These three faculties of the etheric body that surrounds our human body are how we stay connected or *tuned in to* the quantum wave, the universal flow of consciousness. Nonetheless, accessing other energy levels or different frequencies does take focused energy and a sincere desire to do so.

Developing these three senses that have lain dormant for too long will allow us to watch our thoughts more carefully. Possibly we can learn to take off the mask we are wearing and just be ourselves. Connecting to this omnipresent energy allows us to put ourselves in the other's shoes. With the "do unto others" philosophy, we know the energy flows in both directions since we are connected to, and not separate from, each other. Neither are we separate from this omnipotent power we call God. Truthfully, and soon to be proven by science, I believe, we cannot hurt another without hurting ourselves as much or more, because we are entangled. Though, if you follow your heart or the path of your highest good with no intention of hurting another, but someone still gets hurt, it is by their own accord, and may be their lesson in life to learn. Moreover, we can actually be interfering with their own spiritual growth by not allowing them to have that experience.

Also, our higher self knows that if we choose to react in the same negative manner as another, we will keep ourselves at that same negative energetic level, attracting even more negativity. If we can "rise above it," literally by changing our energy or vibration to a more positive or spiritual one, we can raise the energy of both ourselves and our adversary. Then in some respects, we will have become his or her teacher. This is not always easy to do because, out of habit, we react more than we act. Quieting the mind and listening with our hearts before acting is the key. I do love the simple Mayan principles handed down to us by Don Miguel Ruiz as the Four Agreements, which are: *Be impeccable with your word; Don't assume anything; Do your best; Don't take anything personal.* Because we are victims of victims, consciously reprograming ourselves to act in these ways is a must if we see that a change is necessary. And more important than what someone may say or do is how we let it affect us...this we know. Ruiz has now released yet a fifth agreement—*Eliminating beliefs as your path to freedom and enlightenment.*

As mentioned, embracing this knowledge can improve our lives dramatically. Our own vibrational frequencies can change from moment to moment depending on how we act or react, but more importantly, how we are "feeling" in that moment. If we are genuinely excited and happy, our frequency level rises; if we are unhappy, sad, or even angry, our frequency level falls. In CT classes, when discussing the general natural laws therein, particularly the Law of Attraction, I learned not to take anyone else's word but to prove it to myself with the simple test of finding missing things around the house. If you are angry over misplacing something, you are guaranteed to spend an hour looking for it or not find it at all. On the other hand, if you are relaxed when asking for help, most times it only takes a second because you quickly and energetically tune in to the misplaced item. Or, you will be open to getting the message from your guides. When you see how it works on a small scale, you begin practicing it on a larger scale, using your imagination or imaging what you want. It should be logical for our brains to believe that we can have whatever it is that we focus on, since belief is a huge part of achieving. However, we cannot place too many limitations on what the universe can bring us because our analytical ego mind is only a small part of who we really are. As mentioned, it took believing that I could have some things as a starting point to make it happen, even if I didn't quite know all the physics. But now, along with our philosophical beliefs, there may soon be a real scientific understanding of how the Law of Attraction works. If we understand ourselves to be more than our physical body, then we are enticed to learn that what we focus on becomes like a magnet for what we will attract into our lives.

To understand how this works on an energetic wave length, here is a simple analogy. If I want to tune in to radio station FM 96.5 but I'm still focused on or obsessed with listening to FM 107.5, most certainly I will never hear FM 96.5. How we focus our energy is the key. We know what we want, but out of habit we may only think about what we have…and in that thinking, we continually recreate only what we have. Now if we apply this same law of attraction into our life, we simply tune in to or give energy to what we want to attract. Philosophically, this is the image or input which equals the output of mathematics or quantum physics…whatever it is we give our attention to most likely will be what we get. The reason I say "most likely" is because we may not always consciously know what our soul has chosen to experience in a lifetime.

Jerry and Ester Hicks via Abraham is one other that teaches us the Law of Attraction today, and my continuation of learning about it from them has elevated my understanding even more. Whether proven or not with accepted physics, the Law of Attraction for some of us is as real as seeing our face in the mirror each morning. And we also know that this law applies to us consciously or subconsciously, focusing not only on what we want, but also on what we *do not* want in our lives. Besides trying to understand the physics behind it, it can get confusing because, let's face it, who wants to see that we are responsible for the things that we *don't want* coming into our life? Interestingly, the law applies either way. We, at times, without paying careful attention to our thoughts, focus on what we don't want simply out of fear. The emotion of fear is energy, which can attract whatever it is that you fear, if you are giving your attention to it. So true the quote by Franklin D. Roosevelt, "the only thing we have to fear is fear itself."

Fear is the cause of all dysfunction in life, and love is all there truly is in this universe, as Abraham has told us, and I learned in CT. All other emotions stem from these two. We all have fear in some way or to some degree because we are living primarily from the human ego, and right now on Earth there is a veil that separates us from truly knowing who we are. This fear seems to affect each person's brain differently. Sometimes, we may not understand why or where the fear comes from and naturally, our self-defense mechanism will try to bury the fear in our subconscious because our ego wants to protect us. Other times we know and accept our fears and may choose to deal with them, overcoming the fears. And at yet other times, we are simply forced to deal with them. Our only real suffering is that of

Love Promised: A Future Life Revealed

ignorance, as we consciously or subconsciously choose to ignore. What we are starting to remember is that fear is brought on by the ego's illusion so it's imperative that we start living from the heart. If we are looking out into the world and criticizing, it's the ego's way of making us feel better about ourselves or keeping the focus off what we need to change in our own lives. That's why it is so important to pay attention to our own thoughts and differentiate between those coming from the ego and those coming from our heart and soul, for the soul only knows love and compassion and sees that in everyone and everything else.

Developing our three *clairs* can truly open our third eye and help us to live more from the heart. Doing so can also open us up psychically to better receive support from those who stand ready to assist us over the horizon. Further development of opening the third eye means mentally and spiritually being able to tune in to the frequency of an object for information, a timeline, or lifeline. Furthermore, a psychic medium can be a conduit tuning in to a soul who may no longer possess a human body but is real nonetheless.

Reprogramming Our Brains

Our fear readily impacts the choices we make. Whether through love or fear, we do have choices due to our gift of free will, but the responsibility lies within, I learned through CT, and we cannot escape the inevitable consequence of that choice. Soon we may also learn that our so-called past has truly programmed us on a very real cellular level and, if so, we can learn today how to reprogram ourselves if need be.

Dr. Joe Dispenza has written a book called *Evolve Your Brain, the Science of Changing Your Mind*. This book is a result of having sustained an injury from which his healing defied modern medical science. What he found and what science is theorizing today is that the brain has neuroplasticity. Therefore, it can be molded and changed because thoughts can create neurons. We are not hardwired after all, he says! Also, the Discovery Channel in a special program portrayed scientists discussing how this is done scientifically. A chiropractor by profession, Dr. Dispenza has also studied neurology, neuroscience, brain function and chemistry, and cellular biology, to name a few. I was fortunate to take a wonderful workshop at the Unity Church in Houston called *Breaking the Habit of Being Yourself* where he outlined neurophysiologic principles, teaching all participants how to reprogram their thinking in order to eliminate self-destructive habits. Dr. Dispenza also explains how changing our thoughts can change our beliefs, therefore rewiring one's brain.

As individuals we are all walking around with our little, and sometimes big, bag of burdens. Everything is relative, of course. But as humans, regardless of how small or large the bag, we do have an emotional need to feel comforted, to be heard, and to be understood, especially when our bag gets too heavy. That's the vulnerability in us, whether male or female. And, even if we chose on a higher level to have those negative experiences or even positive ones, it's not always apparent to us on the physical level on which we do most of our day-to-day thinking. Loneliness and despair can overtake us if we are not careful with our thoughts. Understanding ourselves, our ego, our past, and possibly even those past lives which may still be affecting us today, can have a huge impact on how we act on, or react to, what happens in our present moment. And the *feeling* with which we react in our present moment is the one that creates our *next* present moment.

Yes, we are more than our physical bodies. Have you ever been reading a book and suddenly noticed that you've continued to read a paragraph but your mind is someplace else and you have to go back and reread? Or, you have been driving the car and suddenly it occurs to you that you don't remember how you got from point A to point C? And you wonder who was driving the car while you zoned out for those few seconds or even minutes. We physically have continued to read on or drive on…but somewhere in the middle, we realize our mind went elsewhere, as though our bodies went on autopilot. As Dr. Dispenza says, we all have attention deficit disorder (ADD).

This thing that we have labeled a "disorder" at times may not necessarily be a bad thing. Quite possibly our minds just needed to wander, or wonder, to bring our creative self back in balance with the technical-thinking part of the brain that has been overused, he says. Or maybe it was the peaceful feeling our hearts needed at the moment. It may be also that these moments are when our mind is open to communication on other levels, because we've set our ego-thinking mind out of the way. Our challenge in being human is to keep both the right and left sides of our brain balanced, while at the same time training ourselves to be fully present. Some of our most profound thoughts of inspiration or guidance come from being in tune to this nonphysical energy. And, as I'm told by Russell and my dad, we exist on many parallel universes at the same time, which most likely accounts for these moments of apparent unawareness.

Love Promised: A Future Life Revealed

We Are All One

Growing up I became aware, as almost all of us do, that our theologies and philosophies have taught us for centuries we are all one and one with God, and the thought of that alone brings a sense of peace. Although my heart knows that to be true, understanding scientifically how we are connected on this subatomic level is exciting too. As an analogy, we don't have to wait for science to tell us how a watch is made, to begin seeing for ourselves what time it is…or how an understanding of being connected to everything around us, seen or unseen, can actually improve our lives at this very moment.

This feeling of oneness within our human consciousness has been experienced and researched for some time. Dr. Edgar Mitchell wrote about his journey to becoming an Apollo 14 astronaut in his book *The Way of the Explorer,* published in 1996. I had the opportunity to ask Dr. Mitchell at a conference what he had experienced. I knew he had left NASA many years before and started the Institute of Noetic Sciences (IONS), which explores human consciousness. So excited to be standing there alone with Dr. Mitchell himself, I asked if it was an OBE he had experienced on his journey into space. Although he felt it was a good question, his experience was one of feeling connected to every living thing…as though there was no separation, "a feeling of total oneness in this universal consciousness." He went on to state what I had heard before, that different cultures refer to it in different ways; in India the experience is known as a Samadhi. I didn't mention to Dr. Mitchell my OBEs as our conversation was quiet and brief while in the midst of hearing another speaker. Also, I wanted to stay focused on any information he might pass along. How wonderful it must be to have had that experience in space, I thought. Today, Dr. Mitchell serves on the board of IONS.

He must have truly felt and sensed that entangled web we weave with everyone and everything, but I do believe it is all in the Divine Order. There are no mistakes, there are only miss-takes and missed opportunities, as stated in Barham and Greene's *The Silver Cord, Lifeline to the Unobstructed.* And through our learning, we are given chances to retake an opportunity in more than one lifetime, if that is what it takes. Seeing our lives as a human through only the small facet of this lifetime, we don't understand why some people seem to get away with murder, literally, while others are falsely accused and will end up serving a sentence behind bars. We may not understand why someone left us, or why we knew in our heart we had to leave someone else. It's hard to comprehend why one child is born with a disease or a missing limb and another is gifted from birth with what we consider a perfect body or a hidden talent. It's hard to fathom why one may die at the age of 2 and another will live till they are 99 or older. This comparison could go on and on. But in the larger scheme of things, the one who murdered was murdered or will be murdered, and the one who was falsely accused may have been serving a criminal sentence for a crime of which he was not convicted the time before. The person whom we left in a relationship may have left us or oppressed us in a previous life. The child who was born with a disease may, in a future life, be a doctor who discovers the cure and receives accolades. Or the child who lived only till the age of 2 may live to be 99 in their next life. Looking at life on Earth with only the human ego mind is like taking a book with a great story, reading only a few sections, and then trying to understand it all. It just doesn't make sense.

"Be Compassionate" Says the Dalai Lama

Being compassionate or having empathy for another's plight is a wise thing to do. Judging another, however, implies that you know God's plan for all. Matthew 7:1 states, "Judge not that ye be not judged." Or judge not, lest ye be judged, as most think of it. What this means, I believe, is not judging *from the heart*. We must use discernment to live in the world of duality on a planet as diverse as ours. We have to differentiate the good from the bad; we have to create laws to protect the innocent; and without interfering, we must try to help those who cannot help themselves. Furthermore, we need to set examples and teach and guide our children to know the difference between right action—a good deed; and wrong action—harming another. I think the real message here is, how do you *feel* about or *view* another's misfortune? Do you rejoice in their sad experience? Or do you have compassion, knowing that somewhere along the line, this soul is still evolving and may have made a bad choice out of extreme fear or because he or she didn't have the same genetics or advantages in this life as another…possibly you. This planet is unique because of its diversity and opportunities for growth. There are highly evolved souls and lesser evolved souls on this plane of existence. But we will never evolve to the potential human beings can achieve if we never move past the "eye for an eye" philosophy. For this is what primates do, those with instinct alone and a strong urge for self-preservation. Forgiveness from the heart could help another's soul more than being judged…though due to man's laws, there remain consequences for every human act, much the same as with nature's laws. To avenge what we may think is a wrongdoing may keep us in a vicious cycle from which there seems no return. That's why we are taught by the Bible, "Let vengeance be mine." I don't believe this means that God punishes, but that the natural laws of our being will draw the same unto us. This is karma.

Humans were given the gift of reason and intellect to evaluate what the outcome will be for each choice made, and we gradually will move out of our collective pit of ignorance. No longer will we want to experience the consequences of our negative choices by giving up our freedom. Living in fear, dissolution, and total separation is pure misery. We've begun to learn that we are all connected, literally, that what we see in one another we have in ourselves, otherwise we would not be able to recognize it, as I've been told. And in seeing ourselves in one another, we understand what forgiveness is all about and how that would benefit us, if we were in someone else's shoes. Forgiveness brings out the God self in each other. And if we feel better, we will want to make others feel better. If just one person can be forgiven, then they too learn how to forgive. And when we have taken someone's hand closer to God, we will have also taken ourselves closer to our God. Russell tells me…*Over here there is a constant feeling of peace and no worries. God provides. Souls forgive all; there is no hurt, no pain, no hunger…only beauty and pure love.* Wow, I can only imagine a world where not even compassion is needed.

The Life You've Only Dreamt of

So where do we go from here to live the life of which we've only dreamed? In our day-to-day interactions with ourselves and those around us (i.e., our journey through this mortal life, the one we are in, *at the very least),* we are not unaccompanied, as God has told us. The aphorism "you never walk alone" that has inspired songs and poems is not just a philosophical one designed to make us feel good. There is a real message here, one our Bibles have told us for centuries, namely, that of having guardians and angels to guide and protect us. But when it appears the help hasn't arrived, we tend to lose faith because, again, we can only see our life or situation from one aspect…certainly not from the perspective of our spirit guides or our omnipotent God. And our lack of understanding why things happen the way they do comes from not knowing the larger plan. We have to go beyond our human mind and stretch our imagination to see with our hearts the *possibilities* of the truth behind this statement. We are also told in Psalms 91:11, "For he shall give his angels charge over thee, to keep thee in all thy ways." And the word "guardian" is used throughout the Bible. If the reality of this does not quite ring true for some, as with any idea, use discernment when it comes to your own basic beliefs, but do not limit yourself, either. In other words, don't throw everything out because you've stumbled upon an idea your mind can't accept at the moment. You too can be inspired by God to know and understand the truths behind words written by man long ago. Simply put any idea on your fact, theory, or fantasy shelf and ask or go within for more answers…and inevitably you will be guided to your truth.

The most meaningful answer does not come from any written material, or any person, place, or thing. It comes from within. Books, documentaries, songs, signs, Bibles, preachers, priests, sages, and avatars may be a good, great, or an ultimate source to lead one to their reality, but one's truth can only come from within. That's the beauty of Jesus' words in the Bible that tell us the Kingdom of God is within. And as Mother Teresa reminded us, "In the end, it is all between you and God." When you can catch that moment of being at one, or atone with God, this infinite power, there is no judgment and one can look out into the world and see only beauty in the diversity of life. It's living as a human and understanding the ego that is our challenge to being in balance with nature. Existing in this dual environment, our ego naturally sees things as either good or bad. And because of that, we have a tendency to think that God does too. However, nothing is good or bad in God's eyes, it simply is. The ego belongs to the human alone. The illusion of our being separated from our creator is the game of life, in which we experience all possibilities. It's like being on God's stage and playing different characters, figuring out for ourselves, with the gift of free will, that we loved that role, or heck, I don't ever want to do that again! When we come here, it may be to choose the opposite experience or role in life to

Love Promised: A Future Life Revealed

better understand what it was like being in someone else's shoes, or simply to help another do the same.

It's becoming a more common belief that we are given the unique advantage of seeing our life in review when leaving the physical body in near-death or death. With love, compassion, and no judgment, we get to see how our choices impacted others and, if necessary, how we could have done things differently. Dannion Brinkley, who has now had three NDEs, told me how during this experience one can see and feel all the pain you ever caused another, as if on a movie screen passing in front of your eyes. Further, he said, you too feel all the love you ever gave to another. It's as if you are being literally embraced in this loving, glowing light with no one to judge you but you. And, this is how we learn and grow as we continue to do over many lifetimes. It's not because we are being punished that we may find ourselves in an unhappy situation. That's not karma. Karma is our own choice on a soul level to experience the opposite of what we may have experienced before (whether this lifetime or another) so we can graduate from our own suffering, ignorance, or just lack of knowing. Or it may simply be balancing our energy, thereby raising our vibration to get closer to God, and realizing the ultimate truth for which no questions are necessary. The natural Law of Attraction enables this balancing act.

The Kingdom of Heaven

We are told that the Kingdom of Heaven is within but we are usually looking without, or outside ourselves. That's okay too, if we are watching for the signs along the way that point inward. We are asked to seek first the spiritual things in life; then all the other shall be added unto us. But why is it that we can be focused on everything else first and seek help from God only in great despair or unhappiness? At times, our ego mind will even try bargaining to get what we want. "God, if you'll just do this one thing for me, I'll...." And when things don't go our way, we even have a tendency to blame God for what has happened to us in our lives, not wanting to understand that it was our responsibility all along. With the gift of free will, we create our own reality...though we are creatures of habit, no doubt, and victims of victims. We can get into a whirlwind of focusing on the negative and by law we receive it. After a while of doing this, we even begin expecting it in our lives. And before long, we've created for ourselves a lifelong habit of being miserable, and pass this mode of thinking along to our children.

It's been said you cannot change your situation in life with the same energy that created it. Rising above it literally means changing one's vibration and we can only do that with thought.

Understand that this statement carries a very real message. It's no different from plugging into the negative terminal of a car battery and expecting to get a positive charge. Our own positive and negative charges in the electrons that make up the nucleus of the cells in our body will attract or repel based on our thoughts. If it seems that it is not working at the time, then know there is a reason behind it that we just don't understand yet. We must surrender our feelings about the situation, or person, place, or thing—and ask quietly for the knowing to become clearer. Then have patience—the answers will eventually come but we must be open to them in many different ways, e.g., signs, songs, messages from a stranger or a friend, a sermon, a presentation, but always with our own intuition. And we need to be open to the truth, though it may hurt; the healing that comes afterward is indescribable. There is plenty of help in the world today, with many who teach how to live our heart's desire through workshops, online courses, personal coaching, self-help CDs, or a progressive learning church. And, of course, we must always be grateful for where we are in our life… for it's the feeling of gratitude that allows or attracts more abundance to come our way.

Signs and Synchronicities

As mentioned, it's important to watch for signs and even synchronicities along the way that will let us know if we are on the right path. I've learned to pay attention to them, whether subtle or not so subtle. As mentioned, songs can bring one an incredible message. Our loved ones on the other side may just want to let us know they are still around and watching over us. While on a business trip to Colorado Springs, I stepped into my hotel elevator, which had speakers playing soft music. The song "Me and You" began to play and brought back a flood of memories of being in Russell's arms at an outdoor Kenny Chesney concert… this just happened to be our song.

Besides songs that would be a surprise everywhere, other synchronistic events also startled me, like when I went with my grown kids and nieces and nephews to play laser tag. In this dark maze of different levels, we were all running and hiding, lighting one another with laser beams that hit the device we each had strapped over our shoulders. Since this game was my first attempt, I was always brighter than the rest, no pun intended! We stood in line after the game to receive a printout of our scores, each ticket having a different personalized character's name. Looking down almost in disbelief, I saw my name was "Ouija"!

Another time I went with family to see an exhibition of *Titanic* artifacts. It naturally made me think of Russell's artwork hanging in our little place, a 16 x 20 inch black and white drawing of this ship that sailed only once. When I walked up to three of the displays, lights started blinking on and off. Knowing Russell was there, I smiled and in my mind said hello. As we exited, each visitor received a replica ticket with the name of an actual person who sailed on the *Titanic*. A broad smile came over my face when I looked down and saw that the name on my ticket was Mrs. Morris. On the way home, I heard the lyrics to yet another song, "Better Life" by Keith Urban: "Someday baby, you and I are gonna be the ones, so hold on...we're headed for a better life."

Regarding songs, I find it interesting to note that in July 2010, the news media was consumed with the story of a Canadian pilot flying an F-18 fighter jet that crashed during an air show. One engine blew out and the pilot ejected four seconds before the plane hit the ground and burst into flames. Spectators were captivated while listening at that very moment to the Bee Gees song "Stayin' Alive," that was on the loudspeakers. Since it was an air show, everything was recorded. What was even more intriguing at the time was that *CBS This Morning* show acknowledged this synchronicity. It seems, as a society in general, we are starting to become more accepting of the fact that there are no coincidences, as I'm constantly reminded.

The afterlife continues to capture the public's attention but perhaps never more than now, with major news channels presenting documentary programs on the subject. For instance, ABC's Primetime *Nightline* featured the series *Beyond Belief* in the summer of 2011. In one episode entitled "The Other Side," prominent people were interviewed such as a doctor, a former skeptic who previously alluded to her patients' experiences as hallucinations but has now claimed an NDE herself. Others, including the show's host, spoke of being separate from their bodies and seemed to have communicated with a higher being or someone who is recognized as no longer existing in the physical.

Also, reportedly, our Western world is moving past orthodox religion to embrace the concept of reincarnation. In August 2010, the *New York Times* published an article about a Cornell-trained psychiatrist, Dr. Paul DeBell, who has a private practice in Manhattan and specializes in hypnotizing his patients in order to retrieve past lives. Fortunately, as the article noted, Dr. Brian Weiss is not the only Ivy League graduate destined to heal the mind in an unconventional manner. The article goes on to state, "According to data released last year by the Pew Forum on Religion and Public Life, a quarter of Americans now believe in reincarnation."

From a scientific perspective and also a philosophical one, it does seem that there are numerous potential paths one can take in this experience of duality—living in the physical. There is free will and there is destiny and, for years, I wondered how the two could exist at the same time and be compatible, as they seemed to be opposing thoughts. Russell states it simply:

As I have been told, destiny is where you are going and free will allows you and others to decide how to get there. Paths are many. Destiny is the end state of one's personal development in each life experience. Free will is God's gift and how you use it determines to what level you ascend.

Love Promised: A Future Life Revealed

Chapter Nine

The Journey's End

All evolution in thought must first appear
as heresy and misconduct.
—George Bernard Shaw

Russell started out our first 2010 session by saying, *Happy New Year,*
as if there is time! Yes, so much to think about now for us humans,
so much to learn! What have you been doing? *Learning more about*
the universe, observing. The secret to it all is so simple, but only everything is
known by God…so bright and intense when seen as a soul, feels complete peace
and love. Heaven does sound beautiful, babe. Tell us more…*It is not cold*
here, always warm, huge place, guarded by angels. Every soul must get permission
to enter…Cannot enter in body. The houses are colorful; skies baby blue, gold
in abundance. Gabriel led us to a really cool celebration, angels I never saw
before, a whole new level. Russell, that is so special. *Guess who I saw playing?*
Who? *Black and white, furry, has big time here…* Oh! Give Bailey a big hug
for me…we miss her. *Sable tries to boss them around, funny. I've been around*
you all a lot.

Russell, you know there were some strange happenings in the sky
recently, in early December. They are calling this the lights over Norway and
a pretty unusual video was made that caught the attention of many, including
news stations worldwide. Supposedly, the Russians are claiming that they
had a failed submarine missile attempt, but that story is being debunked
by many on the Internet. Can you tell us what this was? *In an effort to hit*
a comet, opened a brief hole, waves seen parallel. They believe that a comet or
asteroid will hit Earth. Just to confirm, was it a failed missile from a Russian
submarine? *No.* Does the U. S. know what they are doing? *Yes, allows for*

potentially moving spacetime. It opens space and ahead and closes behind to provide speed faster than light. They have captured antimatter naturally. The material to do it is not man made. Something they used to try to hit a comet? Laser propelled by antimatter. What non-made material did they use and where did it come from? Crystals inside cave not in Russia. What about the Large Hadron Collider (LHC) in Geneva, Switzerland, aren't they trying to create antimatter as well? But it would take hundreds of years that way to get enough naturally occurring antimatter. That's right, you said the Fermi lab in Chicago, for one, has created antimatter but it is under the influence of gravity, a huge difference. It will be revealed that there is a speed faster than light. It is possible, laser boost by Russians tested. They discovered a way to collect antimatter without accelerator… Used lasers to boost antimatter. Wow! The cold of space hitting antimatter speeds it up. First attempt was in March 2008. Well, the video was pretty amazing; these beautiful blue lights perfectly spiraling in a circle, then outlining a dark hole in the center. Actually, the lights generated had broader spectrum than man could see… colors bled thru 4 a moment. Almost like opening a wormhole. For one thing, it is a sign that the veil is thinning. We also saw a YouTube video showing what looked like the Chinese trying to do something similar, oddly the white spiral changed direction in midstream, so to speak. They are working on it. Interesting, thanks.

Gifts Come in Strange Packages

Knowing the book needed to be finished this year, I was starting to feel behind on my self-imposed schedule of getting our experiences documented and ready for the time capsule. Russell said we could bury just the manuscript if the book was not yet published. However, I was wondering if even the manuscript would be ready. I was very busy at work and spending any spare time just documenting our sessions…and then there was family. Once I asked Russell, "You told me you saw more freedom, a change in my life to work on the book, can you tell me what this change is going to be?" Not just yet; can't say. Not even a clue? Right… We are all very proud of you for your writing. It is challenging but I'm enjoying it when I can find the time. My father chimed in to also say, Thomas told me that he often watches with Russ over your shoulder while you write. Well, I can use the help, so thanks to all of you.

Before long, I found out the reason they could not tell me, for the news would have been devastating. And, racing 90 miles an hour downtown to the Medical Center in the back of an ambulance was not on my bucket list of things to do, either. On Saturday, March 20, I awoke and soon realized, with all my severe symptoms of nausea, vomiting, weakness, and diarrhea, that something serious was happening. My sister Rebecca arrived shortly before the EMTs, who suspected a stroke by means of the simple test of raising both my arms in the air and telling me to hold them up. By then my vision had become blurred. My left arm fell like a cooked spaghetti noodle. Within seconds I was intravenously given an anti-nausea drug and my heart was monitored with an EKG. As it turned out, the year before I had had what is called a transient ischemic attack or TIA, and had been unaware of it.

While in the Methodist Hospital ER with family there to support me, for some reason I asked the name of my attending male nurse, who surmised my stroke must have happened during the night. He was trying to determine whether a clot-buster would be necessary as time is critical during a "brain attack." Answering my question, he kindly looked at me and said, "It's Michael." Right away, I thought of Archangel Michael, which started me thinking that all was okay. Also, I was starting to feel physically better, though my eyesight was not quite normal. Later, in the hospital room my female nurse introduced herself as Thomas and, knowing my spirit guide was there too, a feeling of peace came over me. All was in divine order regardless of what had just happened. As I was considered young to have had a stroke, the doctors checked my heart the next day for a patent foreman ovale (PFO), suspecting that one could be the cause. My PFO was a congenital heart defect, they said, a small valve opening where the baby's heart is connected to the mother's lungs, which is supposed to close at birth. Fifteen to 20 percent of all people are left with this opening. My brain scan showed acute damage in my left cerebellum; everyone told me how very lucky I was to completely recover in less than a few days. I knew, however, that luck had nothing to do with it. The doctors put me on blood thinners temporarily and told me to take it easy…which I did for seven weeks. When coming home from the hospital, I couldn't help but notice two large street lights going out on the 610 Loop at different times just as my son's truck approached them, and a light on the street where I lived went out before we pulled in my driveway. I knew my guardian angels were following me home.

What better way to take it easy than sitting with my laptop, alone and at peace. It took only a few days for the three fingers on my left hand to start catching back up with the rest. However, one week later, an arc of severe pain formed from the location of the damage to the center of my eyes. I took my blood-thinning medication and was able to go to sleep that night despite being very frightened. Still concerned the next morning, and in pain, I called my doctor, who ordered an MRI. Fortunately, everything was okay. Russell would soon tell me…*Baby girl, MRI shows a narrowed vessel, pain will go away. Your brain is redirecting the blood flow. Stay on meds, will get better.* Several days later after the pain subsided, I thought how wonderful it is that our brains do just reprogram themselves. Russell then told me…*Your leg felt like it weighed 200 lbs.* What? Wait a minute, what are you saying? *How do you think you got back and forth to the bathroom that morning?* Oh my, yes, my left arm was totally paralyzed and my left leg was feeling numb as well. I also realized then that it would have been impossible for me to walk so easily back and forth to the bathroom twice, or to have grabbed my mobile phone to call someone for help. Rebecca helped me back to the bed just moments before the paramedics arrived. "How *is it* you do that?" I gasped.

For the next six weeks, aside from some bad headaches every now and then, I was able to relax and focus on writing, accomplishing much.

Important Messages from the Other Side

Also in the spring of that year, I noticed online that David Wilcox, who co-authored the book *The Reincarnation of Edgar Cayce,* whom he professes to be, had a weekend event planned in Austin, Texas. Since I had found his book to be quite fascinating, something enticed me to attend. Russell, is he really the reincarnation of Edgar Cayce? *Heck yes.* With limited funds for this $300 event, I went on to ask if this was something to consider. *Go, the money is on the way.* Surprisingly, two days later, in the mail was a check for $300 from my mortgage company, thanks to an overage in my escrow account. I then purchased a ticket online, as did my sister and Judy, our dear friend from Oklahoma, who met us there.

One of many interesting ideas shared at the event is that there are electromagnetic meridians all over the world that intersect; at some places, David said, the veil is always thinner. When talking about this with Russell and Dad, they said…*Historically, yes, and one very significant place you have been.* Is that Stonehenge? *Yes.* I've watched programs on TV where people have used this metal L-shaped device, what is it called, Russell? *Divine Rod.* Yes, that's it. And in these locations, when holding one end of the rod in your hand, it actually will move and turn on its own in the direction of these meridians or what they call ley lines. *The veil has opened many times at Stonehenge.* Oh, so it's not open all the time? *Right.* Can

Love Promised: A Future Life Revealed

you explain that one? *The soul must be alone with like-minded people and want to see across there. The energy floats all around the area. There are other places.* Which ones are you referring to, as David showed a world map and talked about some. *There are several, such as Delhi, Tibet, Mayan…* Where in Mexico? *Ixtapa…I have to step aside for a minute.* Hmmm…okay. The oracle stopped, then changed directions and started moving again. *Bless you my dear…* Whispering, I said, "Oh, who is this?" *Thomas.* Oh, thanks so much for coming. *I am a fan of yours, Russell speaks highly of you. A word for you…Although the path may appear dark, rest assured that your guardian angels are lighting the way, be full of life, dear. You have achieved much. Your soul is blessed, I must leave.* Tears began to form in my eyes as the message came through. At the time, I didn't realize how much worry had filtered through my body—not just the anxiety of my own physical health but over family issues as well. It was a true release of emotions and after the session, I felt much better.

Around midsummer, during one of my checkup appointments, my neurologists offered me an opportunity to participate in a clinical trial for PFO closures. If agreeing to participate, I would have a 50-50 chance of being selected via randomization to have the closure performed, or just be monitored for several years. The procedure seemed very risky, according to the documentation provided, and there were no guarantees. However, if selected, I would have an excellent cardiologist from the DeBakey Center in Houston to perform the procedure. Still, the risks involved outweighed the potential benefits, and I didn't quite know what to do. I asked Russell and Dad for more advice…*Long term u will have more energy.* Is it true your body doesn't get the oxygenated blood to the extremities? One lady told me her doctor said this was the case but my cardiologist says no. *It does cause a lower capillary refill pressure.*

A second time when asking for confirmation, I was very moved to have this guest…*Be at peace, this is Michael.* Archangel Michael? *Yes, the boys are busy.* Oh my, thank you, may I ask you a question? *U may.* Explaining the situation, as though I really needed to, I asked what size this opening was and if the procedure should be done. *Minor no. linear point 4 cm congenital, u should fix it. It is in need of repair, my dear. I must leave.* I was still in awe when Russell popped in…*Hey, wasn't that cool, he is very tall. When he is around here it is warm. He has come to Earth b4, descended from sky, seen by Mayans.* Well, I do know that many have professed to see angels and this experience must be extraordinary. I'm just grateful for the repetitive number sequences that continue to show up everywhere.

Russell, by any chance, do these numbers that we see from our angels have anything to do with the parallel universes that are also numbered? *Yes, all science and communication is based on numbers, same events can happen on more than one level. You are experiencing a duplicate event happening on another level when u notice the numbers 11:11.* What if you just see 444? *When u see 444, it means that your soul is only on one plane.* But how can that be if I am on Earth in parallel universe 11 and 444 is in another parallel universe? *U have left body for what seems like a second but was longer. As Thomas told you, remember, souls are multifaceted and the answers are in the light.*

Challenges, Changes...and Dad to the Rescue

In July, one afternoon while sitting in my office at work, I pushed myself away from my computer and exclaimed to the universe, "I'm ready for a change in my life." Two hours later, my director called me into his office and told me that as of October 1, I would no longer be employed with the company...my job function was going away. Whoa?! That was quick. Maybe I should have been more specific with my statement to the universe? Quickly, I had to remind myself, as I so often would do—All is in Divine order; just because it's not apparent at the moment doesn't mean it's not so. I went back to my office, sat down, pushed myself away from my computer again, and respectfully stated to the universe, "I want to win the lotto!" Hmmm, I'm still waiting on that one. So along with approximately 1500 other people, just at my aerospace company alone, I would walk out the door in three months. Due to the space shuttle era coming to an end my company, which operated the vehicle, would endure a significant downsizing.

One week later, I received a call from the Methodist Hospital saying that I had been randomized to have the PFO closure. This didn't come as a surprise for Russell had told me Archangel Michael would arrange it. Two weeks later, in mid-August, the procedure was performed. When released from the hospital, I was told to go straight to the emergency room if any unusual symptoms occurred. When symptoms did arise two days later, my sister Lee Ann graciously drove me very quickly back downtown to the hospital. They took me in right away and many tests were performed.

One test in particular was an MRI of my heart. I was positioned on the table and just before I was guided into the small, looped tube full of powerful magnets, the electricity in the whole hospital shut down. All of a sudden, I was staring up into total darkness. The power was out for only a few seconds, then everything was back up and running again…except for these MRI machines. In the middle of the confusion, one technician spoke to me saying, "I've been working here for 23 years and not once has this ever happened." She very kindly apologized but my only inconvenience was lying on a comfortable bed waiting for the test, as my symptoms had now dissipated. About 30-45 minutes later, they took me to the floor above (which housed an older MRI machine) to perform the test as the newer machines would need an outside technician to restart them. Yet another test was performed on my heart the next day and when everything checked out okay, I was released to go home.

Our next session, when I asked about the freaky power outage, Russell surprisingly told me *Your Dad worried and you know how protective he is but there were other reasons. Time was not right, so we stopped time to catch up with your frequencies. Your blood was not thinned, etheric body low vibrations.* The machine upstairs looked older. Was it less powerful? *Yes, different frequency.* Trying to understand more, we were told…*Time is a human concept. No one realized the brief stop of time. Took a series of steps to shut down; to you all, it appeared fast. Actually four steps to shut off power.* Oh my, well, I do have a card to carry in my billfold now to show technicians if I need an MRI. Evidently, the metal implant in my heart is safe at strengths at or below a certain level, but most likely, I surmised, this is once the heart tissue has grown around the device. Would something have happened being in the newer, possibly more powerful, machines? *Yes, heart rhythms would go wrong, heart stop.* So my dad actually shut down the power? *Yes.* That's incredible! I can't even imagine how many little miracles are performed every day. *Am going to call Wick…Let's see how fast the old fart gets here.* The oracle switched directions and started moving so quickly, Ron and I could hardly keep our fingers on it. *OK, Sonny boy, here I came from across the universe in a nanosecond.* We all laughed…*Daddy Warbucks here.* What have you been doing lately? *Checking out new intelligent life.* Speaking of the universe, Dad, in the news it stated the Swift telescope took a picture of the largest gamma-ray burst ever. *169 million light years.* Wow, that wasn't specified in the article. *How's my girl?* She's fine, Dad, I'm sure you've been to see her lately. We knew Dad was talking about Mom, now 81, as her Alzheimer's had worsened. *She visits me a lot now and is talking about coming over to this side.* Is she actually seeing you, Dad? *Honey, we visit all the time, yes.* I sit beside her in the bed, Dad, and she acts like a little girl when I bring her ice cream. I love to see her like that. *Me too, it really comforts her to see you girls. I really appreciate you all taking care of her.* My sisters and I agreed that even though it will be hard to see Mom cross over, we know how happy she will be to rid a body that no longer works for her. But more than that, she will be home and with her soul mate again.

It seemed I was praying often in front of the little altar for my mother, other family members who struggled and for myself. Thomas very kindly opened a session soon after...*My dear, be patient, for this life is just one of many, you have much more to experience. Good will come to pass 4 u. Angel Serrena was by your side last night. She said a prayer with you.* I've been doing a lot of that lately, thank you...that is so special. *Yes, it is. Here are your souls to talk. Goodbye.* As soon as Thomas left, I let out a sigh, trying to be grateful for what I did have in life while forgetting all the rest. For I knew it was those moments of fear, or thoughts of not having, that kept me stagnant and not moving in the direction of my highest good. Another session, I was curious to know the truth about some previous experiences in life.

And oh, By the Way...

Hi honey, Dad here. Oh good, hey Dad, may I ask you a few questions about past incidents which I've always wondered about? *Go.* One is the time driving home one night from college in a snowstorm on that two-lane highway and the headlights went out on my little '69 VW. *There were two spirit guides leading u, lights were a vision that guided you.* Wow, so there was no car there? *No.* That was truly a miracle, Dad; I didn't know enough to be truly grateful at the time. I just thought it was by coincidence that a car pulled out in front of me. *There are no coincidences.* Yes, we are learning that more every day. There are two things that I would like to clarify. *Ask.* The nurse in the hospital while I was delivering Matthew...the one that kept patting my hand telling me to push, when the doctor screamed from across the room telling me not to push. *She was your great-grandmother.* Oh My! I never knew my great-grandmothers. Dad, what would have happened if they had performed an emergency C-section, as they were getting ready to do? *Asphyxiation, bad outcome...* Yes, the cord was wrapped around his neck twice. So you are saying he would have died? *Yes...* What a miracle, I would have been devastated and, for sure, he was supposed to be here. Can you tell me also, Dad, when my OBEs started? *You were 3; you and Lee also had friends as children.* You mean as in the unseen kind? *Yes.* Okay, just one more that I can think of right now...just to be sure, was it really the space station in the sky that I saw that day in Austin, Texas, at Sonia's workshop a few years ago, when I was asking for a sign? I just know it was but I would like to confirm. *Yes, real thing, a sign to stay with program and let fate take its course.*

Russ coming but 1ˢᵗ u have a special visitor. Oh? *Thomas.* Oh, thank you for coming. *My dear, put the past behind you and get all experiences that this life affords you. Go forth with a smile and a loving spirit.* When you say put past behind me, Thomas, am I still supposed to be writing the book with Russell? *I am referring to once you have completed the task; you are a bit of a perfectionist. Proceed but do not get mired down with love for this side. I am closing with love from this side.* Of course, my guide knew me only too well. Not only was it my desire to complete the manuscript, I also loved communicating with the other side, as did we all. And, there is nothing wrong with this. However, too much focus on the other side keeps us from living the life we came to live. In addition, I also wanted to ensure our story was documented accurately. As with everything in life, however, all should be kept in balance. And I knew my guide was gently nudging me to do just that.

Russell's Surprise Message

Before Russell left that day, he surprised us with some news. I was not prepared for what he was getting ready to say. He started out as he had many times…*Baby girl, I just had to say it.* Oh, how sweet…What's up? Then, immediately I began to sense his emotions and seriousness. *I want you to know that I will be beside you, behind you, above you, for rest of this experience. But not interfere. There will be a time when this will subside…that's okay.* This did come as quite a surprise as we always looked forward to our sessions. Ron took the news much better than I expected. He said, "I'm okay with that," and I said somberly, "When will that be, babe?" *End of November…I need to run thru agreements and complete work here.* November is not far off. *I will still come back to visit, I will just not be following you both around all the time. Besides, there will be another man in your life, Kent. When time, I will be right here to welcome you over, babe, you still have things to do…don't think for 1 minute that God lets you rest. Ha. Enjoy this while we have it, ours is a love that is timeless, forever, and meant to be, baby girl…*Knowing in my heart this could not go on forever, I was somewhat emotional as I would miss our sessions with him terribly. *Peter is summoning me…a plane crash.* Where? *Don't know yet, there is a group on the way to cross.* Is Thomas here to talk, I just had one more question? *No, Thomas is orchestrating that.* Oh, okay. *Hugs and kisses.*

Two hours later I turned on CNN only to see that there had been a plane crash in India. The pilot had missed the runway. Everyone on board had been killed, except for one passenger who was found aimlessly walking down the runway. Well, I thought, there was at least one person whose time was definitely not up here on Earth...and an angel walking with him who most assuredly made certain of it.

Now, after 22 years, leaving my company would soon become a reality. As my Dad used to always say, "It's not so important what happens to you in life, as how you let it affect you...try to look for the good in everything." And in this moment no longer under my control, I knew what that was and possibly that this all happened for a reason, allowing me to complete what was now my heart's desire. With 22 weeks' severance, I could focus on finishing the manuscript. After coming home from a spiritual workshop in Santa Fe, New Mexico, in early October, I realized that was where I should return to finish writing. Russell had said we could wait until the spring to make our last trip to Toronto and bury the capsule.

Heading to Santa Fe

Before heading back out to Santa Fe, this time by car, we spoke once more on the board. You mentioned, Russell, some other things to put in capsule besides pictures, manuscript, and family genealogy? *Strands of hair for DNA, my beaded bracelet from Watershed* (rehab facility), *our shirts and also put an artifact to prove you went to Ireland.* Ron quickly offered to put in the small stone taken from the Ferry Carrig castle. *Great idea, Dad... carries energy.* Yes, and the certificate with Mark's and Eva's names. *Perfect. Baby girl, I'm proud of you. Keep it up; Toronto will be here before you know it. Have I said today how much I love you...I do.* It was times like this during our sessions that made my heart skip a beat. *I will be with you on trip. Don't worry about job, babe...the fat lady has not sung. Another will be waiting for u...either way, u will be okay. It's time to finish the book.* Russell started reminding me of things to do in order to prepare for the trip, almost as though he was concerned. Hey, I didn't think you worried over there? *We are only concerned that humans won't listen to their guides.* And in fact, I didn't. In planning the trip, I jumped ahead and picked a place to stay that wasn't in my best interest. However, my friend Judy, who had moved there with her husband, offered me a room in their home, once I had made it to the Land of Enchantment. This worked out to benefit us both.

Thomas and Russell Offer Advice

In spite of the minor setback, my writing indeed flowed in Santa Fe, this tranquil part of the country. Thomas would soon come through with a beautiful channeled message after I arrived. As Judy began the session, she told me St. Thomas was crossing his hands over his heart and saying… *One of my children…Many tasks are before you that are done to help humanity toward greater understanding. You've accepted a lot of experiences and in doing so you have been given opportunities for growth. Your most intense times are over, for your experiences came fast and hard, and you are now part of becoming a teacher. Once you accomplish what you've set out to do in this journey, it will unfold beautifully because you took the courage to set out on an unknown journey with only trust and faith that it was for your good, as well as leaving behind all that was familiar, stepping into uncharted territory. You have demonstrated your willingness to serve and graduated from the need for struggle. The next step in your life is flowing easy. Look for signs all around you, such as the bluebird. What better way than the bluebird of happiness. Miracles occur in the natural flow of life when you are awake and take notice. This was not a perfect journey, there were moments of discomfort that you are aware of…but you will find your true self, which is what most humans spend their life searching for. You will welcome an epiphany and revelation of the highest order. There we will welcome you home and you will be the peace you seek and become a great teacher. Persevere…much love to you. Amen.*

This message was surreal and warmed my heart. Early that morning, I awoke and fixed my morning coffee, feeling much better after the long journey there. It was quiet and peaceful. Once again, I was mesmerized by the beauty of these mountains. Then, outside the sliding glass door, three bluebirds landed on the deck!

After Thomas left, Russell showed up. I was excited to hear from him too. Judy said, I'll just repeat what he is saying…*Hey, babe, lots of reasons to doubt and feel afraid. But just let go of that need, we've got your back. Sometimes I watch you worry and overthink things, but I get it because I was just like that. From here I can see it's a waste of time. I am not going to be here much longer, our time together is about up for now. The more I stay around, the less you live your life and I want you to be happy, babe. Thomas has assured* me he will take care of you, and your Dad is not going anywhere. It's been a beautiful journey and I'll come back now and then, but not so you can depend on me. Just to remind you I'm still around and I love you. I have more work to do. Be happy because I finally graduate. Tell Dad I graduate with honors or so they tell me. I'm going to a different level, ready for my next phase before I come back in. We need to put the plan in action, babe, or else all of this would have been for nothing. I don't want to leave but I understand I have to and you need to understand that too. As far as other men coming into your life, of course they will. You are beautiful…go for it. What I learned from this side is have all the experiences you can without damaging yourself or someone else. Because being physical offers many opportunities for that. The longer I'm here, the less I remember what it was like to be in the body. So some of the things I said to you when I first got here are not worth remembering. Just know the only thing left between us is love. Follow your heart. When I leave, when I'm not here anymore, your life will open up…but we must finish the book, babe. What is that book about—present moment of now—everyone is talking about, good way to stay human. We've learned that on this side. I wasn't so good at it when I was in my body. I wish I had known as much, and seen as much, as I'm able to do now, but that's why I'm here. I wish I could hold you again before I go so I'll just do the best I can. Do you ever feel me lay there by you? Yes…Good. I do everything, so I can. It takes lots of focus to do these things when you don't have a body. Focused energy, one of the things I've been learning when I go off to school. I like it here too, just miss my body sometimes. What about my OBE when Thomas took me by the hand…Do I still go there, that place you said was ours on that side? *Of course, how do you think we stay so connected? But it's very hard for me too. So my giving up the body and you staying in yours is hard for both of us, but we do get to talk there. And I usually try to calm you down and comfort you. It's when you are going through your most difficult times that you come to me. Yes, you get to go. One of these days, babe, after I leave and come back, we'll make arrangements for us to meet.….one that you'll remember. Because you'll be in another relationship and it won't hurt so bad. I'm glad that you are willing to move on, that helps me out…because I have to go, they keep telling me that. I just don't want to leave you feeling stranded and you won't be. Your Dad is here and he thinks you are pretty special. I wish you could see how many people love you. And I wish you could see how much you are loved from this viewpoint. You always have lots who surround you; you just forget that we are here sometimes and then you remember and you are fine. The ups and downs of being in the body, I didn't know there were so many…The good with the bad, all of those things. I'll do better next time. I promise not to abuse the next body I get. I won't *need drugs and I won't need all those experiences that I put you and my dad through...didn't know better, now do. And I promise to remember in the next life. I'm going to have to go now...Thank you for loving me.*

For the next several weeks, I worked intently, did my research and hoped the right words would come through me. Writing a partial memoir with all the notes taken over the past five years was like putting together a huge puzzle, with even more puzzles embedded. When feeling frustrated and needing help, I would take a long walk and it would eventually come. I was determined to finish, if for no reason other than Russell, my father, and Thomas, who had diligently been beside me with such patience while I constantly badgered them for more understanding. And, furthermore, I truly wanted to finish this project for Mark and Eva, whose life I have only dreamt about; one with which I am so enamored.

Russell Says Goodbye for Now

In this linear world, endings are sometimes indescribably sad. Before I knew it, it was November 30, a day that I had dreaded. But Russell and my family were right...I had grown to depend on him and now it was time for that to end. In my heart, I knew other doors would open, as they've always done before. There will be another job in my life, another man in my life, another "time" in my life because the gift of free will is a beautiful one. We undeniably create our own life and happiness. Also, my faith in God has always been colossal and through my struggles, I had earned the right to cherish this beautiful connection. But soon it would be time to say goodbye. Russell would speak once again...

Baby, we have a very short amount of time before I leave. Just want you to know I'm going to prepare for our future life together and that I've stayed longer than I thought would be necessary but I forgot about all the distractions in your life. When I go, you are going to feel a little different without me there and I'll come back from time to time and catch up with what's going on in your life. I'm going to ask some things of you that are going to be hard but will make it easier for me, and that is...that you put away all of my pictures, all of them. Judy gets emotional, sensing Russell's feelings, and almost starts to cry, saying, "This is really hard for him," and it was for me as well. *Make a memory box of me and put everything about our life together in that box that you treasure. And get rid of everything else. This is as hard on me as it is you, babe, because I wanted us to be together forever. And we will be; I'm just taking a leave of absence from this* life we had. *The stronger we both are, the better this is going to work. Thomas is the one that will take me. So it will be easier for both of us knowing I'm in good hands. Look at it this way…it leaves more room for another man to come into your life. I take up too much space.* I used to be so concerned, Russell, about the way in which you crossed over; since you were not at your best. *It's different for each individual. Because you and Dad believed in me and wanted to do the work with me from this side, I was given special dispensation from all my misunderstandings about life and life with drugs. That's how I got rid of my addictions, I really wanted to and you were willing to help. I was given the opportunity to work with you or live out my pain in the old way. I was put on a fast track because we were willing to help others understand how things work better…from both this side and that side. Thomas was there to meet me and radiated the love I needed to make my decision. From the moment we met till the moment I died, I felt like you were my angel on Earth. When I crossed, I saw how much you loved me and I asked for help. Thomas arrived and gave me permission to make things better for you and me. You came to this Earth in this life to help others, including me, and the book is going to do that. You didn't really need me for the book but I wanted to help. I wasn't ready to lose you. So I was shown our future together, which is what the book is supposed to be about.* But I thought we were supposed to write this book that may possibly prove the theory of reincarnation? How could we have done that if you hadn't worked with me? *This book, yes, but you had other stories to write that could help humans…Other stories to share, to inspire. Proving reincarnation is not as important as reaching hearts—that helps them open up to greater possibilities… including reincarnation. Anything to break the old bonds of limitation helps the world. I want to give you my blessings and thank you for being a wonderful life partner even when we weren't living together anymore technically…it has been wonderful to be around you and still sense what it was like to love you. That brought me more joy in life than anything I can remember, it was better than a good drug high, and sorry I put you through all of that. I tripped myself up and brought a lot of people down. One of the missions you can help humans with is to understand that not every case is like mine. I was given special dispensation to work together and in my desperation to agree, I was given the gift of eliminating my addictions. Addicted humans need to know it's not easy even if you die, and it's really bad if you take your own self out. You never get away from pain, it follows you everywhere you go…if you are in hell on Earth, you are in hell on the other side. Addiction keeps you from knowing the light because the mind is so focused on getting high, it stops growing, the consciousness ceases to exist and only the five senses are what's important then. Tell Beth to get out of her mind and start being intuitive about what's best for her. Tell her every time she wants to drink, to meditate instead, developing her sixth sense. It's been a long journey, babe, and I want to tell you how much I love you, how much I have loved you and how much I will love you.*

Thanks to Judy, Russell would have a chance to visit with his dad over the phone as well. *Hey, Dad, I'm so happy you can join us today because, as you know, I'm getting ready to go and our times together won't be like this anymore. I know I've told you* (sensing Russell's sentiment again, Judy couldn't help but cry for a moment)…*since I've been on this side, that I love you. But I need you to know that I appreciate you over here more than you can imagine. You did more for me than you needed to and I didn't tell you how much I valued it at the time. I guess I was pretty spoiled but you made me that way. Thanks, Dad. I didn't realize how big your heart was until I saw how much you do after I got over here, not just for me but other people. You are one in a million. Just want to say it while I have the chance. I'm very happy that you were and are open to staying in touch with me. You and Kent have done so well in keeping my memory alive, which gave us a stronger connection. I went so suddenly, and wasn't ready to say goodbye. It's funny over here because part of me is staying but another part of me is already gone. I'm going to be teaching others who have the same troubles I had or difficulties in being on the planet. Thomas says I'm one of his best students because I was so ready to stop the insanity that I had created. Dad, you work too hard. And I don't like to see you get so worn out. You need to rest more and teach yourself how to be happy again. I think you forgot what that feels like so you just take what comes…*Judy then asked Ron if he liked to build model airplanes because Russell was sending the message to get a specific model. Ron said he had always wanted, but never built, a DC-3 and said he was just thinking about that the other day. *Yes, go get that, have fun again. Build that one for me…and when you look at it, remember me. I will leave and come back around and tell you what colors I want where. Also, play with the dog more…do things that bring your heart joy. I worry about you getting too caught up in business; you let days go by before you play.* Judy told Ron that Russell was showing her a stick horse. Ron says, yes, he had one… *Dad, play like I did when I was a little boy. Some of my happiest memories of you were when you watched me play.* Judy asked Ron if Russell ever rode the stick horse in his underwear and Ron told her yes, he even had a picture of it and he was also wearing a cowboy hat…*Dad, laugh like you laughed then. Also, I'm going to ask you to do what I asked Kent as it will be easier for me to go and that is to put my things away…all but one picture. And you know the one, you just talked about it. So that it will remind you to play. You sure did* *love me a lot, by all the things of mine you kept. They are wonderful memories but that was the best of me, I gave you some bad times, Dad, but you remember the good ones. Do something for me...write down all of the good memories of me, put that away and get it out on my birthday each year and read it. I have to go now Dad, I love you...never forget that. And now I can see how love goes and goes and goes and never stops. And that's how much I love you.*

Heading for Home

Just before my journey to New Mexico would come to an end, eleven inches of snow fell in Santa Fe. I had purchased tickets to attend a musical Christmas event at St. Francis Cathedral and meet some new friends. Most of the larger streets were cleared as I carefully drove downtown. Though I had planned to get there early for a parking spot, the streets were very crowded with tourists as well as many locals with last-minute Christmas shopping on their minds. It was nighttime and not being totally familiar with the area, I drove in circles, it seemed, looking for a parking place close to the cathedral so that I wouldn't have to walk in the ice and snow. The thought came into my head, *Drive to the plaza's paid parking area,* so I did just that, even though my analytical brain was telling me it was still far to the church. Earlier, my heart had asked for some guidance when I was feeling slightly frustrated. As I drove in, the kind attendant asked where I was headed. This sounded rather strange since I was pulling in to park. I mentioned having a ticket to attend the church event. "Ma'am, the church has a free parking lot and this security guard here will lead you there," she said. After showing my heartfelt gratitude, it was a relief to be following someone who knew where they were going. It was good to finally get settled in the church parking lot, which was obscured from the beautiful front entrance; I knew finding it was not an accident. After parking and turning off my engine, I looked up at this square, rather large security light right in front of my car, which astonishingly started getting brighter and brighter. Suddenly, it went out completely! I looked up at the light and, smiling once again, thanked my spirit guides and angels not only for getting me there, but also for giving me this sign that I was not alone—my prayers had been heard.

The next day, I was able to begin my long journey back home, grateful that my car battery died before I left and not while I was on the road. But it would be dead again in Dallas where I woke up at Ron's apartment the next morning. Long before now, we had become like brother and sister,

Love Promised: A Future Life Revealed

and I was thankful he would arrive later that day from Houston to help me buy and install a new battery. That day, before heading back to Houston, I pulled out the board to talk with Dad, but we had a surprise visitor first. Archangel Michael had beautiful words to say, then also told me, *I do have a message for u from that energetic soul Russ, he likes how you sing.* I couldn't help but laugh. Having had only four hours of sleep before leaving Santa Fe for that 11-hour trek, singing galore to the radio and my CDs, as well as downing a 5-hour energy drink, sure helped in keeping me awake!

Over the course of our five-year-long communication, we would often ask some questions for pure entertainment, not knowing what answers we might get. However, some very interesting information did come through and I was given permission to include it here. Our first discussion was prompted by Russell himself when he let us know that he had been to see a very important historical artifact, which raised our eyebrows.

The Oldest Artifact on Earth

Considered to be the most important religious artifact in history, the Ark of the Covenant remains a mystery today as no one seems to know its whereabouts. Therefore, some have even questioned the Ark's existence. Biblical history tells us that it was built by Moses to house the stone tablets inscribed with the Ten Commandments. Nevertheless, it came as quite a surprise in one of our sessions when Russell excitedly announced that, along with others, he had been to see it. *Hey, babe, we got to see the Ark of the Covenant, in a very holy temple.* Wow! Is there a known place where it can be found by us Earthlings? *It can be found, only a few know.* Interesting, will more of those on Earth be able to see it? *Someday.* My, is the secret kept by a religious sect? *Yes.* I naturally became excited and curiously wanted to know more. The following conversation was held over more than one session as he stated, *I will need to get permission,* when I started asking more questions. *I have to go now, babe, newbies crossing over, I'm being called.* Who by? *The Angels, love you, goodbye.*

A subsequent conversation followed. Russell, what can you tell me about this fascinating subject? *It is underground; one nation has it hid from another. It is still there. Many things have been kept out of the Bible. One church has not served God well in all aspects.* Where is it hidden? *Buried in temple, it is not under the dome.* Oh, the Jewish temple dome, suspected by many? *No, buried in Damascus, deep under an old market.* So one church hid it right beneath the feet of the other? *Yes.* Who hid it? *The Templars on behalf of the Catholic Church...*When did this happen? *1355 A.D.* But how did that happen, history tells us the Templars were forced to disband more than 100 years before this time? *Some Templars continued underground and were paid a large amount of money to take care of this matter.* Where is it, again? *Under market in Damascus, old market and near a well.* How many feet underground is it? *190 feet.* This is incredibly interesting. Since you've seen it, what are the dimensions of the Ark and what does it look like? *Winged handles, over 5 feet long and 3 wide.* How deep? *31 inches; it was built by the Egyptians, wings of Ra.* That's thought-provoking, I believe most have been told they are wings of cherubs and it was built by Moses. Okay, what does it contain? *Scrolls and the handle of the cane of Moses...*Wow! Does it contain the stone tablets with the Ten Commandments, as documented in history? *Not so.* Really?! Okay, sorry, Russell, I am asking questions so fast, I'm not sure you finished what else it contains, go ahead, babe...*blood of Jesus on cloth and sacrifice of spices; Mary used it to wipe feet when he was on cross.* Oh, my…and just to confirm, was that Mary Magdalene? *Yes…folded neatly in paper.* Who placed these articles in the Ark? *King David, except scrolls, and gold ring with lamb on it…* Whose ring was it? *David.* Does it contain anything else? *No.* What about the scrolls, what are they? *Directed by God, a written biography, life of Jesus as told by Peter...*The apostle? *Yes, he was the scribe.* Amazing! There are many different stories about the life of Jesus, which that would certainly clear up. Also, Russell, if there is the blood of Jesus on a cloth, then it would contain his DNA. *Yes…very powerful.* You mean because it has his energy, why so powerful? *It's like bringing him back. It's a part of God and is energy. God instructed Egyptians to build Ark and store energy. He She exists in all universes.* You mean God and in reference to the fact that this omnipotent energy is neither male nor female? *Yes. Opening the Ark opens link to all universes. Only if opened after being sealed, it can open parallel universes.* How could it open a parallel universe?! *The energy expands rapidly, sucks other parallels into it. It is the opposite of a black hole. Like nothing seen before.* This is absolutely bizarre. So it must have been true that it was carried into battle to help win wars thousands of years ago? *It was powerful and still is today. And, babe, he really did send visitors before...*You mean God, sending other avatars before Jesus? *Yes, and others too, to train ancients, spacemen.* You mean as in ancient astronaut theory? *Visitors.* And the location of the Ark again? *Damascus, originally the cave access was a well. Cannot give exact location, 39 meters NW of altar, near well. Catholics gave coins of gold to well owners to build over it.* What is built over it? *Altar.* When will it be found? *99 years after 2012.* Is

this because of the magnetic poles slightly shifting? *Yes, shifting poles.*
Soon after, I researched Wikipedia online and was concerned when I found the following information:

> Due to the rapid decline of the population of Old Damascus, a growing number of buildings are being abandoned or are falling into disrepair. Between 1995 and 2005 more than 20,000 people moved out of the old city for more modern accommodations. In March 2007, the local government announced that it would be demolishing the Old City buildings along a 1,400-metre (4,600 ft.) stretch of rampart walls as part of a redevelopment scheme. These factors have resulted in the Old City being placed by the World Monuments Fund on its 2008 Watch List of the 100 Most Endangered Sites in the world. It is hoped that its inclusion on the list will draw more public awareness to these significant threats to the future of the historic Old City of Damascus.

In another session, we told Russell how much we enjoyed seeing the movie *The Da Vinci Code.* We suspect there is some real truth there? *Some things cannot be revealed yet. About 80 percent right... Yes, a little off.* Again, we were getting some very specific information, some of which prompted even more questions that have been speculated upon by mankind throughout centuries. Some of the answers aligned with information we had previously heard about.

The Past, Present, and Future

Okay, Russell and Dad, in this game of life there is another question I would love to ask. Was there really a lost civilization called Atlantis; I've always thought this was truer than fiction? *We can tell you this, there has been advanced life on Earth before, life as you know it. All continents were joined together at that place, near Bahamas. Very advanced, Atlantis had use of laser technology. The Egyptians had equipment, some, but not modern. They had technology we don't know they had, powers given by God.* Did everyone have this power? *No, some.* Can you tell us about this technology? *U will find out one day.* You mean when we cross over? *Yes, other side.* Well, then, let me ask it like this... When will our society on Earth discover this technology again?

*Only when the majority is enlightened...*I'm not trying to be pessimistic, though I honestly don't see that happening any time soon. It does, however, remind me of a quote by Ralph Waldo Emerson: "Before we acquire great power, we must acquire wisdom to use it well." This area near the Bahamas, would you also be referring to the Bermuda Triangle where, supposedly, ships and planes have either disappeared or had their instruments quit working, showing that time was actually lost? *Folds in time...*Can you explain more? *Dimensions touch on occasion and always laws of physics change...Bends in space and time, folds and touch. Those that have experienced it have lost way on this plane. But still exist on another level.* So, as an example, is this what happened to Amelia Earhart? *Yes.* Her plane too? *Yes.*

Well, now, let's just start from the beginning. Just how old *is* mankind on this planet? *Mankind started way before. There have been 3 evolutions on Earth of mankind. As a transplant, God of everything brought his creations to Earth; man did not come from monkeys. And God and angels have visited in body. You must know that advanced life existed b4 you. Egyptians had light bulbs and Atlantis, computers. That period was one of them. It was the second of 3.* With us being the third? *Yes...and there have been nonEarth beings visiting always. You do know that the world you exist in was destroyed twice.*

Okay, this is *very* interesting but let's back up a minute...Who or what was the first evolution of mankind on Earth? *Martians.* Really, now?! *There was a civilization on Mars that migrated to Earth. God allowed use of Earth as an experiment. Mars cooled and could no longer sustain life with no atmosphere. They were also called the Alpha.* Well, that makes sense, it means the beginning; hopefully, we aren't the Omega or the ending! *No.* How was this civilization destroyed? *Alpha by fire...*Wow, you would think there would be too much water on Earth for that to happen. *No... There will be irrefutable evidence of life having existed on Mars. You can't possibly think u are alone.* And next were the Atlanteans? *Yes, and also the Lemurians and Egyptians.* Did they all live at the same time during this second evolution? *No. The Atlanteans also had lasers but their civilization ended abruptly.* How? *They created too much heat with fission.* Like a nuclear weapon? *Yes, exploded entire continents, died instantly, not much left.* So their remains are under the sea around the Bermuda Triangle, you said? *Very, very deep...As they ended abruptly a new civilization arose.* Okay, so next were the Lemurians in this second evolution? *Yes.* And I heard once the tip of their continent was what we now know as the Hawaiian Islands? *Yes.* And they were considered to be more spiritual beings whereas the Atlanteans were more technically advanced, from what I understand? *Yes, Lemurians evolved into Mayans.*

Interesting, how did the Lemurians die? *End of Ice Age and Egyptians arose after the Mayans.* What catastrophes hit the Egyptians? *Floods and disease, the Egyptians were the last.* Are you talking about the Great Flood? Was there really an ark built by Moses? *Kind of, flood was regional; certainly not every species was taken. Many believe in the dogma.*

And what was it in the Mayan civilization that caused them to think the world would end in 2012, since their calendar ends at this time? *They were shown future by visitors.* Spacemen? *Yes.* Where did they come from, and what did they show the Mayans? *Came from M204 Star system, left atomic calendar, traveled faster than light, showed future solar events.* Wow! *But you know better.* That the world is not coming to an end like some think? *Right.* Yes, I want to talk about that too in another session soon. In which parallel universe is M204? *11.* The talk of space visitors reminds me of a documentary I saw the other day. It referred to the Shag Harbour incident, which is also called the Canadian Roswell crash. Supposedly aliens crashed into the harbor and there was a big government cover-up, both U.S. and Canadian, about what they found. *There are many others out there and that did occur, Earth has been visited several times.* And the Roswell crash, what can you tell us? *2 spacecraft, 3 aliens, 2 died, 1 lived for 3 weeks...a female, died of a virus.* Did we try to save her? *Yes.* Wow. Jokingly we said, "Are we aliens?" *That depends on who you are talking to, ha ha.* Okay, you have a point! So as you said, we really were transplanted here from other star systems? *U all were, surely intelligent people don't believe that there is no other life in space. All life came to Earth from other places...Evolving slowly.*

Getting back to the so-called past, can you tell us, then, the answer to that age-old question about how the pyramids were actually built? *Slowly.* Russell! *I have the same devious humor, babe, took many to do it.* Well, you know there are numerous speculations because we do not know how the Egyptians had the means of moving this large, heavy rock at that point in time. *Okay, I have permission to say now. Levitation, only through enlightened beings, those who had lived before the Egyptians designed them; the knowledge came from past experience and spirit guides...during Atlantis. And they had light.* You mean the Egyptians? *Yes, how else could the builders see inside the pyramids? Truth is still buried with Khufu family.* Is that a tomb, I'm guessing? I've never been there or studied Egyptian history, but I've always wanted to go. *Yes, Khufu Valley... Google it.* So there would be proof inside these tombs? *Yes, light diode buried...* The equipment itself? *Like a light bulb.* And where did they get the light diode? *Brought by space visitors...* This is fascinating. [That night, I did in fact Google the name "Khufu," as we've done for other information provided, only to find that there was indeed an Egyptian family and tombs with this name.]

One other time, we spoke with Russell and asked about any personal past lives during the Atlantis civilization. Did any of us live there before? *Yes.* What did we do there? *Lee Ann a teacher of faith…like a church. She goes way back on Earth. After, I was a legal expert…u were a business owner there.* What kind of business? *Oldest profession on Earth, ha, ha.* What? As in ladies of the night?! *Ha, I am joking with you. Kent, u liked jewelry.* Yes, and I still do. *What is your favorite color?* Turquoise, was that it? *Yep, you had a jewelry store.* Well, that makes sense. I didn't realize, though, that I have liked turquoise jewelry for quite *that* long! *You were also a high priestess in another life there. Flash! Becky was on Atlantis.* Oh, please tell; she will get a kick out of this. *Yes, owned stables, very wealthy.* Wow, her passion for horses is still with her today. *We must go. Don't be gone so long…miss talking to you.* Okay babe. *Although I talk to you all the time, u just don't always hear me. Thank you and love you both.*

A Few Notes of Interest

Every now and then Russell and Dad did offer some interesting comments about the future, some of which are included here.

1. *There is a scientist in Germany who will turn back the aging gene.*
2. *There is proof that the Knights Templar arrived in the new country a short time after the date of 1362 and before Columbus. In Kensington, Minnesota, there is buried a hook and arrow 160 feet below what is now a sacred Indian tribal ground. There are stone steps underground leading to it.*
3. *A living mammoth will be cloned from frozen DNA.* (Ron and I had never heard of this but in researching, we found the idea has been conceptualized.)
4. *There is proof that you are not alone in a melting glacier, Finland Fiord.* Will this be proof of what we think of as an alien? *Yes, tools that were used to help before current life forms.*

Love Promised: A Future Life Revealed

5. *The Supercollider in Geneva, Switzerland, will be fast enough to create dark matter. Create antimatter and you have dark energy as a by-product. Scientists are about to make a major discovery but it will be kept secret for a while.*
6. *Proof of parallel universes will occur in 2019.*

Our Commitments to God — The Most Important of All

Russell, once you mentioned that God did not give man Ten Commandments, but only commitments. And thinking back to reading *Conversations with God* by Neale Donald Walsch, there too they were referred to as commitments. You stated before, "*Why would God command people who could not live up to it? He gave us free will but laid out the goals.*"

If indeed it is "committing" and not "commanding," I believe it is essential for us to know the original words of God, so that we can understand the intent behind them. I was told to look up the definition for these words and, indeed, there is an enormous difference between the two meanings. Webster's dictionary defines the word "commitment" as "an agreement or pledge to do something in the future, to carry into action deliberately"; while the word "commandment" means "the act or power of commanding." Furthermore, the definition for "command" is "an order given, the ability to control, the power to dominate, to direct authoritatively." One allows for agreement and choice whereas the other lets us be controlled and gives us no freedom to choose. Thus, it makes perfect sense to me why God would not command us, having given us the gift of free will. So when the two words are juxtaposed, there is an obvious contradiction.

Therefore, I would be ever so grateful if you and Thomas could give me the list of God's original commitments. Russell gave me the first three, then said…*Thomas is here now*. Thomas continued the list. *Let me add, the words were changed slightly by the Catholics. There are 12.*

1. *Don't wish for something you don't have, God gives us all power to have all we really want.*
2. *Don't covet.*
3. *Honor parents for they are teachers.*
4. *Don't lie; bad karma.*
5. *Love your neighbors as yourself.*

6. *Honor the body given to you.*
7. *Do not purposefully take a life.*
8. *Trust the inner soul.*
9. *Do not take from another what is not yours.*
10. *Believe in a higher force and have faith together.*
11. *Open your mind's eye.*
12. *Love the Earth as your Mother.*

Russell then tells me...*He has left now, babe.* Guiding over 5,000 souls, Russell says, St. Thomas stays pretty busy. I'm always appreciative that I can call on him knowing he is there, whether on the board or not...and knowing that my prayers are being heard.

Russell went on to say, however...*They are not written down, mental.* All not written, just mental, you are saying? *Right.* So, just to be sure, these words were not really inscribed on Moses's tablet written about in the biblical story? *God spoke to Moses. Many stories evolved that were put in the Bible. Baby, one religion alone does not own the whole story. Many of the popes were corrupt.* Did St. Thomas back in thirteenth century believe in reincarnation? *He did. Pope did not.* Did he want to write about reincarnation and the pope wouldn't let him? *He would have been killed. Many were persecuted in the name of the church.* Well, that certainly violates commitment number seven, hence the corruptness. Can I put this in the book? *Yes, but don't slam them.* Just to be sure, who? *Catholics.* It's confusing to me that you say we *must* experience it all, but then also we are given the commitments. *Yes, how does a soul reach the ultimate ability to live by the commitments?* How? *By failure.* Dad, then...have I killed in a past life, or stolen and pillaged? *Yes, LOL.* I guess you are laughing out loud at the shocking way that I have asked this question, not at the fact of what I did in a past life. *Yes, of course.* (Russell chimes in) *Long ago, not very evolved, you did so in battle, but you were mean, ha.* Really? *Just not as nice as Eva.* So, I guess this is all part of the game, part of God's experiment, as you've referred to it before? *Yes.*

One other time when talking with Dad, I asked if Satan was actually an angel cast out of heaven. *Just like people, there are angels who have not yet reached love. There is no satanic hell.* Was there an angel called Satan? *I'm telling you that there is so much left out of the Bible. As interesting as it is, there are 41 missing chapters.* Unbelievable! I had heard there were some but not that many. Where are these missing chapters? *12 are found but not included.* Were these books removed by Catholics in the 1500s as some suspect?

Love Promised: A Future Life Revealed

Yes. And reincarnation is part of what they took out? *Yes, the majority of religions accept reincarnation.* Why did the Catholics take so much out of the Christian Bible? *They wanted control and to bring all the religious factions under one set of rules. Jesus reincarnated 40 years after he died on the cross.* Who did he reincarnate as? *A Jewish prophet...He also raised the son of a woman from dead. There is a book by Judas missing from the Bible that speaks of this event. Book of Judas is one of the 12 found, it is opening their eyes.* You mean the Catholic priests who are now reading it? *Yes.* Does the book of Judas speak of reincarnation? *No.* Dad, is there an anti-Christ today? *A leader of many lower souls institutes war in middle...I cannot say who. The land of Abraham will prevail.* What about the rapture that is talked about in the Bible, Revelation? *Many people believed the world was flat. It is not as bad as many think. The world will not end, Earth goes on and God will end the experiment at some point but live for today.*

Saints and Angels

On January 1, 2011, we planned a session to wish our soul buddies a Happy New Year, hoping also to get some answers to questions. The following conversation ensued...*Dear, this is Saint Catherine. The others you requested are not here.* Oh, hello, we've not spoken with you before... *No, not directly.* Is it just you on the other side? *Yes.* So you are saying that they will not be able to come today? We are just surprised, this has never happened before. *Souls not here, won't be available, they are on upper level.* Would you be able to stay and answer questions? *I came as an emissary. I was asked to let you know one unanimous wish from all is Happy New Year.* Well, please tell everyone thanks and sorry they couldn't come today. *The souls you seek are planning their return.* Oh, back to Earth? *Yes.* That must be a large working-group session, to plan lives together. I can't even imagine. *Many...I am familiar with you as Eva.* Oh! Did we share that lifetime together? *In England.* From what I understand, King Henry II brought me to the Tower of London, away from the war in Ireland, when my husband, Richard de Clare or rather, Strongbow, died, as it was not safe for me to stay. *I led you out of England...London. I gave you an emerald necklace.* Oh, what a beautiful gift, and this was when I moved to Northern England? *Yes.* Were you a female then? *Yes. Heidel surname, Ann.* So it was Catherine Ann Heidel? *Yes.* Could I Google the name for that time period in history? *I think so, I do not Google.* But of course you don't, my apologies for asking. Was that your last incarnation? *Yes, I serve on a higher level.* My, so you are a saint too. I had some confusion about angels and saints as guides and was trying to clarify for the book, maybe you could help me out. *Angelic souls do not incarnate, saints can. My dear, the souls ask me to leave the answers to them. Goodbye.* Knowing how "time" is different over there compared with here, Ron and I tried a few minutes later. *Not now, honey, Dad here and now gone, luv u…* and the oracle very quickly swept across the bottom of the board…*Goodbye.*

Another time Dad answered our questions about saints and angels. *Angels have no wings; the description of wings came about in the 1300s, metaphor started by Catholics. Glow or aura can appear as wings. They are teachers, the highest guides. There are several levels of angelic service. Archangels never enter body. Neither do guides, but 7th-level angels can enter body only temporarily to facilitate channeling.* So angels can be guides? *Can serve as either.*

The Stage of Life

These commitments or goals all made sense. And I do love the two not previously mentioned throughout history. Yes, it is high time we started using our third eye, the one which our soul uses to see. And it's no secret today that Mother Earth, who has provided us our beautiful home to live, should be taken better care of. Since humans are considered to be imperfect beings, God would not command us to be perfect. Though our soul is a perfect spark of creation, we arrive on Earth as an imperfect human. On a soul level, we are not only aware of this; we also chose it to be this way. It's part of the game. We open the curtain or veil and step onto the stage of life with purpose and, being mindful, we get in character, forgetting who we really are. Then after what is sometimes a long play, we step off the stage and return to God, who loves us unconditionally and understands the drama this life experience on Earth entails. Knowing the lives and roles we choose to create for ourselves, God knows we will have miss-takes. We elected to experience the burden for whatever reason, but if we are not open to our loved ones on the other side—our spirit guides, angels, and God—then we remain separate and block the energy, the help we need, and continue to suffer more than necessary. Hence the famous poem "Footprints" that was so beautifully written some time ago.

Like a parent, God is sitting in the audience watching us play our roles in life, knowing quite well we agreed to the script and even practiced it beforehand. But the real challenge is how well we play these roles when we get on that stage of life because we are also given the right to improvise, to choose using our God-given free will, once we get here. Families choose to come together because it is these souls who are our allies before coming here. We choose to take on the difficult role of helping one another learn forgiveness and acceptance of who we are. With that comes compassion and love...our path home. Forgiveness has to start with oneself, and for some, this is extremely difficult.

Through study and personal experience, it is my belief that as multilevel beings, we each leave our bodies at night, stepping off the stage—an intermission of sorts to ask our assistant directors, or spirit guides, "Hey, how am I doing? What can I do differently or better?" Quite possibly, the likely reply is, "Just listen, I'm guiding you every step of the way!" for we get wonderful counseling upon returning and awakening. It is not by coincidence that when we are faced with a difficult decision, someone may say, "Just sleep on it." *Life has a mysterious way of leading us to our destiny,* I'm told.

Sometimes we just can't see the larger picture from where we stand. Though we, with God, may have a better plan down the road, if our fear of the unknown or fear of change causes us to remain stagnant or frustrated, we might miss the opportunity which leads to our happiness. Over-anxiousness could be creating the fear of not having, and actually pushing away from us what it is that we want. Naturally, sometimes we don't play these roles to the best of our ability. But not trying is our only true mistake or missed opportunity.

God will allow us as many performances as we need till we get it near-perfect, and to our own satisfaction. The curtain closes with each lifetime, we step off that stage and all the antagonists and protagonists who were with us in the play are there cheering us on. "Good job! That is probably one of the most difficult roles you've chosen for yourself." Isn't it true that after a big theater production, the actors and actresses all celebrate and later feel the comfort of being at home? I tend to think it is very much the same with our lives. And possibly someone like Shakespeare was given the insight to attempt to show humanity what life is really all about. And, are we possibly just pulses of light going on and off so fast, beyond the speed of light, that it appears we are moving from a past to a present and then a future? When you run still pictures through a movie camera do you see still pictures or pictures in motion? For those on the other side, watching us may be like watching a movie in 3-D. And I'm sure they would like to tell us, if we could hear them better, "Hey, don't take your life so seriously this time, enjoy it more. If you only knew...it's just a movie."

When we begin to see ourselves for who we truly are, we will change the perception of ourselves and the human race will change as a result. True, we are but caterpillars beginning to plow our way out of the cocoon on the way to becoming a beautiful butterfly. So don't be dismayed by what you see and hear on the news today, there is a lot going on behind the scenes. We know about our conscious mind and even the subconscious mind, but what about cosmic consciousness? We are slowly becoming enlightened beings, and some are already there, just waiting for the rest of us to wake up. We should never stop questioning and, with an open mind, never say never to the possibilities that can be, just because our little minds cannot yet conceive it. As William Shakespeare said, "There are more things in heaven and earth, Horatio, than are dreamt of in your philosophy."

Now, on a scientific level, we're beginning to have an inkling of how all this works. We don't have to use our little mind to make every decision, for it resides in the world of duality and the ego that wants to think it is in control. Our decisions must come from the heart, or within, using our third eye, the part of us that is connected to God. For there is no second-guessing; you feel it, and you know it. Because we have been victims of victims for so many years, we've programmed ourselves on a very subatomic level—possibly even during past lives of which we are not consciously aware. And because of this, we've grown to accept our anxieties, shortcomings, depression, anger, our self-defeating way of life, not even realizing what we are doing to ourselves. Thus we keep recreating the same event and the same mistakes all over again. And I would venture to say, we have a collective consciousness that has created everything that is happening on planet Earth today. We are evolving, and most large-scale change doesn't happen overnight in our dimension, where we do measure time and space. But it does start with each and every one of us—one person, one thought, one image, one belief at a time. And we can only do our best to live by this beautiful message from St. Thomas, "*With self comes love of self, with love of self comes trust in self, with trust in self comes great peace.*"

As everyone keeps telling us, it's that still, small voice within…the gentle nudge, the quiet thoughts when your mind is at peace. Now we know how to change that negative programming. We know it is a game…games are fun! As humans living in this fourth dimension, it's inherent in us that we challenge ourselves. We understand that we deliberately came here to experience duality of life, to embrace one another, to play, to learn, to grow. When we've balanced our karma and experienced it all, we no longer need to come back to this dimension of duality. But we may choose to come back

Love Promised: A Future Life Revealed

and help another along their path of knowing. Eventually, we lose our desires and only aspire to be home, at peace, at one with God. There is nothing left to achieve. We have reached our pinnacle. Then, as stated in the *Silver Cord, Lifeline to the Unobstructed,* "How do we know, as a soul, when we have completed the evolutionary process? How do we know when we are ready to merge back with our source?" And the simple answer was: "Oh, you know, do you know when you are thirsty?"

A Very Humble Thank-You

Words can't describe my gratitude for the assistance in writing this book and the information provided herein. Russell; my father, Wick; and Thomas were called many a time over the last six years. Furthermore, by request, they would often offer advice regarding the personal situations of a few, even when free will may have altered the path one was on and the possibility or prediction given no longer existed in this dimension. *There are many roads to one destiny. Sometimes we see them all,* they would say. As bittersweet as our "talks" were, it is wonderful that personalities continue on to the other side, as they also love to joke and tease. Our sessions could be quite entertaining. In our communications, we are often reminded that their existence is like a duplicate of being on Earth but without all the poverty, killing, pollution, and negativity. *We are free to create whatever it is that we want,* they say. And I think on our level we can too, we still just have so much left to learn. Watching over all of us has been my faithful spirit guide, St. Thomas, who, I'm told, has been my guide in many lifetimes. I am humbled by his servitude and also that of Archangel Michael, who graced us with his presence on the board several times. And, I'm told Archangel Gabriel watches over my family's lifeline, as I'm sure he does many others'. We've been told that when we shed the denser body, the appearance we take on is that of our last life incarnation, healthy and vibrant, appearing to be approximately the human age of 30. For this reason, included below is a picture of my father as a younger man, though he crossed at the physical age of 76, in 1995. Russell crossed at the age of 31 in December 2005. Also pictured below is a seventeenth-century sculpture of the young Thomas of Aquinas, located in a museum in Bratislava, Slovakia. Thomas was an Italian priest of the Dominican order who lived, this lifetime, in the thirteenth century and is still considered today the most influential philosopher and theologian of the Catholic Church. I'm told this was his last incarnation on Earth. Much of his work, better known as Thomism, is, according to history, based on metaphysical philosophy carried over from Aristotle. Russell and Dad tell me that although Thomas was very knowledgeable about many previous works, his was directly inspired by God. Also known as the Angelic Doctor, he was declared a saint by the Catholic Church 50 years after his death. The pictures of Archangels Michael and Gabriel are ones I took in St. Michael's Church, in Sitka, Alaska. They both gifted me with an orb, Michael showing me his heart, Russell said, and Gabriel too. Each has left us a brief message that is included below their picture.

Russell Morris
"You are the writer of your own life"

Wick Smith
"Love, laugh, and learn"

Archangel Gabriel
"If you are not happy
with your life on Earth,
you have only
yourself to blame"

Archangel Michael
"Go and spread love"

St. Thomas of Aquinas
"With trust in self
comes great peace"

Love Promised: A Future Life Revealed

Future Life Synopsis

Over the course of these past six years, I was given details about Russell's and my future lives as Mark Wexford and Eva Stone. Much of this information was revealed all throughout the story, as it was received; however, all details have been compiled below.

CANADA (beginning in 2023)

Mark Allen Wexford (Russell) (to be born January 28, 2023) and Evangeline Marie Stone (Kent) (to be born May 11, 2028) will grow up together as childhood friends on the corner of Pine and Little Oak Streets in, Oakville, a small suburb of Toronto. They will each have a scooter and have a pile-up, with Eva getting a scar on her leg. Eva's nickname in school will be "Em." They are of Scandinavian and Norwegian descent, tan with blond hair, and good features. He is 6'2", good-looking, and she is 5'9", fair skinned, hot. Eva's father, Ben Stone, is a lawyer and her mother is Heather Stone. She is a housewife. Heather will be 2 inches taller than Ben. When Eva is 10 years of age, she will visit her father at his office in the Flatiron Building. It will occupy the entire third floor. At first Eva will be afraid of this historic building, but then she will remember it from this (a previous) lifetime. Eva will have one brother, two years older than she, named Karl, and a much younger sister, Mary Helen, born 14 years after Eva. (Kent's mother, Jane Smith in this lifetime will be her brother, Karl.) They will be very close as siblings. Mark's father, Andrew Wexford, is a pediatric surgeon, and his mother's name is Olivia Wexford. Andrew will come from Ireland to the US with his parents at the age of 17, but he will live temporarily in Pennsylvania before moving to Oakville. Mark's father, Andrew, has a twin. They are called Andy and Adam. Mark will have one sister 3 years older (8 years older than Eva), named Yvonne (to be born 2020), whose spirit is his Aunt Vickey in this lifetime. Mark will have a birthmark on his right leg that looks like a star or maple leaf. At the age of 17, he will spend a summer in France attending school.

Mark and Karl (Eva's brother) will be best friends. Together with Eva, they will have fun ice-skating as teenagers—the three of them will be "great buddies." One day, Mark and Karl will pick Eva up from a birthday party in honor of twin brothers Rick and Nick Lowderback, at 1890 Beach Walk. Along this street not far from Little Oak, a new seawall will be built because the water level will rise over the years. Yvonne, Mark, Karl, and Eva will attend Trafalgar High School. Foolish kids—Mark and Eva will fall for each other but she will be too young, so their parents will keep them apart. Mark will go to college at the University of Quebec and Eva will have a "wild hair" and eventually go to Brigham Young University in Utah with her best girlfriend, for one year. (Eva's best friend will be the reincarnation of Susan Etheridge, Kent's first cousin in this lifetime.) Eva will enjoy mountain climbing while there. She loves mountains and the snow. One Thanksgiving, when Eva is of age, the Wexfords invite the Stones over when they learn Mark is bringing Lucy, his girlfriend, home. Mark's mother, Olivia, knew that sparks once flew between Mark and Eva. She hopes to rekindle the attraction that was once there. (Also, Olivia doesn't care for Lucy.) Eva makes cookies and brings them to the dinner. She will be like a spark that reignites Mark's heart. The next day, Friday, Mark, Karl, and Eva spend time together ice-skating, just as they did when they were growing up. That night Eva slips while standing next to Mark on the top step of the plaza at the skating rink in downtown Toronto. He catches her and they kiss. Russell says, "It is like magic." They will not be able to stay apart and are "head over heels" for each other as they mature; he is 24 and she is 19. Mark and Eva will like to ski. They will one day dance together in the snow in downtown Toronto. And on Church Street, they will walk holding hands in the winter snow, wrapped in each other's arms to keep warm. One of their favorite places is the old Flatiron building.

Mark will give Eva a 3-carat, pear-shaped diamond engagement ring. They will be married when Eva and Mark are 20 and 25 years of age, respectively. They will have a grand wedding in downtown Toronto at St. Paul's on Bloor Street, a beautiful, historic Anglican Church associated with the Royal Commonwealth Society of Canada. The wedding will be held Saturday, August 22, 2048. Eva's younger cousin, Cammy Braken (Kent's sister Lee Ann in the current lifetime) will also attend this grand wedding as a 13-year-old with her father, a successful businessman and owner of the Drake building in Montreal. Cammy will wear a blue dress to the wedding and have blue flowers flowing in her golden locks of hair.

[As adults, Kent's daughter Beth and her niece Chloe (Lee Ann's daughter) in this lifetime will see an article featuring elaborate weddings planned across

Canada and will visit Toronto as tourists. They will bring Eva photos of Kent, and a daffodil, knowing she will like yellow. Eva will get their addresses and send them a thank-you card.]

After the wedding, limos will take everyone to the wedding reception at the Sky Bar in the CN Tower which overlooks Toronto. They will honeymoon on the island of Bali in Indonesia. Eva will join Mark "hand in hand" at the University of Quebec. They will live in an apartment while they are in school. Their parents will be able to help them financially. Mark will get a degree in literature with a minor in journalism. Eva will get a degree in corporate finance and public relations. Eventually, Mark will become a writer and work for a magazine and also part-time for the British Broadcasting Company (BBC). He will write guest articles for the Toronto Star. Eva will become an elected official and work at City Hall downtown. Later she will move up to the state house or the Federal building and have a seat in Ontario's parliament. She will be an alpha female. Having worked in the aerospace industry as Kent, Eva will be a big supporter of Canada's involvement in space. Karl will be a college counselor and Yvonne will be one "bad ass" attorney. She will work in the criminal building in downtown Toronto, which was the original City Hall, and will be married to a man named Maxwell H.

Mark and Eva will live in downtown Toronto because it is close to where Eva works. By the time they are 36 and 31, they will live between 8 and 12 on Washington Avenue, where they will remain for 19 years. They will attend a church called St. Thomas at the end of Washington Avenue. (There is a connection to this church—Kent's spirit guide in this lifetime, who is St. Thomas of Aquinas.)

While living on Washington Avenue, they will have 3 children—twin girls 8 years of age named Cambell Jane Wexford and Rachel Hanna Wexford, and a son, 3 years of age, named Derrick Julian Wexford. (Derrick will someday be the father of who is now Ron Morris, Russell's father, in this lifetime.) Mark and Eva Wexford and their family will also have a nanny, and two cocker spaniels named Winnie and Mack, and a cat named Cassie. Cambell, Rachel, and Derrick will have straight blond hair and will be tall for their age. They will learn to ski and will go on family ski vacations. They will also learn to ice-skate. Mark and Eva will buy a scooter, like the ones they had, for their kids. Like her dad, Rachel will have a birthmark that looks like a star. Their home on Washington Avenue will have the smell of lemon and will have family pictures all over the walls. Eva will have the inside of the house painted yellow and it will have a beautiful stained glass window on the front. Yellow is Eva's color. They will someday build a lake house off Lakeshore and 8th Street in Oakville, which on one side, extends 15 feet out over the water, with a beautiful view.

The kind of marriage and family life that Mark and Eva will have will be one most couples only dream about. They met as Russell and Kent in this lifetime to get the agreements for their next life carved "in stone."

In 2007, a clear acrylic plaque was left in Canada, which will be found in the future. The plaque is inscribed with the words "Mark and Eva Wexford, aka Russell and Kent 2007." At some point in Mark's and Eva's lives, they will begin to research the names Russell and Kent.

An event will open the door for this book, *Love Promised: A Future Life Revealed*, to be found by Mark's best friend, Julian, 41 years of age. He will find it in an off-the-beaten-path bookstore in Toronto. Julian will read it, be amazed, and then give it to Mark at his 44th-birthday celebration. They are skeptical but fascinated with the specific details that align with their lives. Two years later, on July 24, 2067, a time capsule will be discovered containing the original first-draft manuscript and many other items that will prove the existence of their previous life. Once it is found, Mark and Eva will "face the revelation together" as events, dates, places, and names that have been foretold in this book, 40 years before it all happened, may prove the theory of reincarnation. The subject, which cannot be denied, will present itself to the public but will cause much scrutiny among the followers of Christianity. An important interview with the media will ensue, of which Mark and Eva will be a part.

To Be Continued...

Note: Russell has said that our lives will be somewhat like those of the couple in the movie *The Notebook*, except reversed. *The Notebook* tells the story of a couple who fell in love in a town called Seabrook. Mark and Eva will live till they are old and grey and will die together the same day, minutes apart, of old age, as did the two main characters in the movie. Russell and Kent also fell in love in the little town of Seabrook, Texas. They became very emotional when seeing the movie in the theater, as they identified themselves with the characters, but it was during this time that they were going their separate ways. Russell says, "Eva loves yellow and her tears will be yours."

Love Promised: A Future Life Revealed

For Mark and Eva — As Time Goes By — Where or When

Ron surprisingly found a CD in the backseat pocket of his Suburban and then he received a message from Russell to tell me about it. The seventh song on the Rod Stewart CD *As Time Goes By* is entitled "Where or When,"[3] with the following lyrics:

> It seems we stood and talked like this before
> We looked at each other in the same way then
> But I can't remember where or when
> The clothes you're wearing are the clothes you wore
> The smile you are smiling you were smiling then
> But I can't remember where or when
>
> Some things that happened for the first time
> Seem to be happening again
> And so it seems that we have met before
> And laughed before, and loved before
> But who knows where or when
>
> Some things that happened for the first time
> Seem to be happening again
> And so it seems that we have met before
> And laughed before, and loved before
> But who knows where or when
> Who knows where or when

A copy of this CD with the song "Where or When," along with the movie *The Notebook*, has been placed in the time capsule.

Epilogue

We are made wise not by the recollection of our past,
but by the responsibility for our future.
—George Bernard Shaw

Someone with whom I worked and who was aware of our communication one day posed what I thought was a logical question with regard to reincarnation, one that anyone might have. Also, he was aware of almost all the information that had come to light about the details of my supposed future life. His question was, "What's the purpose of us being here if our life is already laid out beforehand?" My answer was, I've learned through a lifelong study of metaphysics that we are here to experience who we really are without a mask of any kind—to know oneself, to love oneself, and to see the beauty in all nature. And to eventually see and understand how we are truly reflections of one another and of this omnipotent power that created us.

Also, there is free will, which, I'm told is almost as strong as destiny. I may have already agreed to on some level, or chosen for myself, where I will be born, and into which family; to whom I will be married and the children I will have; where I will go to school and my future profession. But these are all roles I will play in life…child, student, adult, lover, wife, mother, politician, grandmother. And, I don't think God is concerned as to whether we play the role of a janitor or the president of some large company. At some point throughout our many opportunities of role choices over many lifetimes, we may have done both. What's really important is how well Eva will play those roles and whether she will accomplish everything she set out to do. In other words, do I know for sure what kind of wife, mother, or politician I will be when I'm Eva? Once we become human, we take on the ego. Do I know how she will react to negative experiences or choices that she may be faced with, or to the negative experiences of others who are just as important to her? Will she eventually understand that her unfounded fears of losing the one with whom she is in love to a tragic accident will have nothing to do with her current life? And how will she let those unfounded fears affect her relationship with others around her? Do I know for sure how I, as Eva, will treat others and whether it will be with love and kindness? Will I adhere to the "commitments" that our creator has outlined for us all? I don't know. I simply don't know.

These are the decisions I will make when coming back to this Earth experience which some call the school of relationships. What has been planned on a soul level is the potential to have a beautiful and wonderful life, a heaven on Earth. I will come back and try once again to live by the rules of the game, our commitments to God, each and every step of the way, and to help others do the same. And the only one who will determine whether or not I've done that is me, with God's unbiased love and assistance. I believe in my heart that God loves unconditionally and does not judge us; consequently, there is no need for forgiveness on his or her part. The art of forgiveness is learned by the soul, manifested in human form, as a useful tool and positive emotion that brings us back in alignment with who and what we really are—pure love in motion. When the majority of our society can learn the art of forgiveness, then and only then, we can raise the vibration of this planet. When we learn that condemnation is born from the ego out of fear that keeps us from seeing the reality in ourselves, we will awaken and won't feel a need to condemn anymore. Intellectually knowing how this works and practicing it are two different things. But you can't even practice it if you don't know how it works. That's why we must understand it, learn it, and then practice it on ourselves first. If we can accomplish this part, forgiveness and compassion, instead of self-condemnation, it becomes easier to practice on someone else. There are no words that can teach us this for it comes from the heart and is something that can only be experienced, which is why we are here.

I think it also must be remembered that the art of forgiving does not absolve one of the consequences of their choices. These natural scientific laws of cause and effect cannot be broken, hence our need to understand them. They are part of God's grand design, always there and always available to help us get back on track when necessary, unlikely though it seems at the time. We humans are such creatures of habit. Sometimes, we are not aware of the change that needs to be made, so we keep having the same difficult experiences over again and wonder why. Then we become more aware and eventually learn to make a better choice for our highest good, and to assist others to do the same. I believe many of these commitments can be experienced within a lifetime, or it may take several lifetimes to learn to live only by these. If there is truly no such thing as time, then we can create, along with other souls, as many lifetimes as we need to grow spiritually. Once we've learned to create our own paradise here on Earth, we will have created one for ourselves on another level. Knowing ourselves is the key. And for every lost soul, there is one who is showing him or her the way, whether it is a relative, friend, spirit guide, or one of God's angels. And who's to say that soul is really lost? Maybe it's your soul mate who, on another level before coming here, chose to help you realize the goodness in someone like themselves when nobody else could.

I thought more and more about what I had said to my friend at work when I told him I thought we were truly reflections of God. When you look into a mirror and you see your reflection, that is not really you, it is just the reflection. So what is it that is doing the looking? Just because we are on this seemingly long journey doesn't mean we are separated from this omnipotent power any more than a pebble of sand is from the beach, or a drop of water is from the ocean. Many years ago one of God's greatest creations was brought here to help bring us out of the pit of ignorance that mankind was experiencing on Earth. And he said, "These things that I do, ye can do also, and even greater things." Maybe it is time that we begin to explore the possibilities and really start using *all* of our God-given faculties, believing in the concept that we can do greater things. Jesus was trying to set an example before and after he died. He told us, showing us long ago when he appeared and spoke after shedding his physical body, that we do not die. Yes, these are the things that we can do also; and even greater things. So maybe it's time to take that leap of faith that is sometimes necessary before one can know. And only you will know for yourself the truth of anything that you focus on…For it is the path that we must all take, but not alone; it just seems that way sometimes. I think there is some truth to the statement that when you can expand your mind, you can expand your possibilities. And it was Ralph Waldo Emerson who stated, "Great men are they who see that the spiritual is stronger than any material force—that thoughts rule the world."

Well, I think it's time now. And what I've come to believe is that what we call the Battle of Armageddon is not at the end, for there is no end or beginning, just infinity and eternity. The Battle of Armageddon, more philosophically, is all throughout the journey of living in this world of duality.

Love Promised: A Future Life Revealed

It is the silent struggle of either listening to our ego mind or that soft voice within. But I don't like to think of it as a battle, for both are necessary to have this experience of being human. The ego is symbolic of the darkness because it is blind to the truth, and the inner voice is the light leading us on the path. The two are interwoven in this fabric of physicality. Sometimes we may need the ego to deal with life situations while living in this dichotomy of being human. But in all cases, our inner voice is the one that, when listened to, will guide us to our destiny. Knowing and understanding ourselves and how we truly operate is the key to loving ourselves. And loving ourselves is necessary before we can truly love another or attract one other into our life where the love is exchanged equally—body, mind, and soul.

It was important many years ago, with the discovery of Newton's laws of motion and their relation to gravity, that we understand the laws governing matter in order to cooperate with nature and to better mankind. It is just as important now, that we must try to understand the laws of the non-physical universe and apply them in our life every day. From a layman's perspective, the most profound impact that the theory of quantum physics may have on the world, when we fully understand the concept, is giving us, as humans, the ability to see ourselves in our daily interactions with others. I sincerely believe this is what can help lift the illusion our ego strives to understand and conquer or accept. It will not only help us to look at ourselves through observant eyes but also out into the world with insightful eyes. It can also help us to focus on what we want or need to change on an individual level. Understanding how this works on a more scientific level can make it more believable for some. Truly, belief is preeminent when creating our lives. And on a global level, any attempt that will bring together humanity is an essential one...The ISS is one of these. In addition to the much-needed scientific research, I do hope that our governments, working together, will continue to support our scientific and human spaceflight programs. It is one positive endeavor that can bring the species on our planet together and rejuvenate on a global scale our sense of wonder, discovery, oneness, and peace of mind. Exploration is our heritage...and our future.

Communication is the key, not just between dimensions, but even more so when it comes to how we, as human beings, verbally and nonverbally interact with one another. When we can do this more effectively here on Earth, one by one we can make this world a better place to live, truly my heart's desire. I do hope that scientists continue to study, prophesy, experiment, evaluate, compare, debate, contemplate, analyze, and test to discover more about the fundamental laws of nature and how things work.

At the same time, there are some very real synchronistic personal experiences happening in the world that should not go unnoticed as they may be trying to tell us something very important.

Again, should we wait for scientists to make a statement about what they believe or agree on as a fact? Or should we listen to our own internal guidance system and choose to embrace what many of us already know in our hearts to be true? I think it is a must because of the sheer implications this knowledge could have for our lives, today more than ever, when changes for the betterment of mankind and our planet are so imperative. Our choices affect our reality, our reality becomes our experience, and experience is often the best teacher.

In conclusion, though we have had many surprises in our search for answers to explain the unexplainable, our findings seem to fit well with the many authors of metaphysical literature and even some theoretical science. And in some cases it has even shed a new light of understanding this impeccable world in which we live. Thomas, Russell, and my father, Wick, tell us that God's world is very simple, but there are some things just too difficult for the human brain to understand.

I appreciate wholeheartedly Russell helping me, along with Thomas and my father, to tell our story, one that will continue throughout time, whatever that may truly be. And to all who have made it to the end of this book, I hope you have enjoyed this journey. Though emotionally challenging and intellectually stimulating, it has pushed my own beliefs to a new level of understanding and through this I have learned to accept much more as my truth. Moreover, I do hope that it will give you, the reader, a new perspective for your own journey in life regardless of where your perceptions begin or your beliefs end. We all have challenging and intriguing experiences and, no doubt, yours have been mysterious as well. For as Albert Einstein, whom I have often quoted, says, "The most beautiful thing we can experience is the mysterious. It is the source of all true art and science."

My constant questioning, however, did lead to an unexpected visitor with a message during one of our last sessions in 2010. *My child, you have done well.* Is this Dad? *No.* Oh, is this Thomas?! *No, it is Archangel Michael.* Oh, my…as with my guide, St. Thomas, I am always humbled by your presence. *There is much you cannot know now but be thankful for what you have learned. You have an incredible yearn to know.* Michael would go on to give me a beautiful message and then, of course, I had another question, which he gave me permission to ask. Archangel Michael, I was told by a monk and my guide, Thomas, that I would have an epiphany…that I would be touched by an angel and my daughter as well. However, a friend told me she thought it had already happened and I'm wondering if this is true. *You have not had that experience yet. It will be unmistakable. Your father is here, I am taking my leave.*

For all those who also continue to have enduring questions in your search for truth...May we never stop in our quest to find it. And may we all be touched by angels.

Kent

Author's Letter
To All Those Who Have Lost a Loved One

I do know the shock of this loss can seem unbearable at times. And when the shock wears off, the screaming and crying eventually subside. Because there are no more tears left to cry, you may stare aimlessly into space or frantically search for anyplace their voice was recorded so you can listen to it over and over again. You somehow manage to fall asleep at night, only to wake up with the reality of what has happened and the tears start to flow once again. The depression and despair can sink in…the trauma leaves a scar on your heart that you think will never heal.

I know they were the love of your life…and still are. I know that no matter how much time seems to pass, in the beginning and possibly for years, your thoughts of them will not be fleeting. They are daily, heartfelt memories of days gone by and you wonder what it would be like if they were still here. Even when you have worked through the grief in as healthy a manner as possible, you can still break down uncontrollably. You try to conceal your grief at times when it comes on without warning, such as when you are in public places. There are triggers that will always be there…no matter how much time passes, it seems. You will think about the moments that they will never show up at your front or back door again, or call again. Your heart sinks when you realize that you can no longer lie beside them. If you lost a child, you may always wonder what they would have looked like while growing up or who they would marry. No more will you get to see them do the things they did so well or buy them a gift to watch them smile. No more will you get to laugh, sing, tease, hold a hand, or hug or kiss them again…or just look into their eyes and say, "I love you." The songs, the special places, the events, the friends…there will always be reminders on a daily basis that they are no longer a part of your life as they once were…I feel your pain and my heart goes out to you.

Please know that your loved one is with you as you grieve. When they are not right there beside you, they still feel your pain because you are linked by heart strings, actual etheric strings, cords of light that cannot be seen with the human eye. They can choose to be with you in a nanosecond if they think you need them there. You may unexpectedly find yourself needing to yawn in the middle of a big cry…Know it is your loved one sending you energy of love and comforting thoughts, trying to ease your pain. You may hear a song on the radio that has a totally different meaning than it once did, or you may awake in the morning with a song or words going through your head. Pay attention. You may even find something in a different place around the house or have lights, or electronic devices, go off and on, without anyone touching the switch. When you are ready, watch for these signs…because they are trying to let you know that they are *not* what you may think they are…*dead.* This so-called ending is a new beginning for them and we may not always understand at the time why they had to leave this dimension. When we incarnate in a physical body here on Earth, we deliberately and consciously shut ourselves off from everything we know as a soul in heaven. Only an aspect of us manifests here, knowing the potential difficulties and challenges that lie ahead, but also the potential joys. This life *is* truly a game and knowing all would prevent us from having the necessary experiences to grow spiritually. The one who crosses over will rejoice with this transition humans call death, together with the ones who left before. It is a homecoming. Eventually we must find it in our hearts to rejoice as well. They have graduated to a new level of understanding and are at peace, with more love than we can possibly imagine, being in the physical. They are home. This is why Jesus tells us to cry at birth and to rejoice at death. Now, that sentence makes sense. Though the whys of losing a loved one are not always apparent, please know there is a reason, and you may find out. No more are we limited to not knowing, evolving as human beings. Your loved one exists on another level that most of us cannot see with our physical eyes. But if you are open to believing, your senses will guide you to the truth of their presence. They may follow you around trying to communicate through signs, songs, coins, and intuitive messages to let you know they are still with you. They will not frighten you. Besides, you have your own guides protecting you always. They see that the world you are in is not real…but they remember how real it was. They understand the pain and drama this earthly experience provides and they now see the much larger picture. They may hang around to try to let you know how sorry they are…or they will be next to you, when you need to tell them how sorry you feel—if those words had been left unspoken. There can be closure after all, in spite of this so-called separation. Talk to them, because they are there listening. They will help you adjust to their being gone…till it is time for them to move on…and then time for you to move on. And you can. If you are the one still here, know that as a soul, there is more you planned to experience here on Earth in the physical. Get busy and find out what that is…allow yourself time to grieve, then discover what it is you have left to do…*and find it in your heart to do it.*

A human being is a part of the whole, called by us
the 'universe', a part limited in time and space.
He experiences himself, his thoughts and feelings,
as something separate from the rest—a kind of optical delusion
of his consciousness. This delusion is a kind of prison
for us, restricting us to our personal desires and
to affection for a few persons nearest to us.
Our task must be to free ourselves from
this prison by widening our circle of compassion
to embrace all living creatures and the whole
of nature in its beauty. Nobody is able to achieve this
completely, but the striving for such achievement is
in itself a part of the liberation and
a foundation for inner security.
—Albert Einstein, Physicist (1879-1955)

Acknowledgments

To my father and mother, Francis "Wick" and Jane Smith, I thank you for being such progressive thinkers and for introducing me to sources of knowledge throughout my life that helped me to look out into the world with observant rather than judgmental eyes. Your inspiration, love, and compassion have enveloped me throughout my life and taught me to love myself in spite of my fears. I thank you for your support still…from the other side.

To my spirit guide, St. Thomas, I've always felt you near…a connection that can only be sensed and not described. Thank you for your guidance always and also for your patience, since the human ego can sometimes take the mind where the heart doesn't want to go, succumbing to fears and insecurities when all we need to do is to let go and be nurtured. Thank you for the countless signs that went unnoticed and—with a smile on my face—for all those to which I did pay attention. You've carried me through some tough times in my life and each one has pointed me closer to home. I thank you for your presence always.

My dearest Russell, I thank you for the time we shared when you were here in body. Your passionate and unconditional love, care, friendship, and deep affection shrouded me and also helped me during a difficult period in my life. Moreover, you made me feel worthy of the love we shared. I'm grateful for your presence still and I humbly look forward to our next life. The peace you brought us cannot be described in words. As difficult as our task has been, I realize it was one that we chose on another level. I pray that it will shed light on life itself.

Ron Morris, my deepest gratitude for not only accepting Russell's and my relationship but supporting it as well. And in the difficult time of our loss (primarily for you as the father of an only child), I'm thankful that we were able to provide each other a beacon of hope that sustained us during this tragedy and the difficult grieving process many humans endure. You have also helped to provide this, unbelievable to most, link of communication to the other side and our friendship has grown stronger with each moment we've shared. Your understanding, love, and support in numerous ways have made living during this challenging time not only bearable but enjoyable as well. Without the four of you—Russell, Dad, Thomas, and Ron—this book would not be possible.

To my children, Chris, Beth, and Matthew, who've seen me at my very best and at my very worst, thank you for your unconditional love, forgiveness, and open-mindedness. You've taught me patience and perseverance, and given me the strength to endure even when you had no knowledge of having done so. To Mark, I'll always be grateful to you for our children and your friendship. And to Laura, my daughter-in-law, I thank you for your support and for being such a wonderful mother to my grandson, Derrick, who brings me so much joy.

My heartfelt thanks to you, Lee Ann, my dear sister, for all your support—especially for the endless note taking during this lengthy project, and for being a part of our last scavenger hunt. Sharing the mystical path with one who has the same passion on this journey called life has been excitingly joyful. And to my sister Rebecca, I thank you for being there when my family and I needed you the most in some crucial moments of despair. You both have helped me to breathe at times when there was no breath left to take. To my brothers Bill and Jeff, our years growing up together were simply more fun because of you. To all my nieces and nephews, you complete our extended family and I'm grateful to have you in it. I'm so glad for the closeness and love that we share as a family.

To all my beloved friends who allowed me to share my experiences, I say thank you. And to those of you remaining nameless, who shared your stories with me, I'm eternally grateful. To my former boss, Maurice Kennedy, you helped in more ways than one, not only by listening but also by reviewing some of my work and constantly giving me more to question and ponder. And to Matt Evans, who had the courage to think outside the box and, with a scientific eye, review my material...thank you. Beau O'Shay, your comments on my work, coming from a physicist, truly inspired me. I'm so indebted to you all. Vickey Morris, thank you for being such a great traveling companion on all our scavenger hunts, not to mention the love and support you gave to your nephew, Russell, and me. To my dear friends, John Vogel and Bob Nanney, thank you for reviewing my material. Judy

Butler-Carder, your love and support is genuine. You provided me a place to stay when I needed it the most, and I'm grateful, too, for the beautiful messages from Dad and Russell.

My sincere appreciation goes to The Book Connection, which now links me to some of my dearest friends. Rita Mills, your expertise in carefully taking me by the hand and guiding me through the publishing maze has been invaluable! Thanks for coordinating this project so well. Peggy Sue Skipper, I cherish your critique—as the first to truly embrace this project, you gave me the courage to push forward. Shirin Wright, many thanks for your professionalism, skill, and dedication to the manuscript for all the necessary edits. Thank you, Vicki Mark, for the cover design, logo, and the continued creativity for all else we are still working on! And to Deena Rae Schoenfeldt, my ebook builder and digital director, a special thank you. I'm so happy you enjoyed the book as you worked on it. To Mari Selby for her sincere help in getting the message out there and keeping me straight. My internal guidance system led me to Mark Dowman; both you and the book trailer are ingeniously awesome. To Paul Elder, Petrene Soames, and Sonia Choquette, who graciously took the time to read and endorse my work—I'm honored, and humbled.

To my dear readers, I hope that you've enjoyed the story, regardless of where your perceptions began or your beliefs end…my best to you in your own journey through life.

To our omnipotent creator, who gives us all the wonderful opportunity of stepping out on this stage of life to discover for ourselves who we truly are and all that we can be—I feel blessed. To my angel, Patrick, and the rest of my spirit team…to the universal angels who assist in helping us always in all ways, and most times when we never know it…my heartfelt gratitude.

For Mark and Eva — A "Clue"

Seek and ye shall find, the love we left behind
It was a moment in time, the stars were all aligned
We approached the border with hesitation and not without trepidation
They had helped us the past, we were able to cross at last!
To find the perfect spot, on to find the lot.

We were being driven with the clues that we were given
A triangle of trees, a single red flower; though stressful it was, we did not cower
To bury the gifts we brought, and not without a thought
That knowing you will discover, one day there will be another
So go forth to the cosmic pearls, for there you will find your laurels

One day all will be revealed, now that it has been sealed
In this next circle of life, Eva will be your wife
When the treasures of the past are unearthed at last
What will we think when we discover this link
The joy that it will bring will make the angels sing

For love has been promised and blessed by St. Thomas
All will have come true, but yet… we knew
So what is time after all, if we are never to fall?
From God's holy grace, we will always have our place
In the heavens above, where there is nothing but love.

"A String of Cosmic Pearls Surrounds an Exploding Star"
Photo Credit: NASA / European Space Agency (ESA)

Love Promised: A Future Life Revealed

End Notes

Chapter One

1. Seeger, Pete, adapted from the Book of Ecclesiastes. (1959). "Turn, Turn, Turn!" Recorded by The Byrds. On *Turn, Turn, Turn!* (Record). Hollywood, CA: Columbia Studios, 1965.
2. Sondheim, Stephen, and Leonard Bernstein. (1957). "Somewhere." Recorded by Barbra Streisand. On *The Broadway Album* (LP and cassette). New York City, NY: Columbia Records, 1985.
3. McKuen, Rod, and Jacques Brel. (1973). "Seasons in the Sun." Recorded by Terry Jacks. (Record). Vancouver, B.C.: Bell Records.
4. Des'ree; and Ashley Ingram. (1994). "You Gotta Be." Recorded by Des'ree. On *I Ain't Movin'* and *Supernatural* (CD). London: Sony Soho Square.
5. Dyer, Wayne. (1995). "Meditations For Manifesting, Dr. Wayne Dyer" (CD). Carlsbad, CA: Hay House.
6. Ryan, Roma, and Enya. (2000). "Only Time." Recorded by Enya. On *A Day Without Rain* (CD). Dublin, Ireland: Warner Music UK.

Chapter Two

1. Nicks, Stevie. (1975). "Landslide." On *Fleetwood Mac.* (Record). Van Nuys, CA: Sound City Studios.
2. Day, Howie, and Kevin Griffin. (2003). "Collide." Recorded by Howie Day. On *Stop All the World Now* (CD). London: Olympic Studios.

Chapter Three

1. Blunt, James, Sacha Skarbek, Amanda Ghost. (2004). "You're Beautiful." Recorded by James Blunt. On *Back to Bedlam* (CD). Beverly Hills, CA: Custard Records; New York, NY: Atlantic Records, 2004.
2. Wade, Jason, and Jude Cole. (2005). "You and Me." Recorded by Jason Wade. On *Lifehouse* (CD). Easton, MD: Geffen Records.
3. Tyler, Steven, and Desmond Child. (1987). "Angel." Recorded by Aerosmith. On *Permanent Vacation* (Vinyl, cassette, CD). Vancouver, B. C.: Geffen Records.
4. McLachlan, Sarah, and Séamus Egan. (1995). "I Will Remember You." On *The*

Brothers McMullen (CD). New York, NY: Arista Records, RCA Music Group.

5. Kroeger, Chad, and Nickelback. (2006). "Faraway." Recorded by Nickelback. On *All the Right Reasons* (CD). Abbotsford, B. C.: Roadrunner, 2005.

Chapter Five

1. Stipe, Michael, Mike Mills, Peter Buck, Bill Berry. (1993). "Everybody Hurts Sometimes." Recorded by R.E.M. On *Automatic for the People* (CD, cassette). Burbank, CA: Warner Brothers, 1992.
2. Thomas, Rob. (2005). "Ever the Same." On …*Something to Be* (Digital). New York, NY: Atlantic Records.
3. Rodgers, Richard, and Lorenz Hart. (1937). "Where or When." Recorded by Rod Stewart. On *As Time Goes By: The Great American Songbook 2* (CD). New York, NY: J-Records, Sony Music Entertainment, 2003.

Chapter Seven

1. Eryn, Brown. (November 18, 2010) *Los Angeles Times* "Scientists briefly capture a form of matter's elusive antagonist—antimatter" Subtitle: About 38 atoms of antihydrogen are stored for about two-tenths of a second by researchers at CERN. With some fine-tuning, scientists should be able to make enough antimatter to examine why it doesn't seem to exist in nature."— It seems there is an assumption that antimatter does not exist in nature, which is the opposite of what I'm being told, based on purely non-scientific data (by today's scientific standards). It will, however, be interesting to see what new scientific discoveries are upon us that may someday validate what is written in this book. http://articles.latimes.com/2010/nov/18/science/la-sci-trapped-antihydogen-20101118
2. Chung, Elizabeth. (March 7, 2012) *CBC News/Technology and Science.* "Antimatter 'atom' measured for the first time" —An antimatter atom has been measured and manipulated for the first time ever, by a Canadian-led team of physicists. "This is the first time that anyone has ever interacted with an antimatter atom," said Mike Hayden, a physics professor at Simon Fraser University in Burnaby, B.C., describing the results published in the journal Nature Wednesday. http://www.cbc.ca/news/technology/story/2012/03/07/science-antimatter-alpha-hayden.html
3. Photographs were taken using a Sony Cyber-shot, DSC-W100, 8.1 megapixel camera. Technical features of this camera as provided by Sony are: 8.1 Megapixel Effective Super HAD(TM) CCD Super HAD(TM) (Hole Accumulation Diode) CCDs allow more light to pass to each pixel, increasing sensitivity and reducing noise. Carl Zeiss lens; 1250 ISO; 2.8 aperture, real imaging processor 14-bit DXP super resolution converter; up to 3, 264 x 2, 448 resolution for still photographs; 3x optical zoom—focal length f= (35mm conversion)—7.9—23.7mm (38-114m). These pictures were taken using auto-focus with flash. Specific details of unique pictures taken: Horizontal and vertical resolution 300dpi; f/2.8; exposure time 1 sec; 150-125; focal length 6mm; max aperture 3; no flash; compulsory; light source unknown; color representation RGB.

Love Promised: A Future Life Revealed

Bibliography

Allen, James. *As A Man Thinketh*. London: Collins, 1902.

Barham, Martha, and James Tom Greene. *The Silver Cord—Lifeline to the Unobstructed*. DeVorss, Camarillo, CA, 1986.

Braden, Gregg. *The Divine Matrix: Bridging Time, Space, Miracles, and Belief*. Carlsbad, CA: Hay House, 2007.

Braden, Gregg. *The God Code: The Secret of Our Past, The Promise of Our Future*. Carlsbad, CA: Hay House, 2004.

Brinkley, Dannion. *Saved by the Light with Paul Perry*. New York: Villard Books, 1994.

Bunick, Nick. *The Messengers: A True Story of Angelic Presence and a Return to the Age of Miracles*. Lake Oswego, OR: Skywin, 1996.

Chopra, Deepak, M.D. *Life After Death: The Burden of Proof*. New York: Three Rivers Press/Crown Publishing, 2006.

Choquette, Sonia. *Diary of a Psychic: Shattering the Myths*. Carlsbad, CA: Hay House, 2003.

Choquette, Sonia. *The Psychic Pathway: Workbook for Reawakening the Voice of Your Soul*. New York: Three Rivers Press, 1994.

Crump, E. L. *Selected Writings of Reverend E. L. Crump*. San Antonio, TX: Concept Therapy Institute, 1990.

Dispenza, Joe, D. C. *Evolve Your Brain: The Science of Changing Your Mind*. Deerfield Beach, FL: Health Communications, 2007.

Dyer, Wayne W. *There's a Spiritual Solution to Every Problem*. New York: HarperCollins, 2001.

Dyer, Wayne W. *Your Sacred Self: Making The Decision to Be Free*. New York: HarperCollins, 1995.

Fleet, Thurman, D. C. *Articles and Essays*, San Antonio, TX: Concept Therapy Institute, 1995.

Fleet, Thurman, D. C. *Rays of the Dawn: Natural Laws of the Body, Mind and Soul*. San Antonio, TX: Fleet, 1950.

Fleet, Jr., George T. *Where There is a Will, There is a Way: A Biography of Thurman Fleet, D. C.* San Antonio, TX: Concept Therapy Institute, 1997.

Free, Wynn, with David Wilcox. *The Reincarnation of Edgar Cayce?: Interdimensional Communication and Global Transformation with David Wilcox*. Berkley, CA: Frog, 2004.

Goldberg, Dr. Bruce. *Astral Voyages, Mastering the Art of Interdimensional Travel.* Woodbury, MN: Llewellyn Publications, 2006.

Hawkins, David R., M.D., Ph.D. *The Eye of the I: From Which Nothing Is Hidden.* Sedona, AZ: Veritas Publishing, 2001.

Hawkins, David R., M.D., Ph.D. *Power vs. Force, The Hidden Determinants of Human Behavior: An Anatomy of Consciousness.* Sedona, AZ: Veritas Publishing, 2001.

Hawkins, David R., M.D., Ph.D. *I: Reality and Subjectivity.* Sedona, AZ: Veritas Publishing, 2003.

Hay, Louise L. *You Can Heal Your Life.* Carlsbad, CA: Hay House, 1984.

Jerry, and Esther Hicks. *The Law of Attraction: The Basics of the Teachings of Abraham.* Carlsbad, CA: Hay House, 2006.

Holland, John. *Born Knowing—A Medium's Journey: Accepting and Embracing My Spiritual Gifts with Cindy Pearlman.* Carlsbad, CA: Hay House, 2003.

Hoodwin, Shepherd. *The Journey of Your Soul: A Channel Explores Channeling and the Michael Teachings.* Laguna Beach, CA: Summerjoy Press, 1999.

The Holy Bible: Containing the Old and New Testaments, King James Version, Cleveland, OH: The World Publishing Company.

Kaku, Michio. *Physics of the Impossible: A Scientific Exploration into the Worlds of Phasers, Force Fields, Teleportation and Time Travel.* New York: Anchor Books, 2009.

Keyes, Ken. *Handbook to Higher Consciousness.* Coos Bay, OR: Living Love Publications, 1975.

McKnight, Rosalind A. *Cosmic Journeys: My Out-of-Body Explorations with Robert Monroe.* Charlottesville, VA: Hampton Roads, 1999.

McKnight, Rosalind A. *Soul Journeys: My Guided Tours through the Afterlife.* Charlottesville, VA: Hampton Roads, 2005.

McMahon, Paddy. *The Grand Design. 2 v.* Charlottesville, VA: Hampton Roads, 2000.

McMoneagle, Joseph. *Mind Trek: Exploring Consciousness, Time, and Space through Remote Viewing.* Charlottesville, VA: Hampton Roads, 1997.

Mitchell, Dr. Edgar. *The Way of the Explorer with Dwight Williams.* New York: G. P. Putnam's Sons, 1996.

Mitchell, Karyn K., Ph.D. *Walk-Ins, Soul Exchange.* St. Charles, IL: Mind Rivers, 1999.

Monroe, Robert, A. *Journeys Out of the Body.* New York: Anchor Books, 1977.

Montgomery, Ruth. *Here and Hereafter.* New York: Ballantine Books, 1968.

Moody, Raymond. *Life after Life: The Investigation of a Phenomenon—Survival of Bodily Death.* New York: Harper One, 2001.

Morrissey, Dianne, Ph.D. *Anyone Can See the Light: The Seven Keys to a Guided Out-of-Body Experience.* Peterborough, NH: Stillpoint Publishing, 1996.

Newton, Michael, Ph.D. *Journey of Souls: Case Studies of Life Between Lives.* St. Paul, MN: Llewellyn Publications, 1994.

Orloff, Judith M. D. *Second Sight: An Intuitive Psychiatrist Tells her Extraordinary Story and Shows You How to tap Your Own Inner Wisdom.* New York: Warner Books, 1996.

Praagh, James Van. *Reaching to Heaven: A Spiritual Journey through Life and Death.* New York: Penguin Putnam, 1999.

Praagh, James Van. *Talking to Heaven: A Medium's Message of Life After Death.* New York: Penguin Putnam, 1997.

Ricard, Matthieu and, Trinh Xuan Thuan. *The Quantum and the Lotus: A Journey to the Frontiers where Science and Buddhism Meet.* New York: Three Rivers Press/Crown Publishing, 2001.

Scientific American, Cutting-Edge Science. *Extreme Physics.* New York: Rosen Publishing Group, 2008.

Smith, Gordon. *Spirit Messenger.* Carlsbad, CA: Hay House, 2004.

Soames, Petrene. *The Essence of Self-Healing: How to Bring Health and Happiness Into Your Life.* Spring, TX: FleetStreet Publications, 2001.

Talbot, Michael. *The Holographic Universe.* New York: HarperCollins Publishers, 1991.

Taylor, Albert. *Soul Traveler: A Guide to Out-of-Body Experiences and the Wonders Beyond.* New York: Penguin Group, 1998.

Tolle, Eckhart. *The Power of Now: A Guide to Spiritual Enlightenment.* Novato, CA: New World Library, 1999.

Trine, Ralph Waldo. *In Tune with the Infinite.* Indianapolis New York: Bobbs-Merrill Company, Fiftieth Anniversary Edition, 1947.

Virtue, Doreen. *How to Hear Your Angels.* Carlsbad, CA: Hay House, 2007.

Walsch, Neale Donald. *Conversations with God. Bks. 1-3,* Charlottesville, VA: Hampton Roads, 1996-98.

Weiss, Brian. *Many Lives, Many Masters.* New York: Simon & Schuster, 1988.

Wilber, Ken. *The Integral Vision: A Very Short Introduction to the Revolutionary Integral Approach to Life, God, the Universe, and Everything.* Boston: Shambhala, 2007.

Williamson, Marianne. *Enchanted Love: The Mystical Power of Intimate Relationships.* New York: Simon & Schuster, 1999.

Zukav, Gary. *The Seat of the Soul.* New York: Simon and Schuster, 1990.

About the Author

Kent Smith Adams is the founder of Universal Life Strings LLC. ULS is an organization that promotes the understanding of death as a part of life, and brings a higher level of awareness where life and the afterlife meet. Kent is a Certified Grief Recovery Specialist®. Her passions have led her on a lifelong study of metaphysics and more recently, theoretical science. A NASA contractor for 24 years, Kent now works as an Operational Psychology Coordinator in the human spaceflight operations program, supporting astronauts and their families. She lives in Houston, Texas.

www.UniversalLifeStrings.com

Index

A

addiction – 67, 68, 71, 89, 102, 200, 266
Akashic Records – 146
Alpha – 15, 164, 272, 285, 302
angel(s) – 16, 17, 44, 50, 51, 62, 70, 73,
    85, 87, 89, 97, 100, 105, 121, 133-
    136, 139, 154, 158, 160, 172, 178,
    191-195, 199, 201, 216, 219, 227,
    236-240, 248, 253, 255, 257, 258,
    260, 262, 266, 268, 269, 272, 276-
    278, 282, 290, 293, 299
antigravity – 222
anti-hydrogen – 211, 223,
antimatter – 15, 16, 146, 187, 211, 219,
    222-224, 231-233, 254, 275
antiparticles – 211, 214
Aoife – 197
Archangel – 95, 96, 100, 156, 167, 195,
    201, 226-228, 255, 257, 258, 269,
    278, 281, 282, 292
Ark of the Covenant – 269
Asteroid – 253
astronomer(s) – 15, 208
Atlanteans – 272
Atomic – 209, 212, 213, 220, 273
Atoms – 103, 146, 209, 210, 223
attention deficit disorder – 244
aura – 98, 135, 183, 184, 216, 217, 278
aurora australis – 274
aurora borealis – 146, 274

B

Bermuda Triangle – 272
Bible – 11, 13, 14, 16, 17, 37, 146, 214,
    247, 248, 269, 276, 277
Big Bang – 16, 223, 231
Black hole(s) – 15, 104, 224, 270

C

Castle – 173, 175-181, 183, 189, 196-198
Celtic – 170, 178, 186,
chakra(s) – 52, 227
clairaudience – 240
clairvoyance – 32, 240
comet – 253
Commandments – 104, 269, 270, 275
Commitments – 104, 275-278, 289, 290
communication – 10, 16, 17, 24, 76, 83,
    85, 86, 99, 101, 102, 106, 108, 113,
    120-122, 135, 141, 152, 161, 200,
    201, 204, 206, 213, 232, 235-237,
    244, 258, 269, 281, 288, 291, 298
compassion – 56, 75, 243, 246, 247, 249,
    279, 289, 296
Concept Therapy – 12, 29
Consciousness – 14, 28-30, 96, 107, 119,
    129, 131, 214, 228, 234, 240, 245,
    266, 280, 296
cord(s) – 36-39, 43, 52, 105, 204, 206,
    213, 215-217, 219, 220, 237, 239,
    245, 260, 281, 295

Cords of light – 215, 295
coronal mass ejections (CMEs) – 274
crossing over – 78, 85, 98, 99, 103, 221,
   227, 269

D

dark energy – 15, 223, 233, 280
dark matter – 15, 223, 280
death – 12-14, 39, 40, 41, 57, 69, 78, 85,
   86, 89, 108, 109, 162, 166
dimension(s) – 43, 64, 84, 97, 145, 161,
   206, 209, 211, 215, 217, 219, 223,
   224, 227-230, 237, 270, 272, 280,
   281, 291, 295
Divine Creator – 224
Divine Rod – 256
double-slit experiment – 209
druids – 276, 186, 187

E

Egyptian(s) – 12, 270-274
electromagnetic activity – 274
electromagnetism, magnetism – 104, 210,
   233
electron(s) – 29, 30, 101, 209, 210, 250,
electronic(s) – 26, 30, 91, 96, 295
energy – 14, 15, 29, 51, 52, 70, 73, 76,
   77, 79, 85, 87, 96, 101, 102, 105,
   112, 118, 122, 126, 128, 130, 135,
   137, 138, 141, 144, 145, 149, 151,
   154-156, 159-161, 167, 171, 173,
   176, 188, 191, 192, 200, 202, 203,
   206, 207, 212, 214, 216, 221-227,
   230, 232, 233, 235, 239, 240, 242,
   244, 249, 250, 257, 262, 264, 269,
   270, 278, 295
entanglement – 210, 219, 221, 224,
entity – 39, 61,
ether, etheric, etherally – 18, 39, 43, 119,
   145, 203, 207, 215, 240, 259

F

Fear – 13-14, 16, 17, 24-25, 34, 36, 40,
   42, 47, 82-83, 104, 107, 132, 134,
   187, 214, 242, 243, 246, 246, 247,
   260, 279, 289, 297

Finite – 17, 126, 224
Forgiveness – 57, 64, 247, 279, 289, 298
Fragmentation – 215
free will – 57, 103-105, 109, 132, 181-182,
   214, 229, 230, 238-239, 243, 248-249,
   252, 265, 275, 279, 281, 288
frequency – 214, 235-236, 241, 243, 259
function – 210, 212, 213, 232, 243, 258

G

Glue – 210, 223, 224, 233,
God – 11, 14, 16-17, 23-24, 28-31, 34,
   37, 39, 78, 97, 100-101, 103-104,
   106-107, 116, 120, 125, 131, 136,
   138-139, 145, 149, 152, 154-156,
   185, 188-189, 200, 204, 209, 211,
   212, 213, 214, 221-223, 227, 230,
   239-240, 245-249, 252-253, 261,
   265, 269, 270-270, 271, 275-282,
   288-290, 292, 300
gravitation – 209
gravity – 104, 208, 210, 220-222, 224,
   231-232, 235, 254, 275, 278, 297
guide(s) – 18, 44, 63-64, 102, 105, 107,
   109, 113-114, 120, 123, 132, 135-
   136, 150, 156, 158, 163, 180, 193,
   201, 203, 217, 224, 231, 239, 241,
   261, 262, 278, 281, 292, 295

H

Hall of Records – 146
Hadrons – 210
heaven(s); heavenly – 37, 42, 94, 96-98,
   100, 104, 107-108, 121-122, 139,
   145-146, 199, 203, 206, 216, 219,
   221, 224-225, 228, 249, 253, 276,
   280, 289, 295, 300
human being(s) – 212, 215, 227, 237,
   247, 291, 295, 296
hydrogen – 212, 223

I

Illusion – 132, 150, 221-222, 231, 243,
   248, 291
image(s) – 72, 84, 99, 116, 213-214, 223,
   226, 242, 280

impingement – 239
infinite – 14, 17, 39, 213, 248
intelligence – 133, 213-214
intergalactic communication – 232
intuition – 206, 210, 250

J

judgment(s); judgmental – 30, 52, 248-249, 303

K

Karma – 108, 109, 127, 247, 249, 275, 280
King – 177, 197, 198, 270
Knight(s) Templar – 28, 196

L

Laser – 16, 250, 254, 271
Law of Attraction – 31, 155, 214, 230, 241, 242, 249,
Law(s) of motion – 208, 214
Lemurians – 272, 273
Levitation – 187, 273,
Lifeline – 39, 106, 122, 128-129, 137, 145, 159, 173, 177, 183, 189, 203, 215-216, 219-220, 226-230, 237, 243, 245, 281
life link – 228
life plan – 128, 228
lifetimes – 18, 84, 106, 107, 173, 192, 220, 228, 230, 238, 249, 281, 288, 290
light – 130, 133, 137-138, 146-147, 154, 159, 160-161, 166-167, 201, 205-206, 207-210, 214-216, 219
light body – 146, 216
light diode – 273
light levels – 222

M

M-Theory – 211
MRI – 255, 258, 259
Martians – 272
Mass – 208-210, 221-224
Matter – 15-16, 30, 137, 146, 168, 208, 210, 221-224, 231, 270, 291
Mayans – 187, 257, 272, 273

Meditation – 52, 189
Metaphysical – 10, 136, 166, 170, 181, 207, 214, 220, 282, 292
miracle(s) – 13, 36, 136, 260

N

nonEarth beings – 272
Nanotechnology – 232
near-death experience(s) – 224, 236
Nobel Peace Prize – 233

O

OBE(s) – 24, 33, 39, 133, 138, 165
Omega – 272
Orb(s) – 118, 138, 144, 153, 146, 154, 159, 176
Ouija – 46, 61, 85, 86, 101, 145, 251
Oversoul – 217

P

Paradox – 210
parallel universe(s) – 221, 223-224, 225-227, 229, 233, 244, 258, 270, 273, 275
particle accelerators – 210
particle(s) – 15-16, 209-211, 223
past lives – 7, 122, 169-171, 173, 244, 252
patent foreman ovale (PFO) – 255
philosopher – 207, 234, 281
photoelectric effect – 209
photons – 208-209, 220-221, 232
physical dimension – 43, 215, 217, 219, 228
physicists – 15-16, 128, 208-209, 211, 213, 219, 233
physics – 9, 15, 46, 128, 137, 208, 209, 210, 220-221, 223, 230-232, 241, 272
planes – 14, 129, 222, 224, 272
plasma – 145
prediction(s) – 32, 33, 105, 229, 233, 281
princess – 169, 171, 172, 177, 196-197
prism – 105, 208, 222
psychic – 10, 32-33, 44, 62-63, 65-66, 74,76, 91, 117, 129-130, 133, 165, 206, 215, 230, 235, 237, 239, 243

Q

Quantum – 208
quantum field – 207, 211, 213
quantum mechanics – 16, 207, 213, 234, 238
quantum physics – 16, 18, 137, 146, 205, 207, 211- 213, 230-231, 242
quantum teleportation – 137
quantum theory – 207, 209
quantum wave – 213, 240
quarks – 210, 220, 230
quasar – 277

R

reflective propulsion – 232
reincarnation – 10-11, 18, 29, 32, 40, 56, 89, 117, 120, 123, 165, 186, 199, 230, 251-252, 256, 266, 276, 277, 284, 286, 288
religion(s) – 9, 11, 13, 18, 28-29, 40, 120, 143, 212, 236, 237, 251-252, 276, 277
remote viewing – 133, 134, 189
Rosicrucians – 28

S

Samadhi – 245
Satan – 282
saint(s) – 107, 113, 120, 155, 156, 193, 199, 277, 278, 282
satellite(s) – 235-236
scrolls – 270
silver cord – 38, 39, 105, 206, 217, 237, 245, 281
SOL – 232
soul(s) – 11-14, 18, 23-24, 30-32, 35, 39-42, 44, 52, 56-57, 63, 65, 66, 87, 89, 91, 95-98, 100, 103, 105-107, 139, 144-146, 154-155, 159, 163, 166, 169-171, 177, 183, 203-204, 215, 217, 219-222, 224, 226-227, 229, 260, 269, 276-279, 289-291, 295, 296
soul mate – 43, 260
space – 10, 14-16, 33, 51, 81, 84, 94, 99, 100-111, 124, 130, 141, 145, 146, 148, 187, 206, 211, 214, 219-220, 225, 230-233, 235-236, 245, 254, 258, 260, 266, 272-273, 280, 285, 296, 300
space visitors – 273, 187, 232
spacecraft – 236, 273
spacemen – 270, 273
spacetime – 209, 254,
special theory of relativity – 209-210
speed of light – 16, 195, 209, 210, 219, 223, 231-232, 279
spirit; spiritual – 10, 16-18, 32, 34, 40, 52, 73, 83, 98, 100, 103-104, 107, 110, 112, 119, 122, 129-130, 132, 138, 142, 144-145, 154, 159, 178, 181, 212, 215, 222, 227, 229, 234, 235, 261, 262, 272, 283, 285, 290, 297
spirit guide(s) – 18, 63-65, 107, 120, 122-123, 130, 134-138, 158, 166, 183, 202, 217, 238, 239, 248, 255, 260, 268, 273, 278, 279, 281, 285
Standard Model of Physics – 210
St. Thomas of Aquinas – 107, 120, 156
string bubble – 232
string theory – 210-211, 220, 232
strings – 160, 210, 213, 219, 220, 221, 224, 295
subatomic – 15-16, 31, 102, 104, 128, 140, 188, 209, 213, 225, 227, 234, 235, 245, 280
suicide – 86, 88, 89
superconscious – 17
superposition – 210, 214
Superstring Theory – 211
Synchronicities – 16, 50, 113, 115, 189, 201-202

T

tarot – 32
teachers – 31, 100, 107, 275, 278
teleportation – 137, 187
theology – 12, 16, 29, 215
theory – 10, 12, 18, 19, 29, 99, 120, 128, 165, 206, 207, 2011, 248, 270
third eye – 236, 243, 279, 280
time – 10, 18, 49, 54, 81, 84, 98-99, 103, 128, 140, 146, 158, 209, 2011, 220,

222, 224. 226, 229-232, 259, 272,
278, 280, 287, 296
time capsule – 10
timeline – 226
toyon particles – 225

U

Universe – 15-16, 39, 128, 146, 206, 208-
209, 212, 220-234, 258, 241, 242,
253, 259, 270, 291, 296

V

Veil – 92, 97, 106, 128, 130, 144, 165,
204, 215-216, 220-221, 223, 234,
238-239, 254, 256
vibration(s); vibrational – 38, 63, 95,
100, 102-104, 122, 130, 132-133,
141, 158, 165, 167, 183,211,220,
222-224, 230, 240-241, 249-250,
259, 289

W

walk-in – 127, 169, 183, 228-229
wave collapse function – 210
wave-particle – 209
wormhole(s) – 224-225, 254

www.UniversalLifeStrings.com